DANIEL DEFOE'S

RAILWAY JOURNEY

A surreal odyssey through modern Britain

Stuart Campbell

SANDSTONEPRESS
HIGHLAND | SCOTLAND

First published in Great Britain by
Sandstone Press Ltd
7 Dochcarty Road
Dingwall
Ross-shire
IV15 9UG
Scotland

www.sandstonepress.com

Editor: Robert Davidson

The publisher acknowledges support from
Creative Scotland towards publication of this volume.

ISBN: 978-1-910985-70-0
ISBNe: 978-1-910985-71-7

Cover design by Mark Ecob
Typesetting by Iolaire Typography Ltd, Newtonmore
Printed and bound by Totem, Poland

To Arwen, Juliet and Ruairidh

ACKNOWLEDGEMENTS

I must thank John, my friend and travelling companion, without whose organisational skills and patience this book would not have happened. I also acknowledge Roy's gentle encouragement and advice. Most of all I am extremely grateful to the 250 innocent passengers who willingly shared their stories with an eccentric OAP.

CONTENTS

PROLOGUE

Every mile of railway in mainland Britain. Ridiculous.

This was the thought that woke me in the middle of the night. The feeling was one of panic and disbelief at my own stupidity.

The rest of the night was spent dreaming of spiders; huge buggers crawling over my hand. Eventually their black thread legs morphed into veins. A vast matrix of pulsing capillaries along which I was committed to travelling. Each bent gossamer of blood represented a journey that I would make. By a process of dreamer's alchemy, my hand melted into a map of the UK. My thumb elongated into Cornwall. My middle finger followed the Pennines and stretched up towards Caithness.

My heart seemed to be beating faster than usual. There was still an element of panic in the thought of what lay ahead. This was not a sanitised itinerary chosen by TV executives. This was to be an act of attrition, an obsessive daunting voyage along every mile of accessible rail track. This was going to hurt.

My motivation for this monstrous task remained a mystery. Partially, I was seduced by an image of myself as a chronicler of the mundane and the surreal; a jovial and eccentric completest; an older sort of *Blue Peter* presenter who would engage complete strangers in jolly banter in exchange for their secrets.

I knew that talking to strangers would be the key to what I hoped to achieve. To an extent, we all talk to strangers, in bus queues, in shops. We have unwanted functional exchanges with unknown people working in call centres; difficult exchanges with traffic wardens and HMRC officials; pleasant exchanges with moonlighting students who take our orders in cafes. But our busy and troubled times offer few opportunities to listen for any length of time, and without judgement, to the thoughts and preoccupations of strangers. In the main our conversations are confined to family, friends, neighbours and work colleagues.

I have fond memories of hitch-hiking the length of Britain from my home in Gloucestershire to my university in Aberdeen in the 1960s. The M6 was unfinished and the M5 only existed in a dreaming architect's pipe. On occasions, when I was feeling seriously homesick, the journey would devour most of the weekend and permit me no more than a quick cup of coffee with my parents before I set off again. But the journey itself was the thing.

Hitch-hiking was an accepted phenomenon; an innocent pursuit untrammelled by tabloid tales of vulnerable people being dismembered and left in ditches. Lorry drivers were the undisputed kings of the road and could pick up whom they wished without fear of dismissal for sharing their cab with non-company employees. And the tales. Truckers, travelling salesmen, and men working away from home, would pour out their hearts to this innocent eighteen-year-old who knew nothing about infidelity, or marital troubles. It was as if my presence alone provided a catalyst for confessional monologues and lengthy anecdotes about politics (I only had the vaguest notion who Enoch Powell was). And of course football, about which I knew much more.

Having climbed down from a warm cab I would stand in a lay-by, reeling from the latest weight of disclosure and trenchant views, and hold out my thumb in the direction of whichever driver next felt the need to unburden himself.

Even then I reflected on what this meant. To an extent we

can choose our identity, or at least accentuate those aspects of our personality with which we are most at ease, when talking to a stranger whom we will never see again. This is not to impute deception, rather it is to acknowledge that, on occasions, there are therapeutic advantages to be gained from stepping away from the mundane preoccupations that consume us all, and project more of the person we would like to be for the benefit of a stranger.

I wanted to recreate these discussions by travelling across the entire rail network of this island, and see what I could glean about people. It is arrogant to imply that somehow I wanted to take the pulse of the nation by talking to strangers on trains, but to an extent this was the truth.

I had few preconceptions as to the mechanics of engaging random strangers in conversation. I had rehearsed a few potential opening gambits in my head: 'Hello, I'm writing a book. Tell me about your life.' 'Do you come here often? I mean, do you travel on this train often?' 'Hello, do you have a moment to tell me your secret preoccupations, your ambitions, your dreams . . .' This was going to be problematic.

From the years spent working as a mental health professional I liked to think that I could give something back to any strangers who were willing to tell me about their lives. I would be an attentive listener; I would do my best to listen with empathy and without judgement to whatever they chose to tell me. Research has consistently shown that being listened to non-judgementally is such a rare phenomenon as to carry therapeutic benefit. This would be the least I could do for the travellers who might contribute to this book.

There was another problem; despite an extrovert persona I remain inveterately shy, and genuinely find it difficult talking to strangers. This will be a challenge then.

There was of course a darker reason for wanting to embark on endless train journeys. Part of me has always felt the need, at all costs, to keep moving; to avoid being found out or held to account, for what I didn't know.

Perhaps I wanted to leave false tracks for the Grim Reaper; keep one step ahead, make him miss his train, 'Sorry Sir, we can't accept scythes in Lost Property . . . against the terms and conditions.'

When all was said and done, I am a baby boomer turned twilighter who had never actually believed he would be this age. Apart from anything else, cowardice forbad me backing out. I had told everybody about my plans and milked their respectful if bewildered incredulity.

In the early hours, it all just seemed silly and indulgent. I could hear John, my travelling companion, moving about in the house. He would probably punch me if I said that, despite his meticulous planning, I didn't really fancy it after all.

There was a third member of our party; I was bringing along one of my literary heroes, Daniel Defoe. After writing *Robinson Crusoe* and *Moll Flanders* in the early 18th century, Defoe published *A Tour Through the Whole Island of Great Britain*. The facsimile title page provides more detail:

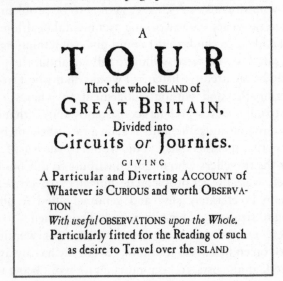

A

T O U R

Thro' the whole ISLAND of

GREAT BRITAIN,

Divided into

Circuits or Journies.

GIVING

A Particular and Diverting ACCOUNT of Whatever is CURIOUS and worth OBSERVA-TION
With useful OBSERVATIONS *upon the Whole*.
Particularly fitted for the Reading of such as desire to Travel over the ISLAND

As a manifesto that would do for me. Defoe's journeys were published in a series of thirteen letters. The chronology of his tours is largely fabricated, and some of the detail is either borrowed or fictitious; a man after my own heart then.

This aspect of his writing deserves further consideration. Defoe would have struggled with the distinction between fact and fiction; the notion of discrete genres would have confused him. He was even reluctant to admit that *Robinson Crusoe* was a work of fiction. In his preface he maintains that 'The Editor believes the thing to be a just history of fact; neither is there any appearance of fiction in it.' This was not a disingenuous literary ploy; such stratagems belong to the century after his. He knew that good storytelling contains universal truths about which there is nothing fictitious, and it was this certainty that led him to exploit ambiguity across genres.

In a more modest way I intend to do something similar in my own account. I would argue that when we listen to someone's tale we automatically create a context to better understand what we are being told. To an extent we cannot help but embellish what we hear. We may reflect afterwards and imagine how things may have turned out. At best, our mind wanders. What is this if not fiction? By way of a small experiment I intend to include some of these embellishments in my narrative.

The world into which Defoe was born in 1660 was in flux. The Renaissance, Restoration and Revolution had changed things forever. The old feudal order was giving way to capitalism. The country was changing, a new London was emerging after the ravages of plague and fire. New ideas in agriculture were taming the countryside while whole forests were being sacrificed on the altar of shipbuilding.

In his account, Defoe obsesses with the details of Britain's trade with Europe while stepping more lightly around the contentious issue of the Union between England and

Scotland. In these respects at least he would have felt strangely at home in this part of the 21st century.

In addition to being a prodigious chronicler of these islands before the onset of the industrial revolution, and ultimately a novelist, Daniel Defoe was also a spy, politician, polemicist and prolific pamphleteer.

Although he seemed quite contained within the 700-odd pages of my well-thumbed Penguin Classic, there was no guarantee that a spirit so passionate, curious and contradictory would be happy to stay there for long.

JOURNEY ONE

The North East of England

DAY ONE

Bellgrove Glasgow – Edinburgh Waverley – Newcastle –
Carlisle – Leeds – Ilkley – Bradford – Leeds

As we stood in the early morning cold on Bellgrove station
in the East End of Glasgow, more doubts crowded in. What
if, by failing to concentrate now, I was to miss something
of importance? At all costs then, I must concentrate. I
must observe my surroundings as if I had never seen them
before.

We stepped onto the first train. The moment should have
felt more significant than it did. Our journey was under
way.

Concentrate. Concentrate on Shettleston Juniors football
ground. Not a venue for the faint-hearted where even the
dogs fight each other, and half time amputations are not
uncommon.

Concentrate on the showman's estate that lines the
track from Carntyne, housing the largest concentration
of showmen in Europe. Neat chalets adorned with Doric
pillars stand cheek by jowl next to mothballed Wurlitzers
and hot dog vans.

Concentrate on the linguistic implications of Coatbridge Sunnyside; the finest oxymoron since Milton's 'darkness visible'.

Perhaps I should say something about John, my large travelling companion with whom I was, for better or worse, destined to spend the next forty days. We have known each other since university in Aberdeen. Now a hermit on a farm in the north of Scotland, he told me this was the first time in nearly half a century that he had travelled for any length of time with another human being. A retired secondary head teacher, John has spent many years developing an impressive capacity for facts and opinions. One of the great mysteries of this adventure was how long we could survive in each other's company without falling out.

So much for concentrating. As we slid alongside Princes Street Gardens into Waverley I realised that I had stopped concentrating several miles back and had, like everyone else on the train, let my thoughts wander without purpose or focus. I had not thought of anything clever or smart to say. By way of mitigation: I had travelled from Glasgow to Edinburgh many hundreds of times before. Every mile was familiar and stale.

Without warning, Defoe burst from page 576! The cloying reek of civet from his perfumed wig filled the carriage. 'I was right,' he said.

'What?'

'About the stale swamp beneath the castle. Were the loch filled up, as it might easily be, the City might have extended upon the plain below, and Edinburgh could be the fairest city in the realm...'

'Full marks for prophecy.'

'And look at the buildings! No blowing of tiles about the streets to knock people on the head as they pass; no stacks of chimneys and gable ends falling to bury the inhabitants in the ruins as we so often find in England.'

According to a large screen above the concourse, 1490 accidents had occurred at railway stations in the United Kingdom in the last year. At that moment, a small toddler tipped himself out of his pram and sprawled howling in front of me, and a CCTV camera nodded in our direction as if saying 'told you so.'

'Platform 12,' said John.

Defoe was tugging at my sleeve. 'Let us proceed to the High Street which is perhaps, the largest, longest, and finest street for buildings and number of inhabitants, not in Britain only, but in the world.'

'No time. We've got a train to catch.'

'Who are you talking to?' asked John.

'Just myself, I'm fine-tuning my perfect prose.'

John snorted.

Defoe snorted.

The man across the aisle on the Newcastle cross-country smelled. 'I got a good shot through her legs,' he said to his thin, equally unsavoury companion.

I stared straight ahead. This wasn't happening. It was too early in the journey. I was still at the stage of playing with the existential concept of peeling back the layers of identity that surround strangers. By subtle eavesdropping and intense scrutiny, I would unravel all manner of subliminal betrayals and vulnerabilities among the itinerant population. I would plunder their stories and somehow make my own soul the richer. But not this.

'I spent ages in that bog,' he continued. The woman opposite clutched her scarf to her mouth, appalled by this shameless admission of sexual perversity.

'Legs like matchsticks,' he said. 'Sublime. *Ardea cinerea* at her finest. With a sprat in her mouth. Beautiful bird.'

'Not as beautiful as the Solan Goose,' chipped in Defoe. 'Over there,' he said, pointing to the Bass Rock on the horizon. 'The Solan Geese are the principal inhabitants ... As they live

3

on fish, so they taste like fish, together with their being so exceeding fat, makes them, in my opinion, a very coarse dish, rank, and ill relished, and soon gorging the stomach.'

'A haven for pirates,' he continued, as the Bass Rock gradually disappeared behind us. 'After the Revolution, a little desperate crew of people got possession of it; and having a large boat, which they hoisted up into the rock, committed several piracies, took a great many vessels, and held out the last of any place in Great Britain.'

Bending over to reach a packet of cheese and onion crisps for John, the trolley attendant revealed a tiny leather holster on his belt containing a hand sanitiser. I could only assume that the company had capitulated to the rail unions and agreed to provide protection for its staff against the dirt and grime of its passengers. Mercifully the germ Taser remained sheathed although its owner looked nervous after handling several coins.

I was watching the long ribbon of the North Sea, waiting for the appearance of Lindisfarne which duly arrived a mile off the Northumberland coast, an enigmatic sliver of land with a castle at its tip, achingly distant from the main line.

The guard played a tape of monastic plainchant over the tannoy and asked passengers to lend a hand to those pilgrims too frail to place their staffs in the overhead racks. I looked at the sky for signs of the whirlwinds, lightning and fiery dragons that were omens of a less than friendly visit from the Vikings in AD 793. The clouds looked benign.

Nothing moves on the undulating land. The tractors are still and the sheep seem to be cast in stone. The brown fields rise and fall with the yellow broom. An air sea rescue helicopter hovers near the coast. All of the horses are wearing coats.

'Can I talk to you?' I take a risk, walk down the carriage and intrude into the world of the woman in her seventies sitting on her own. I invade her thoughts.

4

'Yes,' she said, 'but I'm not a very interesting person.'

She listens patiently as I explain my strange mission, though I keep to myself any thoughts of garnering people's souls.

'I went on a good journey once,' she said. 'It took me four years between 2008 and 2012. You see, my husband had died and I lost all my confidence. I knew that unless I did something, I would never get it back. So I went on a walk. From Lands' End to John O'Groats. Not in one go, you understand, but in chunks. 847 miles but it was probably more as I did my best to avoid roads. I preferred cycle and canal paths ...'

I dared not ask, but wanted to know if her husband had been with her every step of the way. Had she got cross with him? Had she spoken out loud? Had she shouted at him as she walked down the hedgerows? After all, how dare he leave her? Had she picked berries and offered him some? Had she moved to one side of the stile so he could sit down next to her?

Had she felt unsafe?

'Only once. On the outskirts of Larkhall here in Scotland. I could see these youths halfway down the path. It was narrow and I would have drawn attention to myself if I had turned and run. They had bottles and were drinking. It sounds silly but I put the SIM card from my phone down my knickers. What if they stole the phone and I lost all my contacts? Anyway, I braced myself for the worst. And do you know what? They were lovely. They were worried about me walking on my own and insisted on accompanying me to a park where there was a statue of a famous footballer. They told me the whole story. They must have thought I was their gran. Anyway, they made a point of giving me their phone numbers so I could phone them later and tell them I was safe.'

I thanked her for the story and returned to John. 'The Morpeth Curve,' he said.

5

'What?'

'Reputed to be the most severe curve of any main railway line in Britain. The track turns approximately 98 degrees from a north-westerly to an easterly direction immediately west of the station.'

I wasn't listening. Part of me was still walking the highways and byways of Britain with the Lost Boys of Larkhall.

Welcome distraction was provided by an announcement. 'If there is a Mr Alexander Goldsmith on the train could he please make himself known to the conductor when he carries out a full ticket inspection.' At that moment the train lurched to the left and my copy of *A Tour* fell to the floor. I bent down to pick it up.

'Hang on,' I said. 'Alexander Goldsmith? Isn't that one of the aliases you adopted on your last visit to Scotland? I remember now. You were a passionate advocate of the union of 1707 and travelled North of the border as 'a spy'. Isn't that right? The mob discovered your address and threw rocks at your window.'

'It was a long time ago,' said a small voice.

'We are now approaching Newcastle. Will all passengers...'

There was a solitary trainspotter on Platform 4. Having time on our hands I resolve to interrogate him within an inch of his life. My questions are ready. Why do you do this? Do you think your natural maturation has been inhibited somehow? How many notebooks do you fill in any year?

Fortunately, perhaps, the trainspotter spared himself this ordeal by disappearing. The platform simply opened up and swallowed him although he might well have been squirreled out of sight by his protective peers and taken to a place of safety for vulnerable adults.

I feel guilty realising that I was quite prepared to make narrative capital from late middle-aged trainspotters with flask and notebook; men still trapped in part of their

6

boyhoods that had perhaps promised much, and then disappointed.

My attention wanders to an elderly couple holding hands in a queue next to the information kiosk. Waiting patiently, they have many questions. Where have all the past years gone? Why have our children grown apart from us? Can we use our senior railcards before nine o'clock? Do you believe there is a God?

The Tyne Valley train dragged itself out of the station and passed a commune of pigeon lofts. A quick search on my phone reveals Pigeon Chat on YouTube, 'following the lives of three courageous pigeons in their daily fight against man', and an invitation to join *Pigeon Craic! Ireland's Ultimate Pigeon Resource*. Later perhaps.

On a pigeon website, a man called Ronnie describes a chilling attack on his beloved tipplers by three Peregrine Falcons; another posts a picture of two deformed birds under the heading 'Don't tell me my boys are ugly'. Then a John D attempts to break my heart by describing how he'd found a baby pigeon that had frozen to death... but wait... 'I reached down and picked up the cold hard little body, and was about to throw it into the ravine when I felt a slight movement in my hand...'

After skirting the car park wasteland of the Metro Centre, we follow the equally grey mud flats of the Tyne. Eventually the flats slap themselves into the shape of a proper river that supports the upper torsos of several fishermen.

On the approach to Carlisle from the East, ancient woodlands tumble towards small streams and duck under stone bridges.

We pass through Wetheral, a commuter village which, despite its bijou appearance, has known difficult days. *The Times* of 14th December 1836 described in graphic detail 'the dreadful accident (which) occurred on the Newcastle and

Carlisle railway by which three persons lost their lives and a great deal of property was damaged ... two boys aged fourteen and sixteen, who had stowed away in a horse wagon, were found crushed to death. The head of the elder youth was crushed quite flat, and presented a frightful spectacle.'

Alighting from the train at Carlisle our attention was grabbed by Billy, a Train Presentation Leader, addressing us from a lurid poster next to the toilet door. 'Did you know,' asks Billy, 'A lawnmower, a park bench and a coffin are just some of the unusual items that have been left on UK trains?' No I didn't.

The Carlisle to Settle line through the Yorkshire Dales deserves its reputation for stunning beauty. Our enjoyment was enhanced by being adopted by one of the Friends who act as unpaid tour guides on the line. Alarmingly, she was wearing a crocheted map of the route complete with drystane dykes, small farm steadings and lumpy little sheep that we were invited to touch. It was a challenge to align the sights visible from the window with the 3D mirror image on her chest. She became especially animated when we stopped at Kirkby Stephen.

'Look out for the macaws,' she declaimed excitedly. 'They came from nowhere and settled quite happily in the trees next to the fire station.'

'That could be a parakeet,' said John, pointing. 'Or a raquet-tailed drongo.' The woman ignored the provocation but changed tack.

'Over there,' she said, 'were the camps where the navvies lived. Over a thousand settled in the shantytowns which they named after Crimean War victories. The three main ones were Inkerman, Sebastopol and Jericho. Two hundred died either from the smallpox or from injuries incurred while labouring on the line ... They had their own schools, and a hospital, and a missionary they called the parson. But they fought a lot. With bare knuckles.'

8

She then drew our attention to the highest station toilet in Britain and became quite lyrical about the knitters of Dent, all of whom presumably crocheted their own jumpers.

We were distracted from the plight of oxygen-starved passengers gasping for breath in the gents, by the guard who announced in sad and apologetic tones, that owing to an equipment failure he would be unable to either issue tickets or accept payment. Essentially this was now a free train. This was concessionary travel at its finest.

The guard however soon had his hands full wrestling with a small ferrety-eyed young man with red hair. 'I don't care if you are Branwell Brontë,' he said, 'and that it was you what wrote *Wuthering Heights*, I'm putting you off at the next stop!'

Branwell tore the cork out of a stone bottle and downed the contents before belching loudly in the guard's face. 'You don't know what it's like, living with those harridans...'

'Next stop. And you can bloody well walk to Haworth.'

'I approve,' said Defoe.

'Of what?'

'The introduction of invention to augment your account.'

Away from the scenery and the poignancy of abandoned hill farms, our train lowered its undercarriage and started its slow descent towards Keighley and Leeds. A feature of this part of the journey was the proliferation of sewage farms. A honeycomb of circular tanks had conquered the landscape, each being conscientiously swept by a languid arm pushing the sludge sideways in a hypnotic choreography.

As part of a related leitmotif, the railway embankments on the approach to Leeds had all been requisitioned as auxiliary landfill sites: armchairs, prams and general domestic detritus tumbled downwards towards the track. It was Osbert Sitwell who sneeringly referred to trains as 'slums on

9

wheels', but it wasn't the carriages, at least not on this trip, it was the toxic route they followed.

A young girl with red hair passed through the carriage clutching a green tank holding a single goldfish.

The train announcer on the Leeds to Ilkley Sprinter was endowed with the richest RP accent audible this side of a 1950s public service broadcast. He effortlessly offered plummy reassurances concerning punctuality and catering to all who hankered for the certainties of Empire and Ovaltine. In the distance a flurry of doves stood out against the black clouds which were in turn dissected by a rainbow.

We left Ilkley station and wandered into the car park. The main archway was flanked by two women distributing *The Watchtower*. Before the week was out we were to pass through many stations being guarded by a similar phalanx of proselytisers; Jehovah's hierarchy having chosen to target depressed and tired commuters on the not unreasonable assumption that they must be desperate for spiritual solace.

I decided to counter my own prejudiced atheism with healthy research. I know I could have asked them about their beliefs but took the coward's way out, leaned against a wall and used my phone to browse *10 Things You Never Knew About Jehovah's Witnesses*. Thing number 9 was their objection to the cross as a Christian symbol because it is regarded (by whom?) as a historical representation of the male genitalia and thus coupling of the reproductive organs.

'Worshippers of Satan!' shouted Defoe who emerged from the gents fastening his breeches.

'What about religious tolerance?'

'Pestilential heretics! Why are you subverting the Word of God? May their nethers be slowly roasted in the fires of hell!'

Outside Shipley, several towers dominate a scrap yard. The first is constructed from the cubes of crushed cars much loved by gangsters and the makers of cheap thrillers. Its neighbour is more impressive consisting of many hundreds of old mattresses. For a moment I see all of the lovers who once inhabited them, sprawled and spread-eagled, some naked, some in pyjamas, all clinging like starfish to the side of the cascade, doing their utmost to resist the final ignominious fall. I hear their voices;

Do you still love me?

Have you wound the clock?

Was that the cat?

Don't leave me.

Did your team win?

Did you hear from the girls?

We pass beneath the walls of Bradford City's Valley Parade stadium, scene of the worst fire disaster in the history of English football. On 11th May 1985, fifty-six lives were lost and at least 265 people were injured. Over 6000 people attended a multi-denominational service part of which was held in Urdu and Punjabi. A giant Christian cross made from burnt beams was erected in front of the stand.

'I remember very well what I saw with a sad heart, though I was but young, I mean the fire of London.'

'You were only six at the time, weren't you? Your father's house was spared, but only just, isn't that right?'

'Yes, but no more mention of fires I pray.'

On the outskirts of Leeds a single white swan was gliding serenely down a canal.

DAY TWO
Leeds – Cleethorpes – Barton-on-Humber – Hull – Scarborough – York – Leeds (via Harrogate)

I awoke from a dream of Jericho. Some of the men had risked dismissal by defying the ganger. Resting their tools against the side of the trench they climbed onto the track that led back to the camp. Several posters had already been torn down by the younger boys who wanted them as souvenirs, and parson Edwards had wisely abandoned his sermon about turning the other cheek. Irish Leary would be no match for Black Jack, the mulatto from Doncaster. The men were drunk and the women loud.

The crowd funnelled its way between the huts onto a patch of hardened earth where shouts and taunts reached a crescendo as Jack, his skin glistening, stepped over the rope and flexed his muscles. Roared on by her peers, one of the women stepped forward and presented him with a lit clay pipe. He bit off the narrow stem, ostentatiously chewed it and spat the white bones onto the ground. He then placed the burning bowl in his mouth and made as if to swallow it. The crowd roared and ... John knocked loudly on my door.

People-watching on the concourse of Leeds station was irresistible and easy. With upwards of forty trains scheduled to leave within the hour, the human tide became a tsunami at the narrowest point. Sikhs in shades, hipsters in beards, a blind man following his stick with a rotating white ball at its point, Lycra-skinned cyclists, wheelchairs and at least two military moustaches. On the periphery, a couple argued, she in tears, he aggressively pointing. Leave him, you deserve better, it's not your fault.

Two lovers were parting as lovers should, in an achingly long embrace. A strikingly tall woman, wreathed in smiles, strode happily towards her train. A magician in a business suit pressed a button on his compact metal luggage whereupon it transformed itself into a fully-grown bike. Applause.

A large orange hand waddled into the tide. A pretty face emerged beneath the forefinger, and a hand from within the hand dispensed leaflets urging passengers to lend a helping hand that could take the form of 'stepping aside if there's a whole bunch of people trying to get off the train as you're getting on.'

We settled into the comparatively empty coach D on the

12

train to Doncaster. This was a great mistake as the guard's announcement made clear: 'Coach D is not working. Could passengers sitting in seats 9 – 72 please relocate to coach C where unfortunately the seat reservations are not functioning. Could passengers in coach B also move elsewhere on the train, avoiding seats 1 – 47 in coach E as the heating system has failed. Remember, Coach D is now a locked carriage.'

This last detail elicited a frisson of pleasure. Not since the days of the old Soviet Union had passengers been locked into a carriage. Eventually the guard, Nicola, broke in and ushered us into a clearly less secure carriage.

We stopped outside Wakefield Prison, a daunting Victorian building. Strange to think that we were only a matter of yards away from 740 inmates, many of whom may have been there since the original house of correction was built in 1594.

As the train seemed reluctant to depart I looked through the thick stone walls of the prison, down the length of B wing, through more doors and into the mess hall.

Michael paused at the counter with his tray. His rheumatism was bad today. In the stainless steel trough, the cabbage had been swept to one side like seaweed on a beach while the green water leeched and puddled unappetisingly. He listened to the distant sound as the diesel units dragged themselves out of the station.

'That's the 3.41 to York,' he said to the trustee who dolloped a wet pat of mashed potato onto his plate. 'Not to worry, better times ahead.'

'Better times ahead,' repeated the trustee, turning his attention to the next inmate.

Defoe shrank back into his seat. He had not enjoyed this last fictional diversion and was visibly distressed by the mention of prison.

By now our replacement carriage was so cold that

13

we anticipated the long-suffering Nicola returning with blankets and hot water bottles. We were still nursing our disappointment when we arrived once more in Doncaster.

Mindful of the advice contained in the Helping Hand leaflet, we stood back as passengers poured out of the train on the opposite platform. Despite our good manners and laudable caution, we were nearly flattened by an ugly phalanx of fat men all wearing T-shirts extolling the values of REAL BRITAIN and the Union Jack. 'Good to see people participating in political dialogue,' commented John.

> *'These are the heroes who despise the Dutch,*
> *And rail at new-come foreigners so much!*
> *Forgetting that themselves are all derived*
> *From the most scoundrel race that ever lived!*
> *A horrid crowd of rambling thieves and drones,*
> *Who ransacked kingdoms and dispeopled towns!'*

'Sometimes Danny Boy,' I said, 'I think you were ahead of your times.'

'It's from my minor masterpiece, *The True-born Englishman: A Satyr,* published in 1701.'

We had intended to travel directly to Cleethorpes but there were delays on the line as a passenger had been hit by a train. This was a more graphic description than is usually provided; normally the travelling public is only offered the euphemism of an 'incident.'

Defoe was looking particularly anxious again. The cockiness he had shown just moments earlier had vanished. He said that he didn't want to talk about it but I remembered a reference in his biography to moments of black despair when hounded by creditors. He acknowledged that he had sometimes considered 'desperate measures' and seemed eager to move the conversation on.

'I saw a sight not far from here. I was passing on the ridge of a hill when I looked down the frightful precipice, and saw no less than five horses in several places, lying at the bottom with their skins off, which had, by the slipperiness of the snow, lost their feet, and fallen irrecoverably to the bottom, where the mountaineers who made light of this place, had found means to come at them and get their hides off.'

My head filled with unwanted images of dead and flayed horses, my thoughts returned to the experience of the train driver who, too late, catches a fleeting glimpse of someone standing on the track.

He wakes in the night shouting and pushing hard on the brake handle that is in fact his wife's arm. 'Sorry,' he says. 'Sorry.'

On the train to Scunthorpe John treated me to a lecture on the resentment felt by commuters in the North East who believe that they are invariably the recipients of railway stock cast-offs. Allegedly, the affluent South sends its ancient and worn carriages northwards as they approach the end of their working life. This would explain the frequency with which we found ourselves in open top wagons, and why we could only leave certain trains by pulling on a leather strap to open the window, out of which we lean to turn the handle.

The landscape changed rapidly; the dales and moors belonged to a different country. The land itself had been reduced to an irrelevant ribbon beneath enormous skies. We crossed a canal that shrank into vanishing points on either side of the track. The sheer emptiness was alleviated only by the ubiquitous wind farms.

This too changed as we gradually entered a vista of urban decay with all colour leached from the canvas. Cooling towers lurched and pylons leant. Bulldozers scraped at the sides of spoil heaps and, yes, a rash of sewage farms was breaking out again. At least the day's *Guardian* cast some light on their proliferation. It has little to do with poor

15

eating habits and the related consequences of obesity and sewage production, rather it is a largely untapped source of wealth. Evidently sewage sludge contains gold, silver and platinum that would be seen as commercially viable by prospectors. Look before you flush.

'A manufacturing opportunity not to be scorned. I attempted something similar myself back in 1692. I knew money to be made from cats ...'

Despite my bemusement, I was glad that he was in better spirits.

'Cats. More specifically, their arses. As you know, the Dutch perfected making musk from the anal glands of civet cats. I spent £850 for the animals but sadly they were confiscated by my creditors.'

Mercifully, Defoe crept back into the book and pulled the pages over his head.

Wealth and poverty nudged against each other in Grimsby docks as collapsing fish warehouses overlooked the yachts in the marina, most of which presumably belonged to sewage millionaires.

We arrived in Cleethorpes, and gazed at the black and white photos taken with a Brownie and neatly slotted into an album. One showed steam locomotives with their excursion trains queuing outside the station. Although a little out of focus, another captured an entire beach colonised by families sheltering behind hired deckchairs and improvised windbreaks. Excited kids were bailing out the North Sea using enamelled buckets, while their parents discussed the cost of ice cream and when it would be safe to return to the B & B.

The sun was shining and several arcades were open. I gifted John a heap of coppers so that we could both play on the Penny Falls. He beat me, the bugger. The pain of my defeat was made more palatable by the *Batman* theme and *Oh I Do Like to be Beside the Seaside*.

In the café where we had our lunch, a woman shared with us the medical history of her dog who seemed unnaturally interested in John's leg, 'He's got a hole in his skull. It affects his spine. He's on medication.'

As we left Cleethorpes for Barton-on-Humber well-wishers lined up at the level crossing as if we were a liberating army, or John was the Pope. The comparison reminded me that when at University, John had frequently written to both the Pope and the Queen offering them advice on a variety of topics.

'A vomit of popery!' declared Defoe for whom the reference to Catholicism had been a provocation too far.

'What a terrible phrase. We have moved on you know.'

'The image is central to my much-lauded reasons against the Succession of the House of Hanover.'

As the train consisted of a single carriage, we couldn't escape the inordinately loud woman proudly descended from a long line of town criers. She regaled her deafened companion with her views on MRI scans (she didn't see the point), mortgages (quite ridiculous) and as for council tax... plus every other trivial topic under the sun. Eventually her friend left, quite possibly to drown herself in the toilet.

John was asleep but Defoe was shaking his head. 'What's the matter?' I asked.

'You are an eavesdropper plundering words not meant for your ears. Go and talk to these agreeable travellers.' He nodded in the direction of a middle-aged couple sitting along one side of a table.

I didn't think very much of being ordered about by a Figment, but grudgingly sat opposite them. After my hesitant introduction, the man declared that he had always wanted to write a book. 'This could be the next best thing,' I suggested.

'I'm a rat catcher. A pest controller if you like, but I've seen it all. And it's not just rats. Squirrels is worse. How do you kill them? That is the question.'

17

I quite liked this surreal adaptation of Hamlet.

'Squirrel traps don't work, although I've had success with a feral cat-trap baited with peanut butter. The textbook says to shoot them between the eyes. Thing is, I can't bring myself to kill them at all. I take them miles into the country and release them. I got an emergency call out once, and was surprised to see an ambulance had got to this man's house before me. The owner had managed to catch the rat between a curtain and the lining. Of course, the rat sunk its teeth into the man's hand and he was bleeding his life away. The social services called me out to see an old man who had suffered a heart attack. Thing was, he was shimmering with bed bugs and the paramedics wouldn't intervene until they had been given protective suits. After they moved the old fellow out, they found thousands of infested bank notes.'

I felt increasingly queasy but it was his wife who excused herself first and ran to the toilet. I would have assumed that she was immune to her husband's horror tales.

'A landlord called me out to investigate the smell in his flat. These students had grown so fond of the rats in their kitchen, they encouraged them as pets and fed them bread. Another flat was a foot deep with pigeon shit in which the rats lived ... I met this family whose flat was piled to the celling with black sacks of rubbish. In the sitting room they had cleared a square metre which they shared with a huge flat-screened TV. Social services had no idea as the small boy was dressed and cleaned by his granny every day before being sent to school. As for cockroaches ...'

I held up my phone and shrugged, trying hard to imply that I had to take an urgent call and returned to my seat. By now Defoe was shaking with mirth.

'Rats are not the only carriers of plague. If I can quote you a passage from the orders Concerning Infected Houses and persons Sick from the Plague, issued in 1666 ...'

'If you must.'

' ...no hogs, dogs, or cats, or tame pigeons, or conies, be suffered to be kept in any part of the city, the owners will be punished according to the act of Common Council and that the dogs be killed by the dog-killers appointed for that purpose...'

I thought of asking what a conie was, and I was intrigued by the notion of dog killers, but on balance thought it best not to engage with him further.

As we skirted a string of lagoons John supplied the unwanted information that New Holland was the home of the combine harvester. I think he had too much excitement at the arcade. I did my best to calm him before wondering idly if Hull Paragon Station would live up to its name. It didn't.

Defoe interjected a bizarre fact of his own. 'They show us still in the town hall at Hull, the figure of a northern fisherman, supposed to be of Greenland. He was taken up at sea in a leather boat, which he sate in, and was covered with skins, which drew together about his waist, so that the boat could not fill and he could not sink; the creature would never feed nor speak, and so died.'

I was lost for words and wanted more than anything to go home. What had I done to deserve the travelling companions from hell? Deciding to ignore them, I concentrated on the sky, where cloud formations swept like retreating armies over the horizon. The foremost tumbling angrily, punching holes in a timid firmament. At ground level the puffy cumulus offered only token resistance. The smoke from their cannons hovered innocuously.

Refreshed by this small change to my consciousness, I turned my attention once more to what was happening inside the carriage. The elderly woman in the seat opposite laid out an entire winning hand of train tickets accumulated over a lifetime of travel.

'It's here somewhere,' she said. Baulking at the challenge

of sorting through the trove of eclectic railway memorabilia, the guard promised to return, but didn't. The woman smiled knowingly.

What she had failed to notice was that her male companion might well have shuffled off this mortal coil. He was certainly a strange colour. I did wonder what the protocol was if a passenger died when in transit, in *sic transit gloria mundi* in fact. Perhaps he would be discreetly draped in a Northern Rail tea towel until the next station.

Our carriage stopped in Seamer Station opposite a poster introducing us to Dave, who was our stationmaster for the duration of our sojourn in his kingdom. He seemed avuncular but with a demeanour tinged with melancholy; someone to whom one could turn in a crisis.

At the very end of the platform was a small plantation of gnomes and a rabbit. Outside, a solitary Clydesdale horse plodded through the rain.

Defoe put down the copy of the *Review* he was working on as we approached Scarborough to pass comment on the local mineral waters.

'It is hard to describe their taste, they are apparently tinged with a collection of mineral salts, as of vitriol, alum, iron, and perhaps sulphur ... Here is such a plenty of all sorts of fish that I have hardly seen the like, and in particular, here we saw turbots of three quarters of a hundred weight, and yet their flesh eat exceedingly well when taken new.'

Perhaps a fish supper later then.

The most disturbing image from the Scarborough to York train was of a man standing in the middle of a field digging a large hole while his dog stood patiently by. Mercifully the train would be out of sight when he chose to strike his faithful but incontinent pet round the head with a shovel and tumble him into his grave.

This unwelcome interpretation stayed with me. Of

course, I may have misread the situation; perhaps the spade was in fact a metal detector and the dog was his best friend. But in my head I heard the man explaining to his friend in the pub what had happened.

'I almost did it. I almost killed him. I felt such anger. But I couldn't do it. I hate the way he pisses on the floor. My slippers were soaked again this morning. But it's not just that. He reminds me of Maude. She loved that dog more than me. She used to talk to him about me. Can you believe that? She would speak in this stupid wheedling confiding way as if the bloody dog was on her side. She would tickle him under the chin. "I deserve better, don't you think?" Why didn't she take him when she left? It makes no sense. Anyway, I took a shovel, to bury him like, after. But I couldn't do it. I couldn't do it. What's that? Yes, thanks, I'll take another pint.'

Having been dozing for several hours, John rallied and unhelpfully decided to deliver a brief lecture on the history of York Minster. 'It caught fire in 741,' he boomed. 'Was damaged by William the Conqueror in 1069, attacked during the Civil War, was subject to an arson attack in 1829, caught fire again in 1840, and was struck by lightning in 1984.'

Defoe covered his ears. 'No more fires, I beseech you.'

Completely unaware of Defoe's presence, John droned on. 'The deeply pious believed the latest fire was God's response to the consecration of the Bishop of Durham whose heretical views included doubt about the physical resurrection of Christ. *Yea, the clouds parted and a vengeful God sent down his lightning bolt proclaiming "don't you dare refer to me as a sky pixie! Take that, you resurrection-denying bastard!"*'

Defoe sat bolt upright and pointed an admonitory finger in my direction. 'No,' I said. 'I know that as a protestant dissenter you have strong opinions on these matters, but frankly, I don't want to hear them. Back into your book!'

Mercifully, he went.

In York Station we were subjected to numerous exhortations to keep an eye open for thieves who apparently steal £43m worth of cabling each year. The York — Harrogate Pacer set out in the dusk. Defoe glanced at a particularly unfortunate pair of lads further down the carriage. 'Lepers,' he pronounced.

'I don't think so.'

'Take my word for it. There's a monastery near here that takes them in. Each leper is given two pairs of shoes yearly, with every day a loaf fit for a poor man's sustenance, half a pitcher of beer, a sufficient portion of flesh on flesh days, and three herrings on fish days.'

'Put my name down.'

Clearly pleased with himself, Defoe closed his eyes. He wasn't the only one. All of my fellow passengers, including John, were fast asleep. Every carriage holds one or two narcoleptics nursing hangovers or grudges against the rigours of the day, but this was unusual. Perhaps the smell seeping from the toilet had its origins in a small vial of sleeping gas. Ruefully, I remembered reading how, in some parts of Europe, thieves spray incapacitating agents on campers and train travellers. It is possible in these countries to purchase alarms that detect such perfidy.

After our flirtation with death by poisoning, we were sorely tempted by the equally fatal attraction of the Harrogate Tap, an undeniably superior station bar with its promise of '14 traditional cask hand pulls and 14 continental swing-handled taps set against a backdrop of over 150 different bottled world beers'. Defoe too was salivating and kept mentioning 'Northern beer'.

'But you're a puritan,' I said.

'We abhor drunkenness,' he said, 'but in our view of the world, alcohol is neither a social or moral evil.'

'Fair play.'

DAY THREE

*Leeds – Sheffield – Gainsborough Lea Road –
Wakefield – Huddersfield – Bradford – Doncaster –
York – Leeds – Barnsley – Leeds*

Deja vu, *Groundhog Day*, or more appropriately, *Sliding Doors* saw us back on Leeds Station concourse at the crack of dawn, where a lone fisherman swam against the tide with sheathed rod, thermos flask and welly boots, oblivious to the looks of envy from peers still ten years from retirement.

John looked up from his paper to observe that the Naked Rambler had lost another appeal. A pity, it would have been great fun to have spied him at some point on our journey, bearded and resolute, genitalia swinging free, amusing children and frightening their parents.

The sun was shining, the canals sparkled. All was well with the world and God was, or maybe wasn't, in his heaven. In the circumstances, I was almost prepared to give Him the benefit of the doubt. The towpaths were crowded with joggers eager for vitamin D.

Both the train, littered with crumpled Metros, and its aged conductor were recovering from the rush hour. Without doubt the oldest employee on Network Rail that we had so far encountered, he was beyond ancient, and prompted the notion of a direct correlation between the age of the rolling stock and guards. Quite simply they grow old together and get scrapped together.

We passed through a station called Outward which, if nothing else, showed a singular lack of imagination.

A large bank of cloud had its origin in the twin towers of a power station.

A wheelie bin served as a wicket on a cricket pitch outside Bolton-on-Dearne.

The train doors initially refused to open at Swinton. Perhaps the town was already full and visitors were to be restricted, as happens in the Lake District during bank holidays. 'Never mind, another time,' suggested a stoical father, consoling his large family for whom this trip was to be the reward for much scrimping and saving.

At least 100 swans jostled for position on a canal basin outside Rotherham. The trees in the adjacent orchard were heavy with a crop of poly bags.

Sheffield station deserves its place among the top ten holiday destinations on the planet, having cultivated a niche function in attracting impoverished musicians. *This piano has been provided for customer use. Please respect this facility.* A young black lad, his trousers at lower buttock level, improvised a jazz tune which he then dedicated, with moist eyes, to all commuters everywhere.

In the car park known as Sheaf Square I wondered at the stainless steel curtain of water raised on the site of Pond Tilt forge. Several hot commuters stripped off, piled their clothes neatly on the concourse and ran happily into the cascade.

Meanwhile John had struck up a promising relationship with the woman in the coffee kiosk. I listened from the side lines as she tried to describe the excitement she felt at the prospect of the Queen's visit the following week. 'I don't suppose she would want a coffee, but you never know. She looks more a tea drinker. Perhaps the Duke would take a flat white. I would happily accept Maundy money, after all I take euros. And, come to think of it, my feet could do with a good wash ...'

'I met them all,' said Defoe.

'Who are you talking about?'

'Kings and queens. I had the honour to serve, and if I may say it with humblest acknowledgements, to be beloved by that glorious prince, William III. I was subsequently presented to Queen Mary at Kensington Palace.'

I made the mistake of approaching a woman who was raising money for guide dogs, and who smiled at me conspiratorially. I told her that recently my younger son had been so impressed by how a guide dog managed to steer its owner across a particularly wet and treacherous floor in the toilet of a Glasgow pub, that he was thinking of making a contribution to the cause.

'That's all very well,' she countered brusquely. 'But what about you? You have to lead your own life. You can't live vicariously through your son. What can you contribute?'

This is what psycho-dynamic psychotherapists do in their spare time. When I expressed a small reluctance to sign a direct debit form she treated me as if I were a puppy-strangler with a sneering attitude towards the visually impaired. I wished her well and, riddled with guilt, joined John and Daniel on the platform.

'This town of Sheffield is very populous and large, the streets narrow, and the houses dark and black, occasioned by the continued smoke of the forges, which are always at work. Here they make all sorts of cutlery-ware, but especially that of edged-tools, knives, razors et cetera – and nails...'

The Sheffield to Lincoln train itself was at the forefront of a national experiment in suspension-free travel and a vigilant and attentive team of osteopaths, chiropractors and Indian head masseurs were in attendance, or should have been. A line from David Nobbs' description of Reggie Perrin came to mind. 'The shaking caused his socks to fall down his ankles.'

A large sign at Kiveton Bridge urged us to 'beware of hazards at platform edge.' Had the notice not been there, few passengers would have thought of approaching the edge. Curiosity combined with a collective death wish compelled otherwise cautious travellers to approach and marvel at the terrible things to be seen down there. Am I the only person

25

ever to have wondered if a train would pass over me if I were to lie between the tracks? Evidently not judging by the correspondence that can be accessed on the subject via Google. Apparently, the one marginally relevant specification is that a train's axles must clear the top of the rails by at least two and three quarter inches, so theoretically ...

The train continued to buckle and lurch, distracting us from the looming nightmare of satanic coal-fired power stations.

A field of geriatric horses invited conflicting interpretations. Either a soft-hearted philanthropist had sunk his savings into a benign sanctuary for clapped out old nags, or a sharp young entrepreneur was greedily catering for the equine tastes of French diners.

'Shame!' shouted Defoe. 'How dextrous the northern grooms and breeders are in their looking after them ...these fellows take such indefatigable pains with them, that they bring them out, like pictures of horses, not a hair amiss ...'

'I don't think we are looking at the same horses,' I said.

A series of totally incomprehensible announcements from the guard led to John's suggestion that the same garbled message had been introduced into all trains to cover all contingencies and all possible destinations as a time and money saving stratagem. An idea not to be dismissed out of hand.

For reasons I don't understand, the network of canals with their floating industrial froth and cargoes of rusty trikes and drowned prams were a source of comfort to me. Hidden, neglected, melancholic, both ugly and beautiful, they are an abiding, somehow haunting, feature of the North East.

Equally neglected was the set of false teeth found under the bench on Gainsborough Lee Road station. More accurately it was a plate containing two teeth. A solitary traveller, who denied that the teeth were his, spent his days crossing the realm delivering cars with trade plates. He really wanted to

26

open a microbrewery in Tenerife, and suggested our next journey should cover the entire Indian network.

'I'll tell you something,' he said leaning forward conspiratorially, 'My wife had a terrible experience of toilets on a twelve-hour journey from Luxor to Cairo ...' He tapped his nose knowingly, an enigmatic gesture hinting at horrors beyond words.

As we entered Doncaster again, the trainspotters were out in force. I determined not to pass up this second opportunity to resolve the mystery of why they do it? I put aside my natural shyness and approached a particularly animated knot of men in their late fifties.

'Is something good expected?'

'No.'

'There does seem a lot of you today.'

'Yes.'

'Have you had this interest for a long time?'

'Yes.'

'You must like trains.'

'Yes.'

'I pressed the wrong button!' said one of the fifty-year-old spotters staring at the Dictaphone into which he had been solemnly intoning the numbers of each passing freight wagon. He was consoled by a friend who expressed sympathy for his loss.

So ended my pathetic attempt to unravel the mystery. John snorted at my failure.

In the bleak underpass linking the platforms I bought a flower from a sad elderly woman dressed as a daffodil. She was collecting for the Marie Curie cancer charity, and only had another two and a half hours of daffodil duty. When she smiled at me I felt I had made reparation for the guide dog incident.

A sign in the doorway of the Wakefield train instructed

27

us 'Not to bring more luggage than we could carry.' Disappointed, we left the cabin trunk, wood burning stove and the set of human sized chessmen on the platform. This hint of overprotectiveness found its echo in a subsequent request to 'bring to the attention of the conductor anything that caused you concern'.

I had a good mind to have a word with him about the African nun sitting smugly next to a large poly bag advertising a menswear shop. Why had she purchased yet another jumper for the bishop?

Equally concerning was the fact that the train was equipped with a carefully stowed wooden ladder. For what possible contingency? It could be laid across the top of a snowdrift while frozen passengers pulled themselves to safety one rung at a time, or perhaps the conductor had a side line in window cleaning. 'Sorry madam, my train is parked at the bottom of your garden and I couldn't help noticing the state of your bedroom windows...'

Huddersfield railway station almost rivals Sheffield for its unexpected sense of style. Its car park opens onto a square that makes it a contender for the annual Piazza del Campo award. Indeed, several horses were being ridden bareback at considerable speed past KFC.

'Where? Where?' asked Defoe craning his neck to get a better view of the concourse.

'Look,' I said. 'Sometimes I make things up. I mix fact with invented nonsense.'

'The delineation between what is observable and the fruits of your odd imagination should be clearer.'

'Look, whose book is this?'

'I suggest Sir, you look again at the title that you have chosen for your narrative.' He smiled smugly.

Deciding I did not need further critical advice from a Figment, I sought refuge in The Kings Head on Platform 4. The station bar is worth a visit if only to catch sight of its principal resident, a late middle-aged punk sporting a purple Mohican, tartan trousers, huge boots and a camouflage jacket.

Having time to spare I tapped Mohican into my phone, choosing not to dwell on the website that announced itself with *Fuck you: A Brief History of the Mohawk*. Good though to see the colon used correctly.

'The Mohocks belong to my century!' said Defoe.

'You're welcome to them.'

'A gang of these violent gentlemen once put an old woman into a hogshead, and rolled her down a hill; they cut off some noses, others' hands, and several barbarous tricks...'

As we approached Halifax, he asked, 'Do they still execute the cloth thieves here?'

'What?'

'If we're quick we could go and view the mechanically operated axe... The custom prevails here that if the criminal can snatch his head off the block after the executioner has pulled the pin, jump off the scaffold, run down the hill, and cross the river before the executioner can catch him, he is a free man.'

'Is that right?'

'Yes, but they showed me the scaffold and the force of the engine is so strong, the head of the axe being loaded with a weight of lead to make it fall heavy, and the execution is so sure, that it takes away all possibility of its failing to cut off the head.'

I was lost for words.

'The Halifax people tell you another story of a country woman who was riding by upon her hampers to Halifax market, for the execution was always on a market day and passing just as the axe was about to fall upon the neck of the criminal, it chopped through it with such force, that the head jumped off into one of the hampers. The woman, not perceiving it, carried it away to the market!'

He slapped his thighs and roared with laughter. Ignoring him, I stared out of the window.

A Vulcan eyebrowed Station Manager threatened us with his brooding presence at several points on the line back into Sheffield. Arguably he would be better employed clearing the rubbish from the embankments on his patch. Furthermore, Brockholes station provides evidence that his hobby is getting in the way of his many duties. An indulgent line of Olde Worlde enamel signs are bolted to the station fence: Colman's Starch competes with Spratt's Ovaltine and Lyon's Chicory Extract.

An anxious looking woman asked if we would keep an eye on her daughter while she went to the toilet. Her initial failure to return seemed to confirm our fear that she had alighted at Penistone leaving John and me with an unwanted child.

Which one of us would bring it up? I had four already and didn't want any more. There was no point asking Defoe who, despite his eight children, wasn't renowned for his parenting skills. John on the other hand was a lonely bachelor with a large, if empty home. Mercifully, the mother returned. I'm sure I saw a flicker of disappointment cross John's brow.

The delightfully named Wombwell Station made me wonder if my by-now heavily pregnant daughter-in-law had yet given birth to my first grandson.

John and I, along with every other passenger in the carriage, had no alternative but to eavesdrop on a one-way phone conversation being conducted by a distressed woman in her late twenties. She had just discovered that her partner had been unfaithful, and howled in anguish while her fellow travellers squirmed, feigned interest in the passing scenery, reread newspapers or hunted in briefcases and handbags. In short, indulged in any activity that would serve to distance themselves from the pain and trauma flooding down the aisle.

'I'll get my solicitor to sort her out. Fucking cow. He'll have to find a new wife. I'm not putting up with this.'

Through the dusk I caught sight of a small boy wandering on his own down a canal towpath. Go home small boy, be safe.

DAY FOUR
Leeds – Darlington – Bishop Auckland – Saltburn
– Middlesbrough – Whitby – Middlesbrough –
Newcastle – Whitley Bay

I am feeling sorry for myself, this is a silly venture. A nonsense. Another day of anonymous trains climaxed by another night in an indifferent B & B, but John still seems up for it. Several of yesterday's images are still with me. Had the woman been reconciled with her errant spouse? I doubted it. Was the woman in the kiosk even more excited as the Queen's visit was a day closer? I hoped so.

My spirits took a turn for the better soon after joining the 9.05 Leeds to Darlington. The moonfaced guard was goodness and enthusiasm personified. His bedside manner was exemplary as he explained the meaning of RESERVED, without a hint of irony or rancour, to an elderly couple, before wishing them the happiest of onward journeys. He told us of his unconditional love of railways and all who travel on them before being distracted by a stooped female scarecrow in a headscarf, apparently frozen in mid stride at the edge of a field.

Our musings were interrupted by a garrulous catering manager as he described the delights on offer; the finest *pain au raisin* available this side of Paris. His was not a buffet car, more a travelling gourmet delicatessen.

John broke the news that the entire *raison d'etre* of our pilgrimage had been compromised by his decision not to travel on the line to Brigg. My hyperventilation was assuaged by the information that the line was only served by one train a week. Evidently it is cheaper in some instances to keep uneconomic lines open by running the occasional phantom train than to resort to closure. He was forgiven.

In a field a man, flanked by two dogs, stood to attention and saluted with a solemnity last evinced by the passing of Winston Churchill's funeral train through the Oxfordshire countryside in 1965. He may of course have been shielding his eyes from the sun.

My heart did manage a small leap when we passed Shildon Railway Museum, and I suppose this is as good a time as any for a small disclosure; yes, Dear Reader, many, many decades ago, I too was a trainspotter. So, for the benefit of anyone similarly afflicted and who has been living a lie since the demise of steam, the locomotives on display were 13079, 69023 and 65033.

Shildon Station is adorned, if that is the best word, with massive tin reproductions of saucy postcards from the 1950s. This explains why Benny Hill was waiting on the platform. Buttocks and beach balls, bosoms and pearly white teeth assault the innocent traveller who is obliged to answer the question, 'Does my bum look big in this?'

I felt that if I had further cause for confessions, Sarah, the new custodian of all stations on this particular route, would be the woman. She seemed much more sympathetic than either Cliff or Dave.

John explained that we were now travelling over the route of the original Stockton–Darlington railway, hence the proliferation of stovepipe hats, and the festoons of bunting and demure cheering from the crowds assembled alongside the track.

Any indulgent nostalgic reverie was interrupted by my proximity to the tattooed calf of a passenger struggling to place his cargo of offensive weapons in the overhead rack. He had made a lifestyle choice that required him to conscientiously fatten his calves until they were wide enough to provide a pair of canvases for the depiction of the two things he loved most: a bulldog and the Virgin Mary. On closer, if unwanted, inspection the image on his left leg may have been of the other, better known, Madonna.

'Do your duty,' said Defoe who was becoming annoyed at my apparent reluctance to talk to other passengers. 'How, pray, will you manage to deliberate on the true state of the nation if you do not engage with your fellow travellers?'

As I was musing on his implied reproach, the train lurched or, more accurately, given the culture of rugby league, executed a perfect side step. This movement also served to explain why the overhead racks were confined to one side of the carriage, at a stroke the risk of collateral damage was reduced by half.

I have never seen a landscape so unremittingly bleak as that which enfolds Middlesbrough. I was unprepared for the scale of urban devastation that breathed new life into the cliché of a scarred landscape.

The prevailing colour was again grey, shot through with the faded ochre of rust as old dried blood dribbled into the grime; a legacy of long past crimes perpetrated by familiar political names. The earth had been scorched by the retreat of both capitalism and pride.

The disembowelled innards of old rolling stock lay next to the track; the result of pragmatic cannibalism by engineers. A flyover to nowhere had been turned into a vast canvas for graffiti artists. Perhaps scrawling your moniker in metre-high garish letters is as much a nod to posterity as this page. Low brick walls marking the outline of demolished buildings were reminiscent of Highland crofts. Above it all stood the blue Transporter Bridge; a metal Triffid straddling the Tees, more beautiful in its own way than its near cousin, the Angel of the North.

The backcloth to South Bank station consists of gasometers, pylons, cranes, silos, scrap coking ovens and snaking pipe intestines all coated in a miasma that is part haze, part smell. A tiny methane pipe pokes its head out of the rounded buttocks of sculptured landfill mounds. The horizon has been replaced by a distant Legoland of multi-coloured containers.

The train slowed to enable us to stare at the random configuration of interlinked cooling lagoons and toxic wasteland that has been arbitrarily, and ironically, rebranded as the Coatham March nature reserve.

Ostensibly a grotty patch of weeds and dampness, subsequent research revealed that the mounds of furnace slag are apparently a fecund habitat for exotic grasses such as marsh orchids, bee orchids, yellow rattle, eyebright and knapweed. Furthermore, had we paid due attention, we would have noticed that the muddy patch of neglect was in fact teeming with foxes and stoats. It was, when all was said and done, a psychedelic sanctuary to all of the flowers and small smiling creatures dreamed of by Disney Associates and Saint Francis of Assisi.

We had, however, passed by blind and oblivious.

At Saltburn the coast is glimpsed at the end of each neat terraced street. John reminisced gloomily about the impoverished legions of coal pickers who still frequent the same coast; bent double putting compacted black dust into sacks.

'They follow the moon,' he said. 'They're dependant on low tides. They still collect 10,000 tons a year from the beaches around Hartlepool.'

On the return journey to Middlesbrough we are both struck by the wide-eyed delight of the toddler whose hair was caught up in the wind from the open door. She gazed with awestruck disbelief at the giants boarding the train. It was a haunting cameo of innocent rapture.

Hold fast the gentle wonder
With which you met the gusting wind
On a forgotten train.
Fix all travellers you later meet
With those wide brown eyes,
Listen to their tales,
But only give to the very best
Your heart.

Defoe harrumphed. 'An average effort,' he said. 'Poetry was but one of my many gifts. Let me read to you from the *Hymn to the Pillory*.'

'A kind offer, but no need.'

The Travellers Rest café on Middlesbrough station more than lives up to its name. The young proprietor delighted in describing how an upstairs room has been untouched for a century and still holds ledgers and top hats coated in a patina of snuff from a tribe of Victorian travellers. Sadly, when asked if we can peer into this time warp, he explained that the station authorities have now barred all access.

We did though witness on Platform 3 a powerful manifestation of customer attentiveness. Two workmen, carrying a large wooden bench between them, seemed to be following an elderly couple in case they wished to sit down.

The journey to Whitby through the Esk valley offers a poignant contrast to the dystopian approach to Middlesbrough. After the driver collected his single line token, we were progressively sucked into an Arcadian idyll.

At Battersby the train displayed the endearing characteristics of an absent-minded uncle and changed its mind about its preferred direction of travel, moving so slowly and serenely through its rural pageant that we were overtaken by a tractor toiling in a field. The leisurely pace enabled full appreciation of several ancient churches and woodlands.

Unfortunately, the serenity was slightly compromised by a dead sheep upside down and spread eagled in a stream.

John volunteered the information that, when a student, he had been employed to kill 1500 male chicks a day. In addition to this daily routine of casual genocide he was also required, by way of respite, to scrape the belly fat from the carcasses of dead pigs. Sometimes this journey really didn't seem a good idea.

Whitby confirmed the impressions I had formed from various gothic prints. The abbey was impressively gloomy. Dracula was strutting his stuff. All of the residents were crouched over small benches, busily carving tiny black locomotives from coal to sell to the tourists. The sign on the harbour wall urged me to report anything unusual I might see on the water. I did wonder what had been reported in the past; dead mermaids, strangled swans, mysterious dancing lights...

The train back to Middlesbrough was ransacked by hordes of schoolchildren all of whom wore their diagnoses of ADHD with immense pride. Squawking and cavorting, they clambered their way over the seats. Homework diaries, phones, E numbers and expletives were bartered by the younger kids while the sixth form boys and their partners snogged happily.

A notice at the back of the carriage held out the seductive possibility of being able to travel on the Whitby 'Music and Ale' train for only £7.40. A bargain, surely.

By dint of a design quirk, the configuration of the seating on the train to Newcastle meant that we sat facing all of the other passengers who were conveniently arranged for our inspection in serried rows. They were staring expectantly at us. What did they want: a speech, a sermon, a poem perhaps?

'I can oblige with all of these,' declared Defoe with an unwanted enthusiasm. 'I am in mind to deliver a section

36

from the original *Power of the Collective Body of the People of England ...*'

'Sit down and shut up!'

I thought of facilitating a discussion about which of our fellow travellers had had the worst day. All of them looked as if they had been ground down by whatever satanic mill, unforgiving office desk or shop counter they had just left.

The beadle in the front row, Mr Bumble's brother, was angrily tapping his stick against the floor. Best to avoid eye contact. I thought that the nice black woman in the second row was smiling at me, but I was probably just hankering for love and comfort after being trapped in John's company. Three of the audience were now asleep, but unfortunately not the two obvious troublemakers at the back. Someone was reading Dan Brown. Unforgivable. As the pacer gathered speed, the whole audience swung to the right, and then to the left.

As the day faded, two figures and a dog were silhouetted against the setting sun atop a coal-spoil heap.

A young woman standing up at the end of the carriage, despite the availability of seats, bellowed into her phone. 'Of course I had to see her. She was having an operation for f**** sake!' The whole carriage listened and empathised. Had her friend been in an accident? Was her illness life threatening? Was this surgery her last chance?

'She was having her nipples pierced! You don't want to go through that on your own do you?'

Defoe looked confused but I waved a finger in case he was thinking of asking any questions, and drew his attention instead to the masts of a tall ship, visible above the monkey-hanging houses of Hartlepool. Somewhere near the harbour, a tiny frightened creature in chains was about to meet its fate, having been identified as a perfidious Frenchman by the paranoid and not well-travelled burghers.

I regretted that our schedule prohibited us from visiting

the Rat Race pub on Hartlepool station where the lugu-
brious barman emerges from a trapdoor; where the table
corners are marked with double yellow lines to prevent the
parking of bums; and where the beers are only ever referred
to as 1, 2, or 3.

At an outlying station, eight cyclists who had sought
asylum after the English leg of the Tour de France slumped
onto the train, blocking all corridors and access points. A
trip to the toilet was no longer an option.

Having been ushered off the train at the next station by
the xenophobic guard, their places were taken by a team of
powerful drinkers for whom Thursday had become the new
Friday and the start of the weekend. The clanking of bottles
in Safeway bags sounded like discordant wind chimes. As if
expecting trouble, the train manager prowled armed with a
purple staple gun, fully prepared to treat stab wounds once
the fighting broke out.

I received a welcome text message telling me that my
daughter-in-law was going into labour.

DAY FIVE

Whitley Bay – Newcastle – Durham – Glasgow

Peering out of my lodging house window in Whitley Bay,
I realised that we had made the wrong choice. By way of
mitigation, we were tired and it was dark. The premises on
the other side of the street proudly announced 'B & B £15 +
Free pint daily.' It was the triumphant position of the word
'daily' that impressed me. The proprietor had a future in
advertising. How soon could you claim the free beverage?
At one minute past midnight? Could it be a breakfast pint on
the morning of departure? So many unanswered questions.

I found it difficult to concentrate in the waiting room
on Whitley Bay station. My grandson had been born at 6

o'clock that morning and I just wanted to get home. The railway staff waved their flags and blew their whistles. A samba band emerged from the gents and celebrated his birth. As the first part of my journey was ending, his was beginning. Good luck to us both.

'One of my children died when I was in Newgate prison,' said Defoe, who had been surprisingly quiet up until this point. When the time was right I would probe him about his incarceration, but now wasn't the time.

'I paid them scant attention. Too much business. Too much commerce. Relations with my wife were not easy. She was a scold, but not without cause. I had such schemes; I imported tobacco from Maryland, I sold beer and wine to Belfast. And of course, there was the disaster with the cats...'

He put his head in his hands and I moved to comfort him but he waved me aside.

'I had a share in a ship which was taken by privateers. I am mindful that I should have persevered with selling hosiery. It was a good market but it was too safe. I worshipped the goddess Chance. I invested £200 in a diving bell. There was treasure on the sea floor, and I knew we would find it. I had to keep moving. Do you understand? I travelled the realm for trade. I knew every byway. I supped at every inn. People told me their tales. And then I travelled for the king. I was his ears. I was his eyes... He looked immeasurably sad. 'But I hope your grandson thrives. May God bless him.'

JOURNEY TWO

The East Midlands and East Anglia

DAY ONE

Glasgow Queen Street – Edinburgh Waverley – York –
Doncaster – Grimsby – Lincoln – Sleaford – Skegness

Who could resist a foray into the land which produces twenty-five per cent of the United Kingdom's cement? The land which produced Isaac Newton, Silicone, antifungal medicine, the Bakewell Tart, the pork pie, Ladybird Books, the stocking frame, the jet engine, traffic lights, the tarmac road, Corgi toys, Triumph Motorcycles, Doc Martens, Fox's Glacier Mints, Saxa salt, Bisto, half of M & S's sandwiches and most of Tesco's ready meals.

Although a little confused by some of the details in this list, Daniel Defoe rubbed his hands with glee. 'Trade,' he said. ''Tis trade that makes a nation great.' I hoped he wasn't going to be too irritating on this trip.

'Dyers wares, Wine, Oil, Hemp flax, Stockings, Wool, lead, Axes, Bone lace, Straw hats, Block tin, nails ...'

'Look,' I said, 'This is not a manufacturing competition between the 18th and 21st centuries.' Defoe, judging by his smug expression, thought he had come out on top.

A surreal display on Waverley station informed us that the average locomotive weighs 400 tons or the equivalent of eighty elephants. This was a comparison I could savour. Indian or African? Big or small ears? How long would it take an elephant hauled train to complete the journey from Edinburgh to Grimsby? What if it got bored and wandered off the track into the nearest housing estate, dragging its carriages in its wake? Evidently an elephant can eat 330lbs a day. I'm not certain your average buffet car could oblige.

The start of our journey south was beneath clear blue skies, and while we all know that skies may not always be blue, the weather cheered our spirits. The colour chart included fluorescent yellow as we passed fields of rapeseed. The accumulative effect was akin to viewing the world through the psychedelic wrapping that used to mark bottles of Lucozade out from its rivals.

Gradually the intimations of euphoria faded and were replaced by an insidious, dumbing sense of blandness. Clouds crept in by stealth, and the carriage turned dark as those passengers who had pulled the blinds down couldn't be bothered hoisting them upwards again.

What landscape we could glimpse had been stripped of all visual distractions. There was not so much as a flailing scarecrow to catch the eye. The east coast horizon lacked definition, and no longer served as a point of demarcation between sky and sea.

'But where is the dung?'

'Pardon?'

'The greatest thing this country wants is more enclosed pastures, by which the farmers would keep stocks of cattle well foddered in the winter, and would, by the quality of their dung, enrich their soil.'

'You're probably right.'

I turned my attention to John but he was still absorbed in

41

the morning papers and didn't welcome being interrupted. It was going to be a long day.

Almost every person on the train had thin white wires trailing from their ears; small electronic worms that filled their brains with music or the soundtrack from whatever film they were watching on their laptops. This was either transcendent or life-denying, I couldn't decide which.

Others, mainly men, were using their portion of the communal table as travelling office space, every available square inch colonised by their computer, phone, papers, coffee cup and pens. I found myself looking for the do-not-disturb signs. However, all of my fellow travellers had made their choice and I was extremely reluctant to yank any one of them back from their private or business worlds to engage with me.

'But what is their trade? We must discover how they make their fortunes.'

'No, we don't.'

To distract myself from the thought that I would never again find someone willing to talk to me, I even briefly considered reading the passenger safety leaflet which-can-be-found-at-the-end-of-every-carriage according to one of the more intelligible tannoy announcements. On reflection that seemed a step too far. After all, how many accidents have occurred on this particular route? Intermittent internet access provided an answer of sorts. In 1870 a wheel disinte-grated causing a derailment that killed six passengers and two bystanders; in 1876 the Flying Scotsman crashed during a blizzard; in 1892 'the signalman forgot about a goods train standing at his box and accepted the Scotch Express onto his line with inevitable consequences.' I decided that the secret would be to survive this particular leg of the journey and resume my mission once we joined the smaller lines.

The Grimsby to Lincoln single carriage train was manifestly unwell; it wheezed and stuttered across the flat countryside.

At any moment it might shake itself off the rails in a fit of coughing, or expectorate horribly at passing cattle. At the very least it seemed likely that Gordon the Engine was being prepared for a rescue mission.

Who would I accost? Whose stories would I steal? The single woman cocooned by the window looked as if she might scream if I sidled next to her. It would be equally unwise to wake sleeping passengers and I didn't want to gate-crash the extended family enjoying a picnic of gargantuan proportions in case they felt obliged to feed me with Bakewell tarts, pork pies and glacier mints.

Eventually I sat opposite two late middle-aged women who were suitably startled. I attempted one of my many over rehearsed opening gambits, 'Hi, I'm writing a book about train travel and wondered if I could have a few words with you.'

'Are you a trainspotter?'

'No,' I stuttered lamely, and prepared to move back to my seat.

'I love trains, but not the ones in Essex,' offered the older of the two. While I digested this unexpected insight, she continued, 'I was approached once when I was a young thing by an old woman in a carriage who asked if I had a partner. Boy or girl, it didn't matter ...' I opened my mouth to say something then closed it again. 'We're getting off now, nice to have met you.'

I watched them leave while straining to make sense of the exchange and returned to my seat. John had witnessed my first foray into sociability. 'Haven't lost your touch then,' he said. Annoyed with him but sensing that, despite the surreal nature of the initial exchange, I was on a roll, I decided to try again.

The next woman was in her mid-sixties. In response to my preamble, she told me that she was a retired social worker and had spent most of her professional life addressing the mental health needs of carers. I relaxed, knowing that I was in good hands, and would be looked after if necessary.

She turned her clock back several decades, describing how she would put her bike on the train to work, and at the end of the day would freewheel home through the dark green landscape. For a moment I could see her, hair swept back, legs out straight, careering down country roads, cheeks wobbled by the wind, eyes smarting, the falling road glimpsed through slits, all of the small tribulations and triumphs of her day departing in her slipstream ...

I was struggling to reconnect with the present. The mood in the carriage had changed and now resembled that of a 1950s charabanc on a stolen day out to the seaside, or one of the magical mystery tours run by British Railways.

They were called Merrymaker trips and ran up until the 1980s. DESTINATION NOT TO BE ADVISED TO PASSENGERS said the platform signs. Families with buckets and spades were sometimes disappointed to find themselves plonked in Birmingham. On a typical day in the late 1960s, two and a half thousand thrill-seeking passengers from South Wales were taken north for a wild time in Barnsley.

The chatter in the here-and-now was cut through with boisterous laughter. Someone had opened all of the windows, the charabanc had mutated into a hydrofoil and the shock of cold air made the stubble on my head stand to attention.

We passed a clearing in a wood which was hiding innumerable caravans, all of which were flying Confederate flags. Probably a re-enactment society but just possibly a haven for neo Nazis and bad folk generally.

Market Rasen station was notable on account of its huge and colourful silhouettes which variously depicted a stern full-sized Edwardian in tails and top coat; a moody picture of ruminating Red Lincolnshire cows; windmills; and a fleet of Wellington bombers. Subsequent research revealed that the display is the work of the Market Rasen Station Adoption Group. In 2006 John Skelton, who was at that time living in the station house, 'disgusted by the neglected and vandalised state of the station' apparently formed a local cult of station worshippers.

An adjacent primary school playground cast further light on the indoctrination methods favoured by the cultists. Helpless to intervene, we could only stare as we passed several lines of children being made to squat in an approximation of the stress position used on terror suspects.

Lincoln station is a repository for commemorative plaques. While one had been placed in memory of the war dead, its neighbour had been nailed to the brickwork to mark the re-siting of the original plaque. The third was the brainchild of a Lord Mayor who thought he should get at least some credit for the 'centralisation of railway provision in Lincolnshire'.

Defoe was muttering something. I leaned towards him.

'Lincoln is an old dying, decayed, dirty city—'

'Why don't you tell it as it is?'

'—an ancient, ragged, decayed and still decaying city; and except that part which lies between the castle and the church on the top of the hill, it is scarce tolerable to call a city.'

'Don't wait for a call from the Lincoln tourist office then.'

On the Sleaford train I approached a man in his early thirties with wild hair and piercings. It could so easily have been Johnny Rotten dumped by a faulty Tardis into the space between the toilet and the external door. One moment spitting and snarling on Top of the Pops, the next on a three carriage Sprinter. He was in a wheelchair.

'I haven't been on a train for twenty-one years. You see this device here,' he said pointing at something that looked like interconnecting bicycle pumps, 'well, when I learn how to use it, I should be able to get on and off trains without

45

assistance.' His friend, an off-duty policeman, was less forthcoming. If he had been a real policeman he would have paid more attention to the young passenger who walked past us explaining to his mate that, 'Just because I can kick your head in, doesn't mean I'm hard!'

'I'm the most boring man on the train, no one who knows me would possibly want to talk to me,' said the man sitting on his own. This was far from the case. He was a probation officer with a passion for his profession. 'Changing lives, making a difference' were recurrent themes. Sometimes he receives cards from the people he has helped. 'Most of the time you never know how things turn out,' he said ruefully. I thanked him and left him to his self-denigrating reverie.

As we hobbled our way through Lincolnshire, I became increasingly disconcerted by the sheer volume of sky. I thought too of John Clare, the peasant poet, who in 1841 escaped from his asylum and set out across this land, determined to find his first love, not knowing she had died in a house fire. He slept in dykes and ditches, begged pennies from haymakers and staggered onwards, lost and depressed. He satisfied his hunger by eating the grass by the roadside 'which tasted something like bread.'

Unlike myself, Defoe was enjoying the dull landscape.

'This part is indeed very properly called Holland, for 'tis a flat, level, and often drowned country, like Holland itself. If you listen you may hear the uncouth music of the bittern, a bird formerly counted ominous and presaging, and who, as fame tells us, thrusts its bill into a reed, and then gives the dull, heavy groan or sound, like a sigh, which it does so loud, that with a deep bass like the sound of a gun at a great distance, 'tis heard two or three miles.'

I thanked him for this bizarre piece of information and ruminated on the unhelpful characteristics he shared with John. There was however little chance of hearing the call of the bittern or indeed much else above the noise of the train.

I distracted myself from the endless fens by trying to make sense of the graffiti etched into the train table, 'I came in like a wrecking ball.' What strange words. A search on my phone revealed not only that it was the title of a song by Miley Cyrus but gave me access to an explicit YouTube clip of the aforementioned singer swinging naked on an industrial wrecking ball while flicking her tongue across the steel links. It certainly made a welcome change from staring at John.

Apologies to Boston; 'a large populous and well-built town, full of good merchants.' You came and went in a tired blur that finally saw us emptied into Skegness.

DAY TWO
Skegness – Nottingham – Lincoln – Worksop –
Nottingham – Bedford – Bletchley – Rugby

'To awaken alone in a strange town is one of the pleasantest sensations in the world.' Freya Stark was not a frequent visitor to Skegness. I have never strangled a parrot but I came close. Every step of our ascent from the front door to our bedrooms was celebrated by gleeful squawking and fatuous phrases of greeting. Even with both belly and brain awash with beer, some of the phrases did seem to incorporate a slurred racial epithet.

Our suspicions were confirmed the following morning when, apropos of nothing, apart from the quality of the morning, our hostess confirmed that she was a UKIP voter, the first I had ever met.

We opted for breakfast in the fabulously run down Palace Hotel. Poignant photos on the wall served to emphasise the decline and fall of a once great institution. In an ornate frame a flunkey doorman in black and white opened the door of a limousine with a crease down the middle. A woman with a dead fox round her neck paused on the running board for the camera. There was however one very tangible, and possibly still living, link with the past. Hunched over the grand piano, an ancient woman, with several bags at her feet, picked out a surreal version of a Brandenburg Concerto with two fingers.

Skegness station forecourt features a statue of the town's most celebrated inhabitant, The Jolly Fisherman, a plump nightmare uncle with mad staring eyes, arms akimbo and clay pipe at a jaunty angle. The image is an embodiment of the poster designed by John Hassall with the accompanying pithy slogan 'Young and old find Skegness so bracing'. Research on my phone revealed that the poster was first displayed over the Easter period in 1908 to help promote the three-shilling excursions from Kings Cross. Evidently John Hassall died penniless at the age of eighty in 1948.

Having settled into the Nottingham train, I decided that I didn't have to accost any innocent member of the public for at least half an hour, and would just enjoy the view and the cloudless day. John had other ideas and pointed to a man in the seats on the opposite side of the aisle.

'Go on,' he said. 'Talk to him. You're just making excuses. You'll never get a book out of this unless you speak to people.'

The man was in his late twenties and wore a lurid yellow hoodie festooned with a peculiar bird logo. Barely had I embarked on my ritual introduction than he interrupted me. 'I knew you would come and talk to me. It was ordained. I will let you into the secret of the crystal panda,' he said pointing to the logo on his chest.

'That would be good,' I lied.

'This picture, which I designed myself, will make all women find the wearer sexually irresistible ...' I looked across at John for help but he just smirked. 'It penetrates their brains and makes them forget the stereotypical images of attractive masculinity that have been brainwashed into them by the media. You can take a picture with your phone if you like. It will have the same effect on any woman you show it to...'

I swallowed hard.

'It works best with single mums. I get to talk to lots of groups. I get invited into further education colleges...Women regain their beauty just by staring at the Panda Rose, and they lose weight. I have just turned Skegness into a happy place. Mind you I had to use the Golden Eye.'

Despite my better instincts, I found myself wondering if I had met any miserable people in Skegness. Alarmingly, the answer was no.

'I'm going down to London, to make it a happier place. A big job.'

I agreed, wished him well and slid back to smirking John. The man, whose name was Luke, had left me disturbed. Was there such a thing as a Messiah complex? If so, he may be suffering from it. How did cults come into being? How mad was the urge to make people happy? What if the logo worked? More things in heaven and earth ... Did he really bring some pleasure into the lives of single mums? Which one of us was the madder? By writing a book about train travel I will make people happier ...

I avoided any further eye contact with Luke by concentrating on the Virgin Cross Country train travelling parallel to us, apparently racing. It got quite exciting, sometimes we were just ahead and then it caught up, and then we went ahead again.

By a small leap of the imagination we were back in the heyday of rail travel when steam locomotives belonging to the North Eastern and North British Railways would slog it out on the route between Edinburgh and Aberdeen; firemen risking coronaries to shovel the coal into the flaming mouths of their respective boilers; drivers refusing to acknowledge each other when the rickety footplates drew level.

Back in the present I caught sight of a distressed young

49

man visibly shaking as he crouched in the space between the two carriages, his face hidden in a woollen cap. Before I could offer help, the train lurched to a halt, he got off and my last sighting was of him flailing at his head as if to beat away the demons flapping around him like unwelcome birds.

These two brief encounters with illness were disconcerting, and I felt unsettled as we entered Grantham. The proliferation of out of town supermarkets prompted the thought that some enlightened municipal decree had obliterated all small grocer shops lest Margaret Thatcher returns. Predictably Defoe approved of these visible signs of commerce.

'A neat, well-built and populous town, has a good market, and the inhabitants are said to have a very good trade, and are generally rich.'

I had my first rebuff from a man who grudgingly agreed to talk to me 'if it didn't take long'. I muttered an apology and moved on to a more willing victim. He proved to be a gem and welcomed someone to whom he could speak out loud about his obsession with the great Grantham Rail tragedy.

'At 11 pm on the 19th September 1906, postal workers pushing their barrows stacked high with mail, could only look on aghast as the Scotch Express ignored danger signals, thundered through Grantham station, left the rails, drove through a bridge parapet and plunged down an embankment. The gas-lit carriages promptly caught fire and became a raging inferno.

'As there was no obvious explanation the event became the Marie Celeste of its day. Was Driver Fleetwood drunk? Did he become unwell? Was he arguing with Fireman Talbot? Were there demonic forces abroad? Certainly not all of the fourteen victims were identified and tales of hauntings abounded...'

In the immediate aftermath of this conversation, I saw from the window a nightmare one-dimensional, fire-ruined stately home. The sun went behind the clouds and I decided

I had spoken to enough people on this particular train. Defoe was asleep and I took the opportunity to stare at him.

'A middle siz'd spare man, about forty years old, of a brown complexion, and dark brown-coloured hair, but wears a wig; a hooked nose, a sharp chin, grey eyes and a large mole near his mouth.'

He opened his eyes, he had obviously heard every word.

'How dare you!'

'Sorry?'

'You stole those words from the *London Gazette*. If you recall, they were prefaced with the invocation, "Whosoever shall discover Defoe so he may be apprehended ..." And all because of a piddling pamphlet that I penned in an idle moment. May your words also land you in deep waters, may you too endure the ignominy of days in the pillory.'

'I don't think that's very nice.'

I took the chance to stretch my legs outside of Nottingham station and was quite relieved to enjoy the company of more modern, and hopefully more sympathetic writers. I was being stared at by D H Lawrence, Alan Sillitoe and Lord Byron from a poster declaiming Rebel Writers. At least I might have some additional companions for the next leg of the journey to Lincoln.

'I was a rebel,' said Defoe. 'I joined Monmouth, I fought at Sedgemoor under the banner *Fear Nothing But God ...*'

'Look, Daniel, this book is not all about you.'

Before our next train gathered speed, I peered into the front rooms of the trackside houses looking for a sighting of two men wrestling naked in front of the fireplace. Presumably they had been distracted by the kitchen sink drama playing angrily in the scullery, or knocked off kilter by the sounds from the bedroom where Byron was rogering Lady Caroline Lamb. Rebels all.

As we passed into the countryside I did though catch

sight of a solitary child's swing in an orchard which was presumably the one where Miriam and Paul Morrell shared an epiphany.

'Nottingham is one of the most pleasant and beautiful towns in England,' ventured a slightly chastened Defoe, now trying to ingratiate himself. 'It's situated upon the steep ascent of a sandy rock into which they have cut vaults and cellars which are well stocked with excellent ale.'

'One of the pubs from your time is still there. It's cut out of the rock. Ye Olde Trip to Jerusalem it's called.'

'I have a terrible thirst.'

'Sorry, Dan, trains to catch.'

Despite his thirst, Defoe continued: 'I was obliged once to make an excursion into Sherwood Forest where I had the diversion of seeing the annual meeting of the gentry at the horse racing, an infinite throng of gentlemen. Nor is the appearance of the ladies to be admitted as fine and without comparison more bright and gay. The train of coaches filled with the beauties of the North was not to be described...'

'Honestly, all you can think about is drink, sex and horse racing.'

There was something strange about travelling for no purpose, embarking on a journey whose destination was irrelevant. Most travellers endure the tedium, or indeed wallow in the small excitements of travel, sustained by the prospect of meeting up with friends or family. We had no business meetings to attend, no deals to broker, no work situations to resolve. The least I could do to justify this pointless indulgence was talk to people.

The off-duty guard would not be drawn into saying anything about his job. 'I'm not allowed to talk about trains,' he explained. I was surprised. What horrible punishments would be visited on those who broke the silence? In my mind's eye I saw a clip of a Laurel and Hardy film in

52

which the villain, tied to the rails, raises his head in horror as the locomotive steams towards him.

Mistaking my disbelief for disappointment, he relented. 'I can talk about statistical aspects,' he said. I could see the flip charts in the room chosen for the induction of new train conductors. One was headed TOPICS NEVER TO BE DISCUSSED and listed were lateness, accidents, suicides, closed buffet cars, engine failure, compensation, the price of tickets, leaves on the line. Under the heading PERMISSABLE TOPICS I read refurbished stations, new rolling stock, all positive comparisons with our European competitors, and any meaningless statistic.

His chosen meaningless statistic related to the number of signal boxes on the Nottingham to Lincoln line. Encouraged by my silence, he then unburdened himself of two particular memories. The first was the time his train approached a small station, the platform of which was crowded with more people than an LS Lowry market place. 'I knew they wouldn't all fit on the train, there would be serious over-crowding, people could be crushed ...' Apparently they were all train enthusiasts waiting for the arrival of a steam locomotive. While we shared his sense of relief at a disaster narrowly averted, his brows clouded over again.

'And then there was the night of the Lincoln market ...' Barely able to control his emotions, he described how hundreds of drunken young people had invaded his train and proceeded to sing – with actions – a flamboyant version of YMCA before lapsing into loud and maudlin renditions of Christmas carols.

If the train had been equipped with a guard's van that is undeniably where he would have gone to lie down and recover from having revealed so much to complete strangers.

John was becoming animated. When I asked if he was all right, he explained that our train was about to negotiate a flat crossing. Evidently this is the term used to describe the point at which two sets of track meet each other at a ninety-degree angle. He explained gleefully how the consequences of a collision would be incalculable. For a moment I considered joining the guard in his therapeutic space.

We were grateful to the thoughtful, compassionate announcer at Lincoln station who urged us not to 'struggle on the stairs'. Did she realise that my patience with John was wearing thin and that I was fighting with the urge to push him down the steps? Perhaps the struggle she had in mind was more of an existential nature. Were travellers to Lincoln more prone to wrestling with the meaning of life than most commuters? By way of contrast, the ambiance of Worksop station was much less compassionate. 'Fuck the police!' screamed the graffiti. 'No lead on roofs,' countered the despairing forces of law and order.

An old man was battling with the toilet door. It was playing a childish game with him, refusing to open then opening but not locking then opening again. Eventually it grew bored and cooperated fully.

'I'm seventy-nine,' he explained, 'and I still love trains. I used to spot engines in my youth, cycling all day to see them with six pence and a bottle of water. In the early 1950s, me and my pals would pretend to be football supporters so we could get the special up to Glasgow which was taking people to the Scotland v England game. I remember looking out of the window and watching the dawn break over the Northumberland coast. We would get a whole compartment to ourselves, see. We would pull the curtains over the window so no one else could look in. When we got to Glasgow it was straight to the engine sheds at Springburn...'

According to the trackside sign we were now travelling on the Robin Hood Line. 'A man of the most licentious and wicked inclination' said Defoe who rose from his seat, clearly intent on searching for the villain among the passengers.

'Calm down,' I said.

'Just read my *History and Real Adventures of Robin Hood* and then tell me to remain calm...'

I thought it would be prudent to let the subject drop.

While the line represents a victory for the opponents of the Beeching plan, there were stations on route whose names were redolent of a later and less successful struggle. Shirebrook still conjures images from the 1980s miners' strike when it was dubbed 'England's Belfast' by one Chief Constable. It was difficult to make the connections between the picturesque towns through which we passed and images of police charges, flying pickets, three-day weeks, braziers, horses, Thatcher and Scargill, pit closures, desperate families, scabs and pariahs. I'm sure I caught sight of Billy Elliot skipping his way along the top of a grey stone wall.

'The miners have my sympathy,' said Defoe. 'They endure unimaginable hardships and dangers. A new pit was being dug close to this place. The workman came to a cavity, which, as was supposed, had formerly been dug from some other pit, but as soon as upon the breaking into the hollow part, the pent-up air got vent, it blew up like a mine of a thousand barrels of powder, and, burst out with such a terrible noise, as made the very earth tremble for some miles, and terrified the whole country. There were near three score people lost their lives, and one or two, as we were told, who were at the bottom of the shaft, were blown quite out, though sixty fathoms deep, and were found dead upon the ground.'

The driver of the Nottingham to Bedford train had the land speed record in his sights, although it was possible that he had collapsed in his cab with his rigor mortis grip firmly clamped on the dead man's handle.

There is something undeniably exhilarating about speed, especially when travelling in backward facing seats, in a cavalier snub to our destination. Adopt the brace position and bring it on. Soon we were swallowing huge swathes of countryside as if a toddler was flicking the pages of his book to make the horse gallop and the soldier swing his sword. The map was being hastily rolled up. Monopoly board houses were being swept into the box. Hedges and ditches passed quicker than the words could be said. There is a child in every test pilot, an adult on every fairground ride. Forget the imperceptible speed of the Eurostar, give me a bone shaker every time. Those passengers who had foolishly placed items of small luggage in the overhead compartments ducked before the cascade of coats and handbags. I'm sure some of these bends were not meant to be taken on two wheels.

As if trying to slow us, the fingertips of long shadows reached out to the carriages. Our faces reflected in the windows were superimposed on fast moving fields. Slowly, as Philip Larkin said, the brakes took hold and the train was reeled in on a rod bent over still waters.

The Bedford to Bletchley train was the greenest we had encountered so far. The carriage livery was green, the internal panelwork was green and the upholstery was green. Even the white rabbits that peppered the fields only served to accentuate the prevailing greenness. Through this arcadia, we watched as two racing sculls were languidly pulled down river before passing a football match being played out in the early evening on a pitch surrounded by trees. Again, the contentment I experienced had something to do with the notion of travelling without real purpose. All profound thoughts and minor anxieties would stay in limbo so long as we kept moving.

DAY THREE
Rugby – Stoke – Derby – Matlock –
Nottingham – Norwich

After the euphoria that characterised the close of the previous day, this particular morning did not feel quite so good. I'm not certain what gave rise to the idea but the friendly Sikh taxi driver assured me that I would go to hell if I pushed John out of the moving vehicle.

According to Sikhi, when a human dies 'jam doots' or minions of death come and take the soul to the court of Dharam Rai. Once in court, the dead person's deeds are read out. There can be no argument, no mitigating circumstances, before sentence is passed which will be a time-limited period in either heaven or hell. This is the good news, because when your sentence is served you are returned to the earth for another shot. This seems an eminently sensible solution, far preferable to an eternity of devils sticking red-hot pokers up your arse.

The comfort I derived from this thought was offset by the prospect of no one wanting to talk to me, but an elderly woman on the train to Stoke restored my flagging enthusiasm. Liberated by her widowhood, she was making up for lost time, and shuffled her pack of tickets until she found the one that would guarantee safe passage into Lichfield and its many pleasures.

Emboldened by the woman's energy and joyfulness, I decided to take my first risk of the day and sat opposite a young woman dressed entirely in pink and wearing a bowler hat. I knew this was in contravention of the rule never to plonk myself down next to young women travelling alone but her demeanour minimised the risk. Kerry-Anne was a media studies student on work placement. Her mission for the day was to stand outside a temporary windmill in Stoke beneath a canopy of balloons. If approached she was to give away free circus tickets.

She was happy to share memories of two train journeys. Recently she found herself travelling in a carriage with a hen party whose pursuit of mayhem and debauchery was compromised by their collective failure to locate a cork-screw. Despite entreaties to the innocent passengers trapped in corner seats, they were unsuccessful. Several bottlenecks were broken on table edges and the situation was only partly salvaged when one of the celebrants sacrificed her front teeth on a bottle top.

On another occasion, the conductor decided that she looked particularly lonely and persuaded a young Australian man to sit opposite and cheer her up. I had realised by now that train conductors frequently went well beyond the call of duty, but assuming responsibility for the mental health and possibly the love life of passengers was a revelation.

I glanced at John sitting in solitary splendour and enjoyed the thought that, any minute now, the guard might suggest that he join the old woman on her tour of Lichfield with a view to friendship, possible more. Sadly, this was not to be. I was stuck with him.

Defoe had gone AWOL. He had abandoned the confines of his book and squeezed himself into the space next to Kerry-Anne.

'Get back here now!' I said. Grudgingly, he returned to his seat. 'You can't go about annoying other passengers. Apart from anything else, you're a Figment.'

'She is so beautiful. She puts me in mind of my oyster girl . . . I miss her.'

'What about Mary Tuffley, your long-suffering wife?'

'She doesn't understand.'

I left Defoe to his melancholic reflections and sat back to enjoy the descent into Stoke.

Countering the early outbreak of Sikhism, Stoke station was flying the flag for Buddhism. A giant sculptured hand dominated the far platform. In its palm nestled a tiny figure: half lion, half man, symbolising mankind trapped in time and history.

I was still reflecting on the significance of the image as we drew out of the station destined for Derby, where commuters trapped in both time and history by delayed trains could wander a hundred yards and choose either to while away the long hours in the Gladstone Pottery Museum or the Pulse and Cocktails Adult Superstore. Stoke was clearly something of a libertarian paradise, catering for all proclivities.

Surprisingly attuned to my line of thought, Defoe snorted. 'You should read my book *Conjugal Lewdness, or Matrimonial Whoredom.*'

'Well, it's a cracking title,' I said. 'It knocks *The Life and Strange Surprising Adventures of Robinson Crusoe* into a cocked hat.'

'Harrumph!'

The middle-aged, respectable man I approached revealed proclivities that challenged my most liberal of sensibilities. The moment I mentioned the word 'railways,' his eyes glazed and I was pinned back into my seat by a passionate account of his relentless pursuit of steam engines across the world.

His wife shared his obsession, and together they had travelled the length of Sri Lanka (three times), Italy, Romania, Peru, Colombia, Argentina, Brazil, New Zealand (twice), South Africa (four times), Zimbabwe, Botswana, Burma. On the overnight train from Rangoon to Mandalay they had camped in the kitchen...my concentration was waning at this point, some of the details became a bit blurred... where his wife showed the crew how to cook a full English breakfast.

In Argentina the narrow-gauge train was seven hours late. It was so cold crossing the Pampas, they had no alternative but to light a fire in the coach. The possibility that he and his wife were international criminals wanted for gratuitous arson across the globe was not particularly comforting. Finally pausing for breath, he said that he also enjoyed real ale and travelled to a lot of beer festivals. I extricated myself by feigning a stomach complaint and locked myself in the train toilet.

There was a very, very comforting aspect to that particular toilet. This may have had something to do not only with the joy of escape but also with the fact that, for some reason, the bowl was a tasteful blue. I looked around for the Toilet Duck and the matching chintz curtains. Giving train conductors discretion to customise their toilets seemed both humane and enlightened.

Defoe was eager to share his memories of the peaks: 'The people here told us of a mountain where a giant was buried. This tempted our curiosity. As we came near the hill we saw a small opening, not a door but a natural opening into the rock, and the noise we had made brought a woman out with a child in her arms, and another at her foot. Says I, 'good wife, where do you live?' "Here, sir," says she and points to the hole in the rock. We alighted and went in. There was a large hollow cave, which the poor people by two curtains had parted into three rooms.

'The habitation was poor but everything was clean and neat, though mean and ordinary. I asked the poor woman what trade her husband was? She said, he worked in the lead mines, with good luck he could earn about five pence a day. Then I asked, what she did, she said, when she was able to work, she washed the ore. This moving sight so affected us all, we made up a little lump of money and I put it into the poor woman's hand. It was some time before she could do anything but cry.'

Defoe, profoundly affected by the memory, started to sob. I patted him on the shoulder.

The train to Matlock offered up clichés of Englishness. *Jerusalem* was played over the intercom as we passed a succession of bijou cricket pitches with white starched pavilions and sightscreens nestling in idyllic communities from which all nastiness in woodsheds had been banished. Much dappling was going on. We glided through bluebell-strewn woods and meadows of dandelions. A derelict platform decorated with primroses confirmed the impression that this route was reserved for the gradual rehabilitation of drivers suffering from the trauma of numerous unspecified 'incidents'.

'Come, quick,' said Defoe taking me by the arm as we drew into Matlock station.

What is it?'

'We must visit the warm springs of Matlock.'

'I had a shower this morning.'

'One of the springs is made into a very convenient bath; with a house built over it, and room within the building to walk around the water or bath, and so by steps to go down gradually into it. The bath is milk, or rather blood warm, very pleasant to go into, and very sanative, especially for rheumatic pains, bruises, etc.'

Such was his enthusiasm that for a while I was tempted to leave John to his own devices, and join Defoe in a hot tub, but the whistle blew and the train moved on.

At Matlock Bath it is possible to take a cable car to the Heights of Abraham, which probably crosses over the Elysium Fields. To reinforce the intimations of paradise, white flowering ivy had been carefully positioned on the cutting walls and the woman conductor passed through the carriage leaving a chorus of joyous laughter in her wake.

Tony and Laura, who looked like well-heeled hikers, were *en route* to a difficult hospital visit. They had no specific rail anecdotes apart from a shared memory of being on a snowbound train where much convivial drink was taken and bonhomie shared. The late middle-aged couple exuded a sense of lives well lived.

'I endured a difficult hospital trip...' Defoe said.

'They're not interested. Stop it.'

'Bladder stones.'

'Too much information. Stop now.'

'I was held down by three attendants, as a surgeon passed a tube through my penis. Sir, I was torn and mangled by the merciless surgeons, cut open alive, and bound hand and foot and forced to bear it...'

'Look, one more word and I will shut that book permanently!'

The conductor did her best to recreate the sense of prevailing goodness by announcing that as her ticket machine had developed a fault, no one would be expected to pay for their journey if they hadn't already done so. This had happened before on the Carlisle to Settle line; a welcome déjà vu.

Soon after leaving Matlock we saw a man in his allotment painting a huge American flag on his shed. It would soon be visible from the moon and would be a small source of comfort to any homesick orbiting astronauts.

As we ground our way towards Norwich I was again aware of an incipient hankering for hills. Almost any small knoll or wold would do. I had not expected to be so affected by the unremitting flatness. If Greater Anglia had any degree of empathy, they would have painted silhouettes of undulating scarps on the windows.

Having recovered from the disappointment of not being allowed to describe his surgical procedures in greater detail, Defoe was already waxing lyrical about Norwich.

'A weaver told me that 120,000 people are involved in spinning the yarn in this populous city.' I resisted the thought that this statistic seemed so unlikely as to give the yarn-spinning phrase a more immediate relevance. 'There is not one hand unemployed here; the very children after four or five years of age, could every one earn their own bread.'

While I was still thinking about child exploitation, he changed tack: 'Look at that prodigious number of cattle.' I looked out of the window and saw not a single cow.

'All of the Scots cattle which come yearly into England, are brought hither. These Scots runts, so they call them, coming out of the cold and barren mountains of the Highlands in Scotland, feed so eagerly on the rich pasture in these marshes, that they thrive in an unusual manner, and grow monstrously fat.'

I sneaked an uncharitable glance at John and, through the window, saw the sky return with a vengeance. Several manmade structures, wind turbines on one side of the track and huge cooling towers on the other, made failed attempts to reach up and drag it downwards. The clouds were playing cloud puppetry. A wild cat caught in mid leap morphed into a voluptuous Goya matron. Tumbling intestine clouds were suddenly backlit by silver spotlights. In the distance a sharp-edged chute of rain funnelled into the earth.

Eager to escape both my real and imaginary friends, I spoke to an older woman who said that her late husband had worked on the railways from the age of eighteen to sixty-five. Her abiding memory was cleaning his overalls. Perhaps she could strike a deal with the Celestial Fat Controller; one more set of dirty overalls in exchange for a few more hours of her husband's company. Her son was also a driver on the Norwich route.

She then lost herself recalling a distant train journey to Manchester during which she met a woman whom she knew could have become a close friend, but she never saw her again. This whimsically poignant snippet stayed with me. She had not been talking about a Celia Johnson *Brief Encounter* with Trevor Howard, just a lost opportunity

63

for friendship. How many journeys are littered with these transient moments?

DAY FOUR

Norwich – Ipswich – Ely – Cambridge – Ipswich –
Felixstowe – Ipswich – Lowestoft – Norwich

We should have read the small print. The Norwich B & B was run by Kafka Associates and had its head office just outside of Guantanamo Bay. The large building had no visible entrance. All of the windows had been whitewashed. Eventually a phone call directed us to a well-hidden keypad. The entrance hall was but stage one in sensory deprivation. Bland, featureless and anonymous, it felt like slipping into a dystopian coma. Our night was punctuated by the sound of distant but copious vomiting from another unseen prisoner.

When we staggered back into the world, John had much to say. 'Never again will you be entrusted to find accommodation. That was one of the worst nights of my life. Henceforth you are relieved of your duties. Sacked. Redundant. Superfluous. Pointless.'

I feigned disappointment but was secretly relieved. We had barely sat down on the Ipswich train than he bullied me into getting up again. 'Go on, don't be a coward. Talk to someone. Try that man over there.'

'I can't think of anything to say, I drank too much last night,' he said.

An already difficult day was then made even worse by the conductor singing loudly 'Diss is Diss and Dat is Dat' when we approached Diss station. Or Dat station. Desperate to talk with a normal human being I spoke to the custodian of the buffet car.

'In case of trouble,' he explained, 'I pull down the grille, lie on the floor and wait for the fire brigade.' Why the fire brigade I wondered? Perhaps he had also been instructed to swallow several cans of strong cider before padlocking himself to the coffee machine.

'Businessmen are the worst. Drunk as newts some of them. They start early in the morning, you see. So long as the train is moving, we can serve them.'

'An Englishman will fairly drink as much as will maintain two families of Dutch,' observed Defoe sagely.

As I returned to my seat the words, ' ... knickers off? I wasn't doing that!' wafted down the carriage, but I failed to identify which principled person had uttered them. A pity, it could have made for an interesting conversation. Otherwise, the day seemed doomed to mediocrity.

This impression was confirmed by John's enthusiasm for the Ipswich Chord which, apparently, was right up there with the Morpeth Curve.

'The new stretch of line, built on the sight of a disused bacon factory, will mean that freight trains travelling to Felixstowe will no longer need to use the sidings adjacent to Ipswich station as a turning point. It cost £59 million and involved the removal of 100,000 tons of earth.'

John sat back waiting for me to absorb this remarkable feat of engineering. In fact, I was lost for words and steadily developing an envy of dead people. Defoe too, put aside the manuscript he was working on, shook his head and sighed.

On balance, I decided I should savour this low key, empty day. It was after all, a day like most others, floating past with little trauma or emotional engagement. Life seemed in abeyance. It was one of those days that we will wish we had savoured when the hourglass finally runs out, the antithesis of mindfulness; a waste of being alive really.

This mood found a soothing echo in the conductor's announcement. 'Thank you for travelling with us. Please collect your thoughts when leaving the train and reconnect with your lives, preoccupations and mundane worries. For those of you not alighting I will provide gentle countryside, nothing unpleasant.'

My appreciation of travelling on the pleasing cusp of melancholy was compromised by the woman who squeezed into the one available seat opposite. To my surprise, she instigated the conversation. A full-time exam invigilator, she was happy to boast about her record of cajoling train conductors into giving her free upgrades.

'Tis no sin to cheat the devil.'

'It's easy,' she said, 'if you know how.'

In my mind's eye I could see her smirking under a blanket in first class with a free sandwich and a G & T. 'How do you manage it?' She wouldn't pass on her secrets, which of course gave me *carte blanche* to speculate. Was blackmail involved? Did she swap sexual favours for tickets? On reflection, this latter option seemed unlikely. She was a large woman; perhaps she would threaten to sit on the conductor until he relented.

The fourth person squashed around our table was a golf professional. He too was happy to pontificate on conductors, casting himself as the hero who remonstrated with a rail employee for bullying an elderly couple. As the climax to his dramatic reconstruction, he bellowed, 'I am not letting you take their money!' Several heads turned.

Now with an attentive audience, he sought to redress the balance by describing the empathy shown by a conductor on a train delayed by a suicide on the line at St Neots. The man had evidently counselled each passenger in turn, offering to drive them all home in his own car if their delay proved lengthy.

I was warming to the narrator until he continued with a sneer, 'The conductor's efforts were appreciated by all the passengers apart from one … who was not of our nation!'

There. Clearly a total tosser. The free upgrade woman cackled her approval.

On the Ely to Cambridge train the day caught fire when we were surrounded by a raucous hen party of ostensibly respectable women in their mid-forties. All eight were behaving badly beneath a miasmic canopy of discordant perfumes, and being bonded by a cat's cradle of earpieces did not inhibit their capacity to talk at the same time. Champagne bottles and glasses were produced from bottomless handbags.

'I'll have to stop drinking or I'll be incapable,' declaimed one, with no intention of following her own advice. A cork shot down the aisle and I was suddenly noticed.

Great Joy! I was offered olives, cheese straws, champagne and several carnal relationships with no strings attached. Well, certainly the straws, olives and drink. To take full advantage of these offers, I moved to the seat behind the party which I shared with a middle-aged Indian woman in a sari.

'My pants are falling down!' explained one of the ecstatic celebrants. I glanced anxiously at my new companion.

'They are having fun,' she said, smiling.

'Come with us on our magical mystery tour,' one of them pleaded. Perhaps the magic logo was working after all. Just as I was preparing to join the hedonistic coven, John sternly moved me out of my seat.

'I'll dance with you in your absence,' promised my new potential life partner.

'I'll pray for you,' said her friend incongruously.

'Get off the train,' said John.

Defoe was eager that we wander the streets of Cambridge, arm in arm, and see if we could find the fair that he remembered so fondly.

'There are sometimes no less than fifty hackney coaches which come from London, and ply night and day to carry the people to Cambridge. The very barns and stables are turned into inns. As for the people in the fair, they all eat, drink and sleep in their booths and tents, which become taverns, coffee-houses, drinking-houses, eating-houses, cook-shops...'

It sounded too good to miss but, because of John's time-table, we couldn't leave the station. Defoe removed his wig and stared at the car park as if he was witnessing a funeral.

Judging by the view from the window of the Felixstowe crawler, all human beings had been replaced by horses. We were passing through Newmarket where horses poked their heads out of stables as if the effect had been contrived with the aid of mirrors. Defoe, who had recovered from his Cambridge disappointment, leaped out of his seat as he recognised the countryside.

'Being come to Newmarket in the month of October, I had the opportunity to see the horse-races; and a great concourse of the nobility and gentry.'

He then tried to interest me in the tricks deployed by a known fraudster, Sir Robert Fagg, who always managed to cheat the bookies by making his thoroughbreds look 'as clumsy, and as dirty, and as much like a cart-horse as all the cunning of his master and the groom could make him.'

My disinterest mutated into boredom that spread to the other passengers, who either fell asleep or moved their hands over the windows like mime artistes expressing loss and sorrow.

I returned from the toilet only for John to tell me that I had missed an interesting exchange between two young girls, one of whom apparently told the other, 'I'm thinking of getting a picture of Jason tattooed on my bum.' Did Jason have a symmetrically cloven face, I wondered.

The highlight of the day was still to come. John nodded sagely in the direction of a thin man apparently performing tricks with his ticket. It sycamored above the table before landing the right way up on the opposite seat for the benefit of the conductor carrying out an inspection.

'Thanks pal,' he said, as I returned the ticket and sat opposite.

'I'm Warren by the way. A rock and roller. I'm fifty-one but you only get one concert man. I've lived my life like a lunatic. I've ruined myself with drink and spliffs.' He was certainly still under the influence of at least one of these.

'Tell you what I really want man? I want to be on a Thai beach with a woman under each arm, a pint and a spliff. I'd be happy then, God could take me then if he wanted. My mum, she's seventy-two, she don't understand. I'm a rock and roller, man. The only person I've harmed is me. I'm OK with acid, a line of cocaine, I could do that. You've got the beard, man. I'm trying to grow a Frank Zappa number.'

He leant across to John, 'Do you take drugs, my friend?' As John struggled to frame his reply, Warren warned him, 'Whatever you do, don't take legal highs.' John promised that he wouldn't. Warren then set off after his mobile phone which had slipped from his hand and embarked on a flying parabola into the aisle. Reunited with the device, he continued. 'That Russell Brand, he's a good man, but he's a wanker, know what I mean?' I said that I did. 'He's been in dark places, like me. I'm restless, all my life, can't stay in the same place.'

As we drew into Trimley, Warren took his leave, but not before gifting the ticket he almost certainly needed to leave the station, to John as a memento. 'Two years' time,' he said, 'I'll be on The Voice.'

With time to kill, and because John and I needed a break from each other, I decided to spend an hour wandering in Ipswich. I also wanted to gauge if the ancient port still deserved Defoe's glowing review. 'I take this town to be one of the most agreeable places in England. It had good houses, it's airy, clean and well governed...'

Defoe makes no mention of the statue of Giles' cartoon Grandma in the station car park. There must be a reason why Network Rail felt obliged to pay homage to this cantankerous octogenarian, inclined to beat small children with black umbrellas.

A quick google reveals that Carl Giles was a son of Ipswich. It also revealed that he had a friendly meeting with the Belsen concentration camp commander who was, bizarrely, a fan of his work. 'I never sent him an original. What was the point? He had been hanged.'

Equally bizarre is the shop at Portman Road, the home of Ipswich Town football club. Although I am not a stranger to the absurd passions the sport can induce, I balked at the startling array of themed products on display which included laundry sacks, chopping boards, door banners, baubles and street signs.

'Trade is king!'

The canal towpath provided respite from the commercial world. There was however something haunting about how its walls and flat surfaces served as testimonies to someone's grief. RIP DAVE read the graffiti, reflected in the canal's calm waters.

The woman on the Lowestoft train only wanted to talk about the scandal of the Lowestoft fisherman statue. I gathered that the statue was dedicated to the local lifeboat men, but I could not persuade my fellow traveller to reveal any details of the scandal itself. Was it financial? Was it facing the wrong way? To distract herself from the undisclosed horrors of whatever it was, she gleefully described seeing a locomotive hit a cow on the track.

Mercifully her narrative was drowned out by a maniacal youth bellowing into his mobile phone. 'The drugs were out of my system by then,' he roared. 'I shagged her for at least half an hour.'

This last revelation was too much for the passenger sitting in front of the priapic prodigy. 'Keep your voice down, son,' he urged, to no effect whatsoever. The carriage was soon flooded with sexual images so graphic that time stood still. Even the statue-and-dead-cow fixated woman was disconcerted.

John eased himself from his seat and approached the loud boy, asking if he wanted to talk to a mental health specialist and unhelpfully pointing in my direction. As the offer was ignored, John explained that as he was increasingly hungry, if the boy did not shutthefuckup, he would be eaten. This threat was so horrific and unexpected that a reverential silence descended. I resolved to have a word with John about empathy.

The conductor announced that the train would terminate at Beccles and we would all have to pick up our belongings and leave. The ostensible reason was a lightning strike. Had other stations been similarly affected? Were there frogs at Saxmundham and locusts at Wickham Market?

On the replacement train a kindly woman, embracing her role as tourist guide, pointed out Sizewell's nuclear power stations and described how she used to swim in the warm waters of the outflow. Suddenly everything made sense; there was an explanation for all the aberrant behaviour we had witnessed. This theory was confirmed by the sudden appearance of a dog, the size of a fully-grown horse, in the aisle.

We enjoyed a lengthy chat with the conductor on the train back to Norwich. There were few passengers and he was happy to talk. He loved his job and never regretted leaving a very high-powered position with a large bank. His new employers were initially incredulous at his willingness to work for significantly less money and found the idea of life-work balance an alien concept. They were still badgering him to apply for senior management positions on the railway but he always politely declined. He liked his work, and he liked people. He admitted to sometimes worrying too much about the more vulnerable passengers, including in this number the legions of scantily clad young women, the worse for drink, who crowded onto Friday night trains. He too had daughters.

His mood lightened when he mentioned the woman in Newmarket who insisted on bathing topless in her garden next to the railway line irrespective of the weather. She always had a cheery wave for the drivers who responded with a blast of the horn. Innocent pleasures.

Ditto the couple he had interrupted having sex in the first-class carriage. He had whistled to announce his approach but they remained completely oblivious to his presence so he discreetly wished them well and tiptoed away.

DAY FIVE
Norwich – Great Yarmouth – Norwich – Sheringham – Holt – Sheringham – Norwich – Peterborough – Doncaster – Waverley – Glasgow

I had only visited the Norfolk Broads via Arthur Ransome's *Coot Club*, and hadn't particularly enjoyed the journey. Saving nesting sites from the damage wrought by the Hullabaloos in their motor cruiser had not impressed my prepubescent self as particularly noble, and I had moved on to *Biggles, Air Detective*. Nevertheless, I resolved to approach the day with an open mind.

From the train I noted the windmills, glimpses of water and the unexpected appearance of boats above hedges; a juxtaposition ominously reminiscent of recent TV images of the Asian tsunami. Out at sea, wind turbines communicated via a languid system of semaphore. The instillation was incomplete, which explained why some of the towers seemed stripped of their wings.

As a treat, John had devised our itinerary so we could

travel on the Sheringham – Holt preserved railway and I enjoyed a quick wallow in the manicured nostalgia that the excursion offered.

Steam engines are always great fun. If I'm honest though, it seemed like a parody rather than a journey in its own right. The clunk of a hole being punched through a card-board ticket is undeniably pleasing, and there is a novelty value to a locomotive impersonating an emphysemic Labrador after a swim, but I found it difficult to connect no matter how many reruns of *The Railway Children* I played in my head.

Perhaps we should have timed our visit to coincide with the annual 1940s weekend which promises air raids, spam sandwiches, jitterbug dances, and all the excitement, fear and bravery of the Blitz. If the excitement proves too much, you can opt for the beer festival on wheels or the chance to buy fish and chips at a local shop and eat them on the train. How different were these experiences from the average Friday night trip into Glasgow Queen Street? Not wanting to upset John, I thanked him profusely.

On the way back from Sheringham, we passed through Cromer. Defoe stood up and stared out to sea, sheltering his eyes with his hand.

'It happened out there, in 1662. (I think it was that year) A fleet of 200 sail of light colliers (so they call the ships bound northward empty to fetch coals from Newcastle to London) were taken with a storm of wind and so were forced to run west. But few could find their way and 140 sail were all driven on shore, and dashed to pieces, and very few of the people on board were saved.'

The impact of his words blotted out all other noise. All I could hear was the sound of breaking timbers as the wooden ribs shot upwards into the dark suffocating waves.

Before the journey back north we had another small piece of the jigsaw to complete, the trip to Great Yarmouth. The journey passed without incident apart from a man who spent the duration of the journey impersonating a chicken.

The truth of the matter was that I was becoming scunnered with trains. This was the forty-first of the week and, at that moment, I just wanted to be another traveller looking forward to being home. I wanted to stop noticing things. It is all very well masquerading as a profound chronicler of human behaviour, intent on catching snippets of conversation with my butterfly net, but it was also undeniably tiring.

There was however one remaining episode that needs to be recorded. We were wakened from our slumbers by anguished cries as we approached Newcastle. 'My case has gone!' A woman in her early thirties tugged at the unyielding stack of suitcases and bags crammed into the end-of-carriage luggage rack. 'Someone's taken it.'

She became a child again. A bully had stolen her lunch money along with the small doll she had knitted for her mother. She was beyond distraught. She breathed new life into the phrase 'wailing and gnashing of teeth'. Our hearts went out to her, as did the hearts of the passengers who offered consolation and the assurance that her luggage must have been taken in error, but Herr Schadenfreude sat among us.

Everyone checked that their cases were where they had been left. Everyone mentally reflected on their inventory of possessions, placing their losses on a scale from inconvenient to incalculable. The woman sobbed her way onto the platform where she ran from one member of staff to another.

As we glided ever closer to Edinburgh, I concentrated on my inner landscape rather than the passing countryside. It was Martin Buben who said 'All journeys have secret destinations of which the traveller is unaware.' Had I found any surprising destinations? For many of the people I had spoken to, and indeed for myself, the past was more of a destination than I had anticipated. It had been easy to tap into people's heads as they sat unfocussed, half dreaming, perhaps enjoying the company of their earlier selves, talking to the shades of friends. I certainly felt richer for my life-affirming brushes with eccentricity.

We passed two more significant blots on the landscape: the Torness nuclear power station, famed for its radiation leaks and a cooling system frequently blocked by seaweed, and the Oxwellmains cement works. I scoured the flat seascape for any redeeming feature and found it in the hunched outline of the Bass Rock.

'Pirates,' said Defoe. 'Remember?'

As Arthur's Seat came into sight, the carriage became crowded. Everyone was there.

Warren lit up a large spliff until the conductor confiscated it and ground it under his foot. 'Rock and Roll, man,' he said, attempting to scrape some of the contents off the floor.

The Panda logo man was staring intently at several young women, to very little effect, growling, 'Stare at my T-shirt, don't you want to be happy?'

The seventy-nine-year-old former trainspotter had struck up a rapport with the man who had travelled the globe looking for steam engines. They were lighting a fire beneath the table, feeding it with tickets.

The probation officer was having his hand rigorously pumped by a grateful ex-offender. 'I can't tell you how much I owe you.'

Kerry-Anne was distributing her leftover circus tickets to the other passengers.

Laura and John had got good news at the hospital and ordered two gins and tonic from the buffet car. They toasted each other.

JOURNEY THREE

South East England

DAY ONE

Glasgow Central – Euston – Watford Junction –
Willesden Junction – Gospel Oak – Stratford –
Highbury & Islington – Dalston Junction –
West Croydon – Crystal Palace – Clapham Junction –
Willesden Junction – Queens Park – Paddington –
Greenford – Paddington

Defoe was increasingly irritating as we walked alongside the Caledonian sleeper.

'London! London!' he declared with annoying regularity.

'Yes, we're going to London. Big hairy deal, get over it.'

We could only afford seats, rather than berths, but £15 did seem a remarkable bargain. There was a frisson of anticipation as we made our way from pub to station. The train was so long, John and I were virtually sober when we found our carriage. Through the windows we could see people settling into their cabins. Others were making their way to the lounge car. There was something conspiratorial about the friendly greeting dispensed by the clipboard-wielding attendants on the platform. It might not be the Orient Express but excitement was guaranteed.

After settling into ancient blue upholstered seats, I left to seek interesting people in the lounge car. There were lots of them, all doubtless desperate to spend the night telling me stories of marital shipwreck, financial intrigue and political scandal: a young woman with a much older man stared into each other's eyes; a louche young man with a bohemian aspect cast a languid glance in my direction. I fingered my notebook in anticipation of much excited scribbling, but first a drink.

'What carriage are you from?' asked the attendant, finely tuned to imposters and interlopers from cattle class.

'Coach A.'

'Then you can't stay here. You can take a drink back to your seat if you are quick.'

I would like to pretend I saw hints of disappointment in the faces of the other passengers but I would be lying. It was, of course, class-driven apartheid at its worst.

When my pride had recovered and I was settled into my seat I noted with relief that we were at liberty to leave the curtains open. And I did wish. I was anticipating a soothing blackness punctuated by the occasional light from the homes of insomniacs, or street lamps in industrial estates. I looked forward to that half sleeping state when dreams can be steered in pleasant directions.

'London!'

Soon after we glided out of Glasgow Central, the attendant seemed unduly attentive as he checked tickets and seat reservations. His gaze wandered to the overhead luggage racks, and he had no hesitation in probing the small tent erected over one of the seats by a secretive passenger. He also checked both toilets at the end of the corridor. A small commotion indicated that he had located his quarry. We had a stowaway. A young man with beard and long hair was pleading for his life. 'I will pay, I will pay!' To no avail.

'Come with me. Now! And bring your bag.' The prisoner

was escorted to a padded cell where he was beaten with a truncheon before being allowed to limp back, his bones broken, to his illegal seat.

'I will be thrown off at Carlisle,' he explained to his new audience, one of whom had already organised a petition on Change.org to secure his release. There is an alarming precedent in *Autobiography of a Super Tramp*, in which W H Davies mentions being forced to jump off a moving train at the point of a revolver.

'Shame,' said Defoe. 'I too have been pursued and hounded by the unreasonable forces of law. We must provide sanctuary for the unfortunate boy.'

'We will do nothing of the sort.'

Another victim of this oppressive regime was failing in his attempt to prise apart the ancient doors that prevented him returning to his seat from the toilet. Like a Marcel Marceau impersonator, he flattened his hands on the glass panels and wailed soundlessly. We all ignored him.

The carriage lapsed into collective unconsciousness and I just had time to reflect on the intimacy of sleeping with strangers before succumbing to the very half dreams I had anticipated.

I woke to experience the carriage gently expiring; the train was slowly dying as its life support systems closed down. The air drained out of the radiator pipes and the silence was near total. We had stopped on the first of several scheduled pauses that ensured the journey would take the full eight hours and not end before daybreak, and were resting in Carstairs station just beyond the State Hospital. What unimaginable dreams disturbed its restless inmates, and might these dreams tumble down the hill to envelop the train in an angry mist? I closed my eyes, but jolted awake again. I could hear a siren.

It was the blood in my veins, a sleep-induced tinnitus, a passing thing. The hospital has an alarm system based on

World War II air-raid sirens. A two-tone alarm sounds in the event of an escape, but all was quiet. I glanced at the stowaway who was colouring in large moons and stars in a child's book. Elsewhere passengers slumbered beneath the black eye masks provided by the railway company.

Waking again as we slid through Carlisle, a perverse part of me anticipated the moment when the stowaway would be hauled from his seat and tossed, arms akimbo, from the moving train into the dark, dark night. There was no sign of him.

'Into the sea with him!' shouted Defoe. 'Crusoe survived, so will he.' Somewhere wires were getting crossed.

'You've changed your tune,' I said. 'And don't bring your fiction into this, it's hard enough trying to make sense of your journeys as it is.'

'Harrumph,' said Defoe.

As we crawled through the London suburbs in the early hours he became animated again. 'Bricks!' he shouted.

'What?'

'Bricks! Bricks! Vindication.' He pointed at the neat lines of back-to-backs. 'I knew I was right. All these dwellings are constructed from bricks.'

'Observant or what?' My sarcasm was lost on him.

'I founded a manufactory of Bricks at Tilbury. You should know that; you've read my biography. The finest pantiles this side of Utrecht. You wouldn't catch me mixing earth with the clay, or burning ash and cinders in the kiln. Half of London would be built from my bricks…I was destined to be a rich man.'

'You were declared bankrupt and put in prison.'

'My enemies were jealous. Perfidy was in the ascendant.' He made angry gestures with his hand.

As I ate my bacon roll at 6 am, I read the Caledonian Sleeper magazine with the snappy title, *Sleeper*, and felt a small resentment that I had met neither Kirsty Wark or Chris Brookmyre who, apparently, always use this service.

John's vindictive itinerary propelled us straight onto the train to Willesden. I was braced for scenes reminiscent of the evacuation of Saigon as commuters fought for a handhold on strap or pole but it was unnaturally quiet. The carriage was virtually deserted. There must have been a disaster. All of London's inhabitants had been instructed to stay at home and construct bomb shelters from spare furniture and doors torn from their hinges. Above all else, they must not stare at the light in the sky.

It was the same on the train to Gospel Oak. The only travellers were sitting in total silence in long lines down either side. The palm trees growing on Hampstead Heath station tended to confirm my view that we had arrived in a strange country.

At least the few commuters on the train to Barking were talking to each other as the train warmed itself in the early morning sun.

'Dfnsdfvhdfvuiu,' said a middle-aged man.

'Vjdjdak,' replied his partner.

At Barking station two train drivers embraced each other on the platform. Their hug was warm and affectionate. This can't be London.

On the Stratford train a young boy sat down opposite the pair of us. He took one look at his new travelling companions and fled down the carriage to find his parents.

A young couple seemed to be smiling encouragingly in my direction. Emboldened, I approached. She was a student nurse. He was doing very little. They were returning from a rock festival in Northampton, and their happiness seemed enviably complete.

'Do you have a shed?' she asked on learning that I was a writer. I opened my mouth and closed it again. A shed was not at the top of my wish list. Perhaps she was thinking of Dylan Thomas' shed in Laugharne. On reflection, Virginia Woolf had a shed of her own, and Sophie Dahl is raising funds to restore her grandfather's shed.

'Yes, you need a shed,' said her companion. I thanked them for the advice and promised to get a few catalogues.

Elsewhere in the carriage, a ginger-haired toddler was swinging happily around a pole while his mother timed her interventions carefully, pushing a banana further down his throat every time he swung past. A man with the dungarees and chiselled features of an old testament prophet stared impassively, listening on his headphones to psalms interspersed with diatribes against fornication and adultery. Two Japanese men sat next to each other, both wearing black kilts and back-to-front baseball caps. Yes, this felt more like London.

An exasperated young man in a sharp suit raised his eyes heavenwards and gripped his phone tightly. 'We're very busy, Dad...I know we should meet up but we're very busy. You don't understand!'

There had been a lot in the papers recently about the alleged discovery of a Nazi train in a blocked-off tunnel near the Polish border. It was allegedly packed with untold riches looted from the Jews. This news made travelling through the tunnels near Gravesend much more interesting. Peering into the darkness by pressing my nose against the cold and unpleasant smelling glass, I saw at least three ancient steam locomotives, the skeletons of numerous SS storm troopers and several brass-bound chests overflowing with plundered jewellery.

'That's why I invested in that diving bell.'

'Pardon?'

'Treasure. Plunder if you like. It was there. Just off the Kent coast. I would be lowered forty fathoms then light the lantern. The ocean would reveal its secrets...'

'Don't tell me, the venture failed and you were declared bankrupt, again.'

'They were conspiring against me ...'

Looking along the length of the train, I realised that the carriages stretched to a vanishing point. It could have been one of those illusions created by the mirrors in changing rooms that feed off each other with myriad synchronised reflections. Fully grown figures gradually diminished and lost colour until they were distant dots. The serpent-backed floor undulated with the contours of the ground; a tame rollercoaster. By way of surreal accompaniment, the concertina connections between the carriages chirruped and gossiped merrily.

The immediate foreground was now occupied by a man old enough to know that falling-down jeans is never a good look, and a young girl staring impassively. If she kept very, very still then no one would notice her. Even better, she might not actually exist. This was perhaps the consummation that she desired. Her face was disfigured by piercings, each positioned to dehumanise and obliterate her attractiveness. Her earlobes were elongated like Dali's watch, and her thin legs covered in an untidy spider web of ripped tights. John saw me staring and told me to take off my professional face, but I was genuinely worried for her. What traumas had compelled her to construct a persona sufficiently forbidding to preclude anyone getting close to her, physically or emotionally? What was she thinking? What was going through her head ...?

'That man's pitying me, I can tell, I recognise that look. He's probably a do-gooder, a social worker perhaps. No, he's too old for that. Retired perhaps. No one knows how strong I feel. Their pity is wasted; it can't pierce my armour. I have a shell. I am protected. I am a chrysalis. When the butterfly is fully formed it will burst into the sun. I will rise on gossamer wings of silk ...'

As we rattled our way towards Highbury and Islington it occurred to me that Defoe had been unnaturally quiet. Realising that part of me was actually missing him, I held *A Tour through the Whole Island* by the front and back covers and shook it, but he wasn't for coming out. Eventually I heard him muttering 'Hackney Fields'.

'Is it a good memory?' I asked.

He re-emerged, checked that there were no sheriffs' officers in the carriage, and cleared his throat. 'The authorities had seized all copies of my pamphlet from the printers and ordered that all copies be burned by the common hangman. I offered to serve in the military for no pay but to no avail. I went into hiding.'

'And?'

'A man discovered me on Hackney Fields. I drew my sword and forced him to his knees, making him swear that if he ever met me again he would shut his eyes and say nothing or...' He chuckled to himself and sat back contentedly.

Perhaps the lack of sleep was catching up with me but much of the inner London routes passed in the cliché of a blur.

Endless small trips, meticulously organised by John to guarantee maximum coverage of the network, only served to minimise opportunities for meaningful connections with anyone. People appeared then moments later disappeared; an ever-changing kaleidoscope of faces glimpsed for a moment and then gone forever. It was like standing on the edge of eternity and watching everyone who had ever existed tumbling head-first into oblivion. Handmade Christmas decorations which, when unfolded, reveal a frieze consisting of hundreds of small identical figures all holding hands. Their brief candles put out in an instant.

It would be simplistic to characterise the abiding impression as one of alienation. It was more complex than that. With one or two exceptions, the passengers rarely exhibited symptoms of hostility or disassociation. They were seemingly content in their self-containment, their inner landscapes more compelling than the outer perspectives.

83

For most, the journey was no more than a brief, irrelevant synapse between different facets of consciousness.

Our itinerary dragged us at speed through the London gazetteer leaving an impressionistic afterglow of famous place names: Crystal Palace, Battersea Dogs and Cats Home, the Oval, Wembley, Putney. 'Alight here for Big Ben'; each name redolent with connotations, heavy with false memories.

I watched smoke curling upwards from tyres burning on wasteland, and became aware of Defoe's profound agitation.

'What's up?'

'Everything's on fire! The red sky is falling. Papa save me!'

'How old were you when the Great Fire broke out?'

'See how the smouldering rafters tumble into the street. A woman has been crushed. Papa save her! I can taste the ash on my tongue. People are running this way, their clothes on fire. A dog is rolling on the ground to put out the flames. Papa save it!'

'Stay calm, old fellow. It was a long time ago.'

'Why was I saved? Why did the flames miss our house? I should have died with the others.'

'We call it survivor syndrome now. Don't ask, it doesn't matter.'

As we drew slowly into Paddington Green I saw a fat fox sunning itself on the track beneath a tree, in the branches of which a magpie was picking at red berries.

DAY TWO
Paddington – Slough – Windsor & Eton Central –
Slough – Maidenhead – Marlow – Maidenhead –
Twyford – Henley – Twyford – Reading –
Redhill – Reading – Waterloo

The day felt full of promise. My good mood threatened to compromise objectivity. It was a pleasure to behold the happy commuters on the station concourse, each one suffused with beatific smiles as they waited patiently in the queue to the underground station. Perhaps the guru with the logo had been successful in his mission to make London a happy place. Even John seemed the best possible travelling companion, and I knew the day would be characterised by an accumulation of small joys and telling insights.

We missed our first train. While I am astonishingly fit and lithe for an old person, John is less so. He lumbered and rolled down the platform reaching for the door as it slammed shut in our faces and the train drew out of the station. When we got on the next train, I found myself squashed next to a woman intent on organising her entire life by phone on the Paddington to Slough express.

'Yes, we put his name down the day he was born, I just need to know if he has to wear his uniform today.'

'Eton College,' interjected Defoe. 'The finest school for what we call grammar learning in Britain, or perhaps in Europe.'

Her next angry conversation was conducted in Italian. After she had brought the discussion to an abrupt end, I glanced sideways at her phone. Her screen saver consisted of the single word LOVE. Surely now was the moment to speak but, as I drew breath, she stood up and got off the train.

I had more luck with three young Asian passengers who were more than happy to talk about their day ahead. *En route* to enrol at Windsor College with a view to resitting A levels, they listened with feigned attention as I trotted out geriatric clichés and truisms of 'the best days of your life' variety. I felt a moment of connection when suggesting that they should choose universities as far as possible from home 'so that they could misbehave.' Smiles all round.

'Poppycock!' said Defoe, who had been listening more intently than I realised. 'Great mistake. Get a trade. My father was a butcher. I learned about life standing in the offal with the smell of blood in my nostrils. Hack off the trotters, twist the sinews until they snap.' He mimed the procedure. 'Shank and brisket. Sirloin and cutlets.'

'All very well, but isn't it the truth of the matter that you couldn't go to university because you were a Dissenter?'

'Fillets and chops ...' said Defoe, choosing to ignore me.

We spent a total of three minutes on Windsor station, long enough to appreciate the external attractions of the castle and the flowing Thames. A sign on the platform urged all parents, guardians and responsible adults to 'keep little fingers clear of lift doors... as they will be chopped off and they will be left with tiny bleeding stumps'.

'And now I am, by just degree, come to Windsor, where I must leave talking of trade, river, navigation, meal and malt, and describe the most beautiful, and most pleasantly situated castle and royal palace in the whole isle of Britain ...'

'Stop right there.' He looked up, confused. 'If I remember, you spend the next twenty odd pages describing the building in tedious detail.'

'You too Sir, as this tome amply demonstrates, are more than capable of describing the mundane and trivial in great and unnecessary detail.'

I had no answer. As we left the station I was surprised to see a Hawker Hurricane hovering precariously on a metal pole above a public park.

In Slough, although initially exhilarating to be buffeted by the blast of trains passing at supersonic speeds, the impression was that no services actually stopped here. This left a sense of alienation and disenfranchisement. Slough had been abandoned in the great exodus from the city. Fat cat brokers would not have had time to sneer at the passengers waiting forlornly on the platform. Among these lost souls

was a stooped Asian man who, wanting directions and/
or reassurance, approached John with sad and completely
unwarranted deference, 'Excuse me, Sir...'

On the opposite platform a young man in a shell suit
jogged his way out of the gents and ran on the spot. Eventually his partner, clad in hijab, waddled her way down the
steps to join him.

A soothing voice on the tannoy offered bland, Big-
Brotheresque reassurance that all underground services
were functioning smoothly. Furthermore, 'world poverty
had now been eradicated and government scientists have
uncovered the secret of immortality...'

The only hint of sanity was manifest in the unexpected
presence, in a glass case on Platform 2, of a stuffed 150-year-
old dog: Dog Jim, and thereby hangs a tail. Beneath that
moth-eaten and rancid coat, stitched together in a sort of
canine quilt, once beat a warm heart.

Dog Jim started his duties as Canine Collector for the
Great Western Railway and Orphans Fund in the early 1880s.
He mastered a great many amusing tricks. He would sit up
and beg, or lie down and 'die'; he would make a bow when
asked; he would sit up in a chair and look quite at home with
a pipe in his mouth and cap on his head; if anyone threw a
lighted match on the ground, he would extinguish it with
a growl; if a ladder was placed against the wall, he would
climb it. His longest jaunt was to Leamington. He was also
spotted in Paddington and once, when placed back on the
Windsor to Slough train, got off, preferring to walk down
the track.

On the journey to Maidenhead, John feigned profound
emotion on spotting a field. I suggested it was artificial
and would be rolled up in the evening before reverting to
its true function as a used car lot. He had a point though,
there weren't many fields and those we did see were being
gnawed at the edges by huge machines and turned into

quarries. Even back gardens were being halved to accommodate I'm-richer-than-you swimming pools.

Our new companion on Maidenhead station was Nicholas Winton, whose statue was an integrated part of a platform bench and engraved with the names of the 669 children he rescued from the Nazis. He arranged for whole trainloads of children to leave Czechoslovakia in 1939 as part of Operation Kindertransport. Eventually one train, packed with children, was prevented from leaving Prague. But what happened? Did someone betray the children? And then I saw the moment...

'Be still children, be still.' The woman moved from compartment to compartment, opening each door with her finger to her lips. 'Hush, babies. Soon the train will move. No Franz, you can't go to the toilet. Hold it in. Alese! Close the curtain! Alese!'

The soldier put his face up against the carriage window, shielded his eyes and peered into the startled face of a small girl...

Needing some respite from these thoughts, I took advantage of the twenty-minute hiatus before the next train to explore Maidenhead High Street.

The highlight of this brief excursion was a race between two mobility scooters down the middle of the road. The ancient custodians were taking no prisoners. Innocent pedestrians fled before joining the others mangled beneath the wheels. The old woman, at full throttle, just managed to finish ahead of her male competitor. She punched the air and sprayed champagne over the delighted crowd.

On the outskirts of Marlow we saw hot black cattle standing up to their knees in the Thames, for all the world like old ladies with their tights round their ankles, staring bewildered, trying to remember how to misbehave.

It was time for me to stop enjoying the view and talk to people. Seeing me hesitate, John took the initiative and addressed the man sitting opposite.

'Excuse me, but my socially inadequate travelling companion is too shy to talk to strangers on trains, and so is unlikely to fulfil his mission of writing a book about the people he has encountered.'

I stuttered and looked pathetic. The man quickly scanned his repertoire of innocuous opening gambits and offered, 'I live in Wokingham on account of its excellent private schools and its complete lack of council houses.' I thanked him and smiled nervously. I would be revenged on John, of that there was no doubt.

My own efforts had similar results. An Italian-born but naturalised South African extolled his place of residence on the grounds that 'It is full of Englishmen. There are no foreigners in the pubs. Not like London.' Oh dear. Perhaps I should steer clear of men travelling on their own for a while.

'That's the hill!' exclaimed Defoe banging his hand against the window. 'The battle.'

'Which battle?'

'The battle between the Irish Dragoons and William's troops. I met a lone survivor hiding in a ditch.'

'"We woke to an arrow shower," he told me. "The men were felled like quoits. The arrows rained silently. Harpooned like beasts, the men pulled at the wooden shafts sticking in their sides. The blood ran down their tunics. The wound grows big when you try to wrench out the arrow. The flesh tears. It was easier to leave the stump in your body, and break off the shaft. Men were spiked like hedgehogs. Michael, I knew him well, he wandered delirious with an arrow sticking from his head, his eyes bulging. Help me, Sir."'

'I don't think that account has been published before.'

'No, but you may use it, Sir, for your own purposes.'

My imaginary friend was turning out to be more sensitive and generous than I had anticipated. As if embarrassed by this thought, Defoe sank back into the pages of Letter Four in which he describes the Berkshire skirmishes.

I next succeeded in frightening two innocent German girls by the mere act of sitting next to them. A frisson of unease clouded both of their faces. They recovered to politely explain that they were attending a local school as they were not yet old enough to work as au pairs. I could think of nothing else to say, and neither could they. The day was not going well. Perhaps I should confine myself to staring out of the window and desist from disconcerting strangers, at least for a while.

Alternatively, we could abandon the journey and head back shamefaced to Glasgow. Then again, I could just relax and see what the day brought.

Inertia suggested the latter course and we climbed aboard the Reading to Redhill train. Our perseverance was rewarded by the sight of a late middle-aged couple who had barricaded themselves into a corner of the carriage, rendering at least eight seats unusable. They had constructed an impressively elaborate barrier of suitcases and holdalls: Little England. Through a gap, I could see them sprawling with their feet up. He had actually removed his socks and shoes. All that was missing was the Union Jack, a basin of Epsom Salts and a cup of cocoa. By aligning my mouth close to a slit, inadvertently left between two bulging cases, I was able to conduct the semblance of a conversation. The husband responded to my disembodied voice with a degree of reluctance but told me they had just retired from a lifetime of teaching and were going abroad for a long, and much deserved holiday.

'The bursar begged me to return for supply, but I told him no. Enough was enough!'

I moved to the end of the carriage where a tanned pensioner was flaunting an impressive chest-length scar visible though his shirt, intentionally left open for the very purpose of flaunting. Pleased to notice my stare, he explained, 'Triple bypass.' He fingered the fleshy zip proudly. 'I keep myself fit though, you have to, don't you?' This rhetorical question was answered by a young woman in a high visibility vest who was nursing her bike.

'Try cycling,' she urged, before revealing that it was her job to encourage people to travel by sustainable forms of transport.

The geriatric bull, provoked by this red flag, lost no time in retaliating. 'Why does nobody wear a helmet?'

'I do,' she said, but he wasn't listening.

'How much is a helmet for goodness sake? Ten pounds? Not much for a life, is it? And what about all this cycling on pavements? Eh? Eh?'

Keen to defuse the discussion, I asked if she had ever encountered resistance to bringing her bike on the train.

'There was the time,' she offered, 'when a man vomited all over it.' I nodded politely and retreated to my seat.

The train stopped for no apparent reason, and the conductor made an announcement. Contributors to the carriage debate divided evenly between proponents of 'cattle on the line' and 'trespassers on the line.' I was undecided which would make for the best narrative. On balance, I veered towards the cattle, envisaging a rodeo round-up in full view of the carriage with lassoes, lanyards and rustler.

Further announcements confirmed that the second interpretation was the correct one. Several young people in the carriage took to social media to glean more information. According to one, ultimately peachable, source, a gang was being chased by police in our direction. This carried hints of much needed excitement. Should we step onto the track and trip the gangsters as they passed? Were the villains propelling themselves towards us on one of those rail bogies with pump-action handles leaving the Keystone Cops to flail in their wake?

The day was hot and in response to desperate pleas from smokers, the guard opened the doors onto the platform.

It was Robert Graves who remembered being given two

hours: 'The wheels failing once more at Somewhere-Nowhere/ To climb out, stretch our legs and pick wild flowers.'

Unlike Graves, and having no wish to pick flowers, I discussed the delay with the guard. There wasn't a gang, just one vulnerable man threatening to harm himself at the station ahead. I felt guilty about my facetious speculation, and sought comfort in the fact that he had not yet thrown himself under a passing train as none were currently passing.

Meanwhile we had been joined by another passenger who said he had worked for twenty-five years in Broadmoor high security prison, and was a trained hostage negotiator. He ruefully offered to come out of retirement if needed.

While the conductor attended to official business, I asked the negotiator about his time in the hospital. I was genuinely curious and to reassure him that I was not just seeking sensational insights into the lives of the truly mad, I told him about my own background working in the mental health sector.

'The most difficult thing,' he said, 'was to remain firmly non-judgemental about the patients, even when it was known that they were sex offenders'. He said that, in the main, he thought he had managed this throughout his career. I asked him about the concept of recovery in the context of Broadmoor. He brightened and said that the average time patients spent in the hospital was seven years, after which they were released back into the community, with safeguards, to lead worthwhile lives. This was a good conversation, only spoiled by Defoe's intrusion.

'The orders for the government of the hospital of Bethlem are also exceedingly good. Namely;

'1. That no person, except the proper officers who tend them, be allowed to see the lunatics of a Sunday.

'2. That no person be allowed to give the lunatics strong drink, wine, tobacco or spirits, or to sell any such thing in the hospital.

'3. That no servant of the house shall take any money given to any of the lunatics to their own use.

'4. That no officer or servant shall beast or abuse, or offer any force to any lunatic; but on absolute necessity.'

I thanked him but suggested he get back on the train as we were about to resume our journey. There was however no indication that the trespass episode had not ended satisfactorily.

Passing slowly through North Camps station I saw a lone man with military style haircut screwing up his cap as if in a degree of distress.

My eyes wandered upwards to the overhead luggage rack as a single feather floated towards me. I had no recollection of the train hitting either a chicken or an angel. John then got cross with me as I wrongly identified a dive-under as a flat crossing. His reaction seemed unfair as I was genuinely doing my best to humour him.

'Get oop and give seat t' young lady!' A stereotypical Yorkshire man with craggy features and a walking stick carved from an oak tree berated an embarrassed young lad who was quite oblivious of any wrongdoing. The lad blushed to his roots and shuffled towards the toilet.

'It's all those laptops and phones,' explained the stereotype. 'It makes them dead t' world. That's for children, not grownoops.' Enjoying his sojourn from the nineteenth century, he continued his lecture. However, my concentration was momentarily compromised by a blow to the head from a passing rucksack.

When the cartoon halo of stars settled, I noticed that almost every passenger was watching a screen perched on their laps. At least five of those nearest were watching films. It was well past six o'clock. It was now commuters' leisure time.

Shortly after the conductor announced that we were about to stop in Egham, the Yorkshireman shouted, 'Don't egg'm on!' and roared with laughter. Realising that his quip had been met with a stony silence, he sought refuge in a can of Guinness before sallying forth again, 'Egg and chips!' he shouted to even less acclaim. Mercifully we were approaching Waterloo station.

DAY THREE
Paddington – Bedwyn – Reading – Banbury –
Oxford – Moreton-in-Marsh – Reading –
Basingstoke – Reading – Paddington

Why was my dad staring at me from the window of the tube to Paddington? He looked quizzical, as well he might. He smiled back at me, but of course he would.

The train was alive with bright chatter. There was an unspoken consensus that this new day would be a good one. An American woman sitting opposite her partner was producing ribbons and bows, knotted handkerchiefs and turtledoves from her magical suitcase. I assumed this was some sort of commercial enterprise, perhaps a private courier service. 'You dial, we shop, wrap and deliver.' It transpired that all the presents were for her daughter, who lived in Dulwich and whom they had not seen for a long while.

We had a pleasant chat about being stopped by the police in America for the heinous crime of walking when you could have taken the car. John's sympathies lay with the police.

Realising that writing about American women wrapping presents was not Pulitzer material, I steeled myself to wander the carriages until I located someone exuding narrative potential. Easy to find, he was standing with Bill Sykes' dog and a stolen bicycle, scowling beneath his stubble, but when he spoke it was with a gentle politeness and disarming urbanity.

Appearances and reality again. He too was American. I should have realised from the shafts of light funnelling onto the concourse, and the proliferation of men in Homburgs, that we had taken a train from Grand Central, not Paddington.

He had left Connecticut at the age of fourteen and was a ceramic potter with a studio in Newbury. Furthermore, he lived on a longboat that he moved every two weeks for a change of scenery, parking alongside a different pub. He had a wood-burning stove and, when feeling lazy, would let his dog pull him along the towpath on his bike. I was consumed with envy. This was the man I wanted to be.

The dissatisfaction I now felt with life clouded my initial impressions of Bedwyn. What a stupid name, and why did every bungalow possess enough solar panels to service a space station? So many questions. The sole justification for visiting Bedwyn (and I suspect that very few people ever have) was the pursuit of completism; if we were to travel on every line in the United Kingdom then we had to poke our noses into some obscure and profoundly uninteresting places.

To make matters worse there was no functioning toilet on the escape train. The new Reading station with its billion pounds' worth of architectural innovation, including several corrugated ski slopes, must possess state of the art facilities. It does, but they are well hidden. My inability to locate a toilet, despite following numerous signs, made me fear for my sanity. The experience was akin to being trapped in an Escher drawing.

The most alarming aspect of the trip to Banbury was passing the site of the recently concluded Reading music festival. Endless multi-coloured tents poked out of a sea of detritus. The garbage pickers of Delhi would make a fortune if unleashed in this particular field of dreams. Yet the Metros strewn about the carriage showed harrowing pictures of refugees, desperate for tents, desperate for anything.

'I have seen similar sights,' interjected Defoe. 'It puts me in mind again of the Cambridge horse fair. In less than a week there is scarce any sign left that there has ever been such a thing there: except by the heaps of dung and straw; and other rubbish which is left behind, trod into the earth...'

Idyllic glimpses of green Ransomesque waterways went some way to offsetting these thoughts. I let myself be distracted by several one-sided phone conversations.

'I think she's fallen out with me. I think she took offence at my reaction. I will visit. I will try to smooth things over.' While applauding the conciliatory impulses of the speaker, I couldn't help speculating about the nature of the discovery that had led her to react so badly ... Perhaps her daughter had got engaged to a convicted murderer. Perhaps she had been disinherited by an aging relative who had changed her will. Perhaps she had joined UKIP.

In Oxford station, three sinister figures on the opposite plat-form aimed long-lensed cameras at us. Paranoia took hold. As happens in the worst of thrillers their aim was instantly obscured by the passing of a freight locomotive. The truth dawned. They were trainspotters. One of them must have been in his mid-eighties. Obsession is a wonderful thing, but their joy was short-lived as they were approached by a man with a tank on his back, wielding a spraying wand. Another train blocked our view. When it had passed, there was no sign of the geriatric spotters; they had been exterminated.

'Beware of the ragwort!' pronounced John sententiously, wagging his finger at me.

'What?'

'Spores escaped from the university botanic gardens and settled on the cinder track beds that reminded them of their home on Vesuvius. They hitchhiked a lift down the line and soon conquered England. Turning it yellow. Very bad for horses.'

'What?'

'Horses. Ruins their liver and turns them blind.'

'Don't say that.' Defoe was visibly distressed.

'Now you've upset him. You know he loves horses.'

'Who the hell are you talking about?'

'Doesn't matter.'

As the train gathered speed, I caught sight of two very frightened old people huddling together in their airline seats. An ancient mother and her son perhaps.

Not wishing to intrude into their private misery, I plonked myself opposite a woman with a not unwelcoming demeanour. She just stared at me. It was not an intimidating stare, but one calculated to loosen my tongue, not hers. I suspected that she was a counsellor by trade, and could feel myself succumbing to the unspoken invitation to tell her my secrets. The confession of murder was comparatively easy, she just smiled in a pointedly non-judgemental way.

In retrospect, I think she genuinely wanted to tell me something important and couldn't decide if I could be trusted. In that moment of indecision lay a paradigm for the myriad times that we almost make contact but the moment is lost. To accentuate this sense of yearning, I noticed that the woman sitting diagonally across had moved to the edge of her seat to better hear our one-sided conversation. She too had a tale to tell, and wanted me to engage with her, but my social ineptitude prevented me approaching her.

These failed encounters lowered my spirits and rendered the countryside less attractive than it had seemed five minutes previously. To shift my mood, I decided to sally forth from Moreton-in-Marsh station for the twenty minutes before our next connection, and in that short time managed to scan the books in four charity shops. I was half tempted by a shelf of early crime fiction but none of the books had dust jackets and, in any case, did I really want to carry twenty volumes for the rest of the day?

The volunteer in the last of the shops directed me to the

book room upstairs which I thought I had all to myself until I noticed a tiny girl on a Victorian rocking horse in the corner. 'It's called Ned,' she explained in an unworldly voice.

Outside once more, I realised that we were passing the Black Bear, one of the last pubs I had taken my dad to. I had failed to make the connection with the small town, which was why he had appeared earlier.

Back on the train, John was bewailing the fact that he had been ignored in the local deli. I suggested this was because he resembled a cross between an escapee from a care-in-the-community project and a refugee from Planet Obesia. He responded to this cruel abuse with a grunt, and sought out the conductor to ask the whereabouts of the refreshment trolley. The custodian dutifully promised to 'send a man along', who intoned in fruity camp tones a full inventory of the delights he could deliver to our table.

'But what about real food?' asked John.

'Crisps or flapjacks?' asked the man, cutting to the chase.

'Bring everything you've got!'

I hoped that John was not going to repeat his threat to eat the next small passenger to pass through the train. Any such threat would not have gestated in idleness.

'He is almost as fat as the Fat Woman of Ross,' said Defoe, pointing at John.

I knew that, unlike Edward Thomas during the First World War, we would not be stopping in Adlestrop, mainly because the station had been closed since 1966. That moment of bucolic epiphany captured in the poem of the same name was irretrievable, but that was the point. The train having stopped unexpectedly, Thomas stared through the heat haze and beyond the deserted platform to the ' ...willows, willow-herb, and grass. And meadowsweet, and haycocks dry'.

To complete Thomas's poignant moment in arcadia, a blackbird sang. The world was at war, and his destiny was to be killed in the cloying stinking mud of Arras two years later.

Defoe, who had been snoozing, sprang into life and stared intently at the countryside.

'Basingstoke has a good market for corn, and lately, within a very few years, is fallen into a manufacture of making druggets and shalloons, and such slight goods, which, however employs a good number of the poor people, and enables them to get their bread, which knew not how to get it before.'

'I am pleased for the poor people of Basingstoke but what on earth are druggets and shalloons?'

'A drugget is a heavy felted fabric usually made of wool, and used as a floor covering.'

'And shalloons?'

'A lightweight twilled woollen fabric used chiefly for coat linings.'

I found myself wondering which of my two travelling companions was the most boring.

I attempted to bring the excitement back into my life by observing two young Japanese travellers who had become unnaturally engaged in a game of paper, stone and scissors. Shouts of disappointment alternated with cries of glee. A quick moment's research on my phone explained their commitment. The game has great cultural significance in Japan where few life decisions are taken without invoking the gods who use this game to communicate their thoughts to mere mortals.

Players start by chanting 'Saisho wa guu' and pump their fists in time. This is quickly followed by 'Janken pon', at which point both parties choose to demonstrate 'Guu', 'Choki' or 'Paa'.

'If I win, we get married.'

'Guu...Guu.'

'Bugger!' (In Japanese)

'Choki...Choki.'

'Shit!' (In Japanese)

'Paa...Guu.'

'Yes, ya beauty!' (Borrowed from Scots)

The young Japanese girl shows her delight by kissing me hard on the lips while the young man shakes John firmly by the hand.

I extricated myself from her embrace and moved down the carriage to admonish a young student who was reading Conrad's *Lord Jim*. I explain that my mission in life is to stop people on trains from reading Conrad. He mutters an embarrassed apology and explains that it had been an impulse buy from a second-hand shop near the Kassam Stadium where he had been watching Oxford United play Yeovil. Another bad mark. Desperate to extricate himself from my opprobrium, he explained that he bought the book in error thinking it was Amis' *Lucky Jim*. The lad was beyond the pale. I admonished him briefly but wished him well with his future studies at Durham.

While having a meaningless conversation about the reason why Great Western carriages have tinted glass, John startled me by explaining that tinted glasses were originally introduced to alleviate the symptoms of syphilis.

'Of course, my own dear Moll Flanders was badly afflicted with the pox ... Furthermore, let me show you one of the notices that I included in several editions of my Review.' He produced a crumpled piece of paper and smoothed out the creases with the back of his hand. 'Anti-venereal pills, which perfectly carry off the infection of a clap, or running of the reins, and complete the cure in a few days' time, without any hindrance of business. They free the body of the remains of any ill-cured pox or clap, and of mercury (unskilfully given).'

Unskilfully given ...

When we slid into Reading station for the third time that day I noticed unmistakable prison architecture towering above Platform 1. The proximity of Reading Gaol also explained why a tall foppish figure with blond hair was passing through the carriage distributing copies of his latest poem. 'Read my ballad and weep,' he said supressing a shudder.

I opened the thin pamphlet at random.

Dear Christ! The very prison walls Suddenly seemed to reel. And the sky above my head became Like a casque of scorching steel;

John looked at me as if I had finally gone mad. Defoe had removed his signet ring and was tapping it on the table in front of him. He looked extremely upset.

'What is it?' I asked. 'No, don't tell me, it's the idea of prison, isn't it? But you were in Newgate, not Reading which wasn't built until 1844.'

'It's all the same.'

'Tell me.'

'It was the pamphlet I wrote. *The Shortest Way.* The shortest way to prison ... That horrid place, my very blood chills at the mention of its name ... tis impossible to describe the terror of my mind, when I was first brought in ... the hellish noise, the roaring, swearing and clamour, the stench and nastiness ...'

I moved to his seat and rocked him in my arms.

The evening was spent recovering from the ordeals of the day in a surprisingly downmarket pub in Pimlico. A huge mural of John Terry and Frank Lampard looked down on twelve shaven-headed pot-bellied men moving in a respectful choreography around a dartboard while the cricket played out on TV. This soporific carnival of Englishness was suffi-cient to send me to my bed where I hoped I wouldn't dream of Newgate prison, nor indeed of John Terry.

DAY FOUR

St Pancras – Gravesend – Sittingbourne – Sheerness –
Sittingbourne – Ramsgate – Ashford – Tonbridge –
Tunbridge Wells – Tonbridge – Dover – Euston

In St Pancras Station we were presented with a twelve-page booklet: the National Rail Passenger Survey. The questionnaire offered us a total of 569 boxes to tick. I guiltily skip-read the options in response to question 48.9, eliciting reasons why passengers might feel uncomfortable on trains. These included: passengers drinking, putting their feet on seats, playing music or smoking. Being accosted by an old person intent on uncovering your darkest secrets was not an option, although it may be in future.

The conductor on the Gravesend train was determined to do his bit for customer relations. Before asking for tickets and rail passes, he placed a comforting hand on every passenger's arm. 'All right pal? OK matey?'

'Back in Blighty soon ... all over by Christmas ... don't worry mate, your missus has already got someone else ... think of all that lovely wine waiting to be liberated ...' Someone hummed *The White Cliffs of Dover*. 'That's right mate, keep your pecker up.' The troop train lumbered through the Kent countryside towards the ports.

An elderly man said he was going to walk from Herne Bay to Margate. He only travelled on foot or by train.

Four young mothers and a squad of excited, tumbling children said they were going to Dreamland in Margate. FAQs in abundance:

Will it be like the Dreamland I remember? We can't promise ...

What happened to The Whip and The Corbiere Wheel? They are being stored by our partners at the Dreamland Trust.

Can we camp at Dreamland? I'm afraid we don't have a camping area.

It's raining today, will all the rides be working? During wet weather it may be necessary to close our Born Slippy slide.

Glancing at the Medway from the bridge outside Rochester, I saw a submarine nestling in the estuary. Surely the craft had not been conjured by my wartime reverie? Apparently, it was U-475 Black Widow, a Russian relic from the cold war, now rusting away while funds are raised for its restoration.

I was startled out of my reverie by the vegetation slapping at the windows of the Sheerness train like a happy toddler running his stick across railings and soon we were running parallel to the estuary marshes where I caught a glimpse of Magwitch dragging his chains across the mud flats.

He was, as Dickens accurately described him, a fearful man, all in coarse grey, with a great iron on his leg. A man with no hat, and with broken shoes, and with an old rag tied round his head. A man who had been soaked in water, and lamed by stones, and cut by flints, and stung by nettles, and torn by briars; who limped and shivered, and glared and growled. He certainly glared and growled at the passing train. If he continued, he would soon stumble across the gypsy traveller encampment hiding beneath a flyover with at least two of the caravans burnt out.

It came as no real surprise that many more people were eager to escape from Sheerness-on-Sea than were preparing to board the returning train. The station itself merged seamlessly into a waste disposal plant.

'What are you doing here?' a lad in his late teens greeted his younger friend as she flounced into the seat in front. Despite wearing more make-up than an embalmer's apprentice, her face betrayed a seething anger.

'I've been sent home, ain't I? That Mr Davies, he was like,

103

"Your skirt is too short". He was in my face, I was like in his face. "You need glasses," I said. And then he touched me on the shoulder. "Don't you touch me!" I said. "I'm calling your mum," he says. "Whatever." So, he calls my mum and she says to put me on the phone, "Come home love," she says.'

Still in the grip of the confrontation, the young victim of injustice made small feinting movements to outmanoeuvre her enemy. Half words formed and dropped away. Her hands pointed, hung in the air and sunk back down again. 'Fuck!' she said, 'Fuck!'

I could tell that John was slipping back into his head teacher persona and was eager to assuage her anger. Defoe too was preparing to intervene. In fairness to him, he had consistently espoused the cause of education for women. Up he rose.

'I have often thought of it as one of the most barbarous customs in the world that we deny the advantages of learning to women. They should be taught all sorts of breeding suitable both to their genius and quality. And, in particular, Music and Dancing. But besides this they should be taught languages particularly French and Italian. They should be brought to read books, and especially history.'

I thought it unlikely that Kent girl would agree.

John and I were both distracted by a marauding dog, an escapee from the eponymous isle.

I glanced out of the window at a line of identical thin houses with pinched porches. Each dwelling had a Union Jack planted defiantly in the back garden as a warning to foreigners.

A swan was craning its neck to get a better view of whatever was happening in the caravan parked over the fence.

A flash of grey sea and a row of faded beach huts showed that Margate was close.

On balance I was getting better at talking to strangers. A gambit that was proving successful was to approach promising subjects and announce, 'I'm writing a book about trains and you are without doubt the most interesting people in the carriage.'

Strictly speaking, the three dishevelled folk and their equally dishevelled dog were between carriages. They had been camping in Canterbury *en route* to an acoustic therapeutic healing convention. Their guru was Tim Wheater. There are magical frequencies and one of the best is 528 hertz which can remove nitric oxide from the body. With a pang of authorial envy, I learned that a key self-help book has the truly magical title *How to Fork Yourself*. It is required reading for all courses on Tuning Fork Sound Therapy. There are other recommended frequencies including the OM, Solfeggio, Cosmic and Egyptian. The Egyptian is especially interesting as there are theories that the pyramids were built primarily as healing chambers. Ailments which are reputed to respond to sound therapy include cancer, arthritis and fibromyalgia.

'This is the work of the Devil!'

'Quiet.'

'I speak with authority. I wrote a History of the Devil.'

The three proponents I talked to outside the train toilet exuded integrity, compassion and general goodness. Few if any of these qualities were apparent in Tunbridge Wells where I had hoped for a chance encounter with Disgusted of... but he was occupied writing a diatribe against lesbians and litter according to the locals.

To my surprise, Defoe had decided to accompany me, and stared bemused at the posh shops on the High Street.

'Tunbridge wants nothing that can add to the felicities of life, or that can make a man or woman completely happy, always provided they have money; for without money a man is no-body in Tunbridge, any more than at any other place;

and when any man finds his pockets low, he has nothing left to think of, but to be gone.'

After the unrelenting geometry of hop fields and several silly little oast houses with pointy roofs, I gazed with yearning at the thin sliver of France separating the turquoise sea from a ribbon of pink sky.

John pointed out a teenage girl, slumped with her head in her hands on the floor. There were plenty of unoccupied seats but she chose not to sit in them. Perhaps she had a phobia of ancient train upholstery, perhaps she was attention seeking, but these facetious projections could not mask my growing certainty that she was unwell. With sinking heart, I realised that I would have to approach her and ask if she was all right.

Just as I lifted my bottom from the seat she rallied, unplugged her iPhone from an obscure socket on the floor of the carriage and took out her copy of *Catcher in the Rye*. I can now pass on Travellers' Tips Number One: 'If your phone is running down look for the plug marked NOT FOR PUBLIC USE, usually situated three inches from the carriage door. Although intended for the exclusive use of train cleaners, no one will mind you stealing some electricity.'

As we paused in Ramsgate, Defoe asked if he had time to visit The English Sampson, a local man. 'No,' I told him. 'You'll miss your train and never find your way back. You'll probably be arrested for vagrancy and find yourself in Newgate.' He chose to ignore my unkind remark and continued.

'It was from the town of Ramsgate, that a fellow of gigantic strength, though not of extraordinary stature, came abroad in the world, and who suffered men to fasten the strongest horse they could find to a rope, and the rope round his loins, sitting on the ground, with his feet straight out against a post, and no horse could stir him ... but his history

106

was very short, for in about a year he disappeared, and we heard no more of him since.'

Despite the anticlimactic conclusion to the story I found myself thinking that a horse might have its work cut out if John was similarly tethered.

We had the shortest of turnarounds in Dover, which seemed to suit Defoe.

'Neither Dover nor its castle has anything of note to be said of them, but what is in common with their neighbours; the castle is old, useless, decayed and serves for little.'

'I don't think a work placement with the National Trust is a good idea, Daniel, old mate.'

Our return journey was on the oldest and slowest train on the network. The man in top hat walking sedately in front should have alerted us. Obscure stations and whole decades crawled past.

By now my incipient inertia and general fatigue was mutating into profound boredom. What a truly stupid mission this was. What a ridiculous idea for a book, and if John drew my attention to another fly-over, fly-under or any other completely uninteresting piece of railway architecture, I would stab him with my ballpoint before eating my own eyeballs. I was determined to sulk for the rest of the journey and would not, for example, deign to make fun of passing stations with names such as Selling.

Mercifully there was hope. The conductor, after a phone call to the driver, announced that the train might have to be evacuated at the next station as the doors in the rear carriage were refusing to close. Evidently several passengers had taken the chance to escape by launching themselves into the ether.

To my profound disappointment, the problem rectified itself and the doors closed.

There is a documented phenomenon known as *angoisses*

des gares: being the anxiety associated with the approaching end of journeys. It may partially explain why passengers will tug at their luggage and wrestle with coats long before their destination.

By a quick sleight of head, I avoided decapitation from a tumbling bag containing several items of garden furniture and an ink printer. I was then smacked across the face by an overcoat, the linings of which were reinforced with lead shot. Cyril Connolly believed that *angoisses des gares* is 'closely connected with guilt, with the dread of something terrible having happened during our absence. Death of Parents. Entry of bailiffs. Flight of loved ones ...' The only one of these directly relevant to my age and stage was the last, but I had no reason to believe that Morag back in Scotland was thinking of leaving for a better life, away from her increasingly eccentric and absent spouse.

With several hours to pass before the sleeper departed, and eager to dispel any lingering *angoisses*, we took to consuming significant quantities of alcohol in The Gentle Tap, an outdoor drinking den close to Euston Station. Defoe had earlier intimations of this moment when he described a visit to an inn where 'the people were all quite drunk, all drinking, stinking, roaring, swearing, sleeping, spewing etc.'

Perhaps knowing that we were about to board our last train made us more receptive to the animated conversation being conducted by several very drunk but alarmingly articulate students. Passionate and principled, they exuded all the values of social inclusion and fairness. Unable to contain himself any longer John intervened declaring that he agreed with every word. Instantly they forsook their chairs and crouched at the feet of the sage like students listening to a portly Sophocles. I meanwhile offered absolution to a young lad mortified and embarrassed that his parents had paid to send him to public school.

There were rumours that Serco staff were thinking of

going on strike because they believed that the conditions on the overnight Caledonian sleeper were deteriorating to the potential detriment of passenger safety. Carriages were either overheating to the extent of spontaneous combustion, or so cold that some travellers had lost digits to hypothermia. The toilets, air conditioning (I didn't know such a thing existed), smoke detectors and overhead lighting only worked if the conductor was prepared to enter a Faustian pact with the devil. By now I didn't care. They could carry me home in an open topped coal wagon if they wished. I would lie back and look at the stars.

Before the sleeper pulled away, I interrogated everyone in the bar area. Talking to strangers held fewer terrors after drink. The fact I could not subsequently make any sense of my notes was irrelevant. I vaguely recall a young woman told me the most interesting thing that had happened to her on a train was meeting the Archbishop of Canterbury. Another couple gleefully recounted seeing a man crushed by a wagon on the outskirts of Cracow.

As I staggered to my seat I squeezed past a young girl talking from the doorway of her cabin to the already ensconced occupant. 'Hello, I'm your cabin mate...' Inside, Hannibal Lector grinned.

JOURNEY FOUR

South West England

DAY ONE
Glasgow Central – Birmingham New Street –
Cheltenham – Great Malvern – Gloucester –
Newport – Bristol – Swindon – Cheltenham

Hearing John pontificate about the limitations of democracy at 5.50 in the morning made me reflect on whatever heinous misdemeanours I had perpetrated in a previous life. Mercifully, he talked himself back to sleep by the Lake District, and I could luxuriate in the Wordsworthian vistas gliding past.

At its best, train travel has something in common with yogic flying; a pleasurable out-of-body experience during which the senses surrender to a mesmeric lantern show of beautiful landscapes.

'Himalayan Balsam,' said John. So much for mesmeric vistas. 'It's everywhere. Worse than Japanese knotweed, also known as Policeman's Helmet, Gnome's Hatstand or Kiss me on the Mountain.'

I wandered to the toilet and was distracted by an elaborate mural of a poppy field surrounding the bowl. From above the cistern, a solitary balloon rose majestically. I decided that on my return to my seat, I would pull the blinds so as not to compromise the image that had set my heart racing.

From the opposite side of the carriage I could just see the long low mud flats of Morecombe Bay. It was over ten years since twenty-one Chinese illegal immigrants were drowned while picking cockles. They had travelled to Britain in containers. Many of them swam in the wrong direction when the tides engulfed them. Four years ago, a fisherman discovered a human skull washed up by the tide. At first, he thought it was a set of false teeth upside down in the sand.

Defoe shielded his eyes from the sun and appraised the Pennines tumbling towards the track.

'Not only are these hills high and formidable, but they have a kind of an unhospitable terror in them.'

To me they were just hills, pleasing to the eye and devoid of all terror, but I wasn't going to pick a fight with him. He also had little time for Lancaster.

'It has little to recommend it but a decayed castle, and a more decayed port.'

Defoe's random pronouncements inclined me to see even more unsettling similarities between him and John; pontificators both.

'I slipped into your bed this morning without you noticing,' said a middle-aged man into his phone. He smirked, snorted and muttered some mercifully unintelligible endearments before ending the call with a series of grunts. He then dialled another number.

'Are you OK? I had to leave early this morning. Mike called a team meeting for eight.'

The man was either a bigamist or a common adulterer. He certainly looked quite tired.

I approached him and started my interrogation. 'So tell me, does your wife know about this other woman? How long has it been going on? Have the two women met? What about the children?' Appalled by my questions he ran

111

terrified down the middle of the train and locked himself in the toilet where he tried to lose himself in the field of poppies. 'I know you're in there!' I persisted. 'Come out and explain yourself.'

The other eavesdropping passengers, monogamous every last one, applauded and gave me the thumbs up.

'I know it's wrong,' came his muffled voice, 'but I love them both and my wife doesn't understand.' The passengers emitted a collective groan.

The outskirts of Preston are dominated by the austere silhouette of Tulketh Mill where doubtless there had been much trouble, and which was probably satanic in its own way. A glance at my phone revealed that the artificially created humidity necessary to stop the cotton snapping had the opposite effect on the workers. In addition, rumours persisted that pregnant women would barely pause from their duties to give birth before laying the infant on the pile of cotton waste next to the looms.

'The people are gay here which is why it is called Proud Preston,' commented Defoe. Again, I chose not to elicit further details.

The descent into Birmingham New Street was accompanied by a distinct plummeting of my spirits. What follows is a vitriolic diatribe against that station.

It is a dystopian, dreadful place of nightmares in which lost souls wander without purpose or hope, with expressions on faces of which Munch would have been proud. There is no colour but grey. All public announcements are made by torture victims from whose throats the vocal cords have been ripped. Under duress they emit tragic guttural, incomprehensible noises. Birmingham New Street is bleak beyond attrition and personifies alienation from all human values. According to the *Midlands Express and Star*, police are seeking a man who punched a complete stranger and pushed him onto the tracks when he refused to put out his cigarette. Any judge would accept a plea of momentary insanity induced by hideous surroundings.

'Well done,' said Defoe. 'There is nothing like venting the spleen.'

'Thank you.'

On the train to Cheltenham I approached a man writing longhand in a large ledger. It was a mistake. He covered his work like a schoolboy fearful lest the class bully copy his answers, and looked at me incredulously as I explained my mission. He had always filled in his work diary in this way but had never been asked to explain himself before. To my further embarrassment, he apologised for not being an interesting person.

Having spent most of my childhood in Cheltenham, I bored John by pointing out the field where a group of us had been admonished by a policeman for trespass and, as we came into the station, the vantage point next to the bridge where my father used to stand and wave his stick when he saw me opening the carriage door.

There was a further nostalgic element to our journey through the Vale of Evesham. In my mind's eye I was seventeen again, kneeling, sunburned and filthy on the brown parched clay beneath blackcurrant bushes plucking the fruit. No subsequent job ever gave me the satisfaction I experienced in those innocent and never-ending days.

Defoe seemed especially pleased to see the Malvern Hills.

'They talk much of mines of gold and silver, which are certainly to be found here, if they were but looked for, and that Mauvern would outdo the mines of Peru.'

I heard a llama bleating somewhere, and the gentle melody of panpipes suffused the carriage. These in turn were replaced by Elgar's cello concerto. There must be a posh term for the instinctive association of places with music. Whatever it is, I always experience it when I see these hills on the horizon. Elgar himself said, 'If you ever hear someone

113

whistling this melody around the Malvern, it will be me.' In fact, he wrote the piece in his secluded cottage, Brinkwells in Sussex, haunted by the sound of the artillery from across the channel in 1918.

'Not to mention the witches of Mauvern,' said Defoe enigmatically.

'What?'

'The witches who would perform their wonders.' He leered knowingly, but I decided not to probe further about the alleged tricks turned by the harridans of Mauvern.

If Birmingham New Street exists solely to satisfy Satan's whims, then Great Malvern station exists for the angels. 'Carry your bag, Sir?' offered the stationmaster, doffing his top hat. 'Charles Dickens alighted here just last week. Appearing at the Hay Book Festival I think.'

The Victorian decorative ironwork was freshly burnished, and an extremely proud station cleaner tut-tutted as she removed a microscopic particle from a bench. 'I love this station,' she volunteered, 'apart from the alcoholics.'

The station houses two charity bookshops, one on each platform. I seized on a facsimile of Aubrey Beardsley and Henry Harland's *Yellow Book* in excellent condition for two pounds. The day could not get much better.

The vendor told me that not much had happened in the last decade since a Buddhist monk became distressed in the car park, having lost his father. I was about to say something facetious about impermanence, but thought better of it. In any case, he was now describing how his shop had been invaded by a party of uncouth Australians all of whom wore hats with dangling corks.

Revelling in his role as surreal chronicler, he waxed lyrical about Lady Foley's private waiting room, now a tearoom on Platform 1. Despite being revered as a local benefactor it appears that, in the 1880s, the old bat found train travel so distasteful she insisted on the tracks being hidden from her view at huge expense. Also, unwilling to sully her nose with the smells of ordinary people, and presumably the occasional alcoholic, she insisted on having her own private waiting room constructed on the station.

I used the sound of the approaching train as an excuse, and stepped onto the Gloucester train. There was however to be no respite from the bizarre.

I sat next to a man in at least late middle-age. Motionless, possibly comatose, he might even have been dead. Either way he was not very clean. I regretted sitting there especially as my every move was being scrutinised by his three companions. A fierce woman beckoned me to join them. 'Why are you talking to him and not us?'

I had not said a word. She leaned forward and told me one of the worst things I had so far heard on any train. 'We are Morris dancers.'

I reeled in disgust but there was no escape. I was caught in the middle of a collective confession. 'We were playing at the Bromyard festival.' I could only think of the news item widely circulated on Facebook the previous week: 'Morris dancers and blind footballers in mass brawl,' the *Suffolk Gazette* declaimed, in one of the great headlines of our times.

I stared at my companions. They stared at me. If I said a wrong word I could be beaten with a stick. 'Why did you talk to him?' persisted the ringleader.

'I thought he looked interesting,' I replied lamely. I thought I saw one of them reaching into her bag for her weapon.

'We are all interesting, my love.' She explained how Bromyard is the festival centre of the known universe, with a marmalade festival, and a scarecrow festival (in June) and I wondered if their companion was a prizewinning scarecrow, and had never been a human being. Anyway, there were *en route* for the Crediton folk festival.

'I was right, you are all the most interesting people on the train,' I suggested with an unhelpful mix of condescension and panic.

'I take exception to that,' said a stranger in the next seat.

'What do you mean?' I asked, now wishing I had been rendered senseless by a Morris dancer's stick.

'I'm the most interesting person on the train.'

'Prove it.'

'Well,' said the new participant in the most-interesting-person-on-the-train competition. 'After seven years as the deputy head teacher of a large secondary school, I decided I wanted to be a train driver. And that's what I am.' Applause from the audience. The train driver nodded his head by way of acknowledgement. 'I started off as a chemistry teacher.'

A perverse part of me heard the cheeky kid in third year ask, 'Is it true you want to be a train driver when you grow up, Sir?' I could at least use his contribution as an excuse to distance myself from the petulant Morris dancers and their scarecrow.

'As a train driver you must have seen some interesting things…' Not the best of opening gambits but it worked.

'Well…' I detected a small glazing in his eyes. 'I was once flashed at by a man in a field near Bedford …' This man had clearly lived. 'And I'll tell you something … sometimes people don't close their windows at night and you see some extraordinary things from the cab.' What had he seen precisely? Naked couples swinging from the light fittings? Human sacrifice? Cannibalism? Unspeakable acts of bestiality? Either way you should keep your eyes on the track, I thought, in the interests of public safety.

The journey to Newport was slow and uncomfortable. The condition of the seats was explained by the presence of a huge moth with a self-satisfied grin, which had eaten the upholstery.

Large trackside signs warned us to KEEP OUT of areas that had been conquered by Japanese knotweed. John's words were proving prophetic. If the train went much slower, it ran the risk of being dragged into the poisonous undergrowth.

The Severn estuary was bleak and the sky was turning dark. The West Country had, the night before, been visited by a tornado. Whether it sucked up small flocks of sheep, disability scooters and innocent ramblers attempting the Cotswold Way was unclear.

Wiping the condensation from the window Defoe pointed out where he thought the village of Aust might be. 'A little dirty place,' he said. He had taken fright there when he saw the state of the Severn ferry boat and decided to take the long way around.

'Not very brave,' I suggested. 'With you being a soldier and all that.' He looked daggers at me.

As the train was now almost completely empty, I could only assume that rumours of my on-board interrogation had spread throughout the rail network.

Obligingly, the connection to Swindon passed through the Baedeker regency splendours of Bath and I caught a fleeting glance of an altercation between several crusties, their dogs and Jane Austen. An oddly slight and prim figure I thought, *en route* to supervise the heritage centre which bore her name. Also to encourage aficionados to dress up in bonnets and shawls before re-enacting a scene of simmering passion between Elizabeth Bennett and Mr Darcy.

Predictably Defoe had to comment on Bath.

'I shall be very short. It has been observed before, that in former times this was a resort hither for cripples; and we see the crutches hang up at the several baths, as the thank-offerings of those who have come hither lame, and gone away cured. But now we may say it is the resort of the well, rather than the sick, and the town is taken up in raffling, gaming, visiting, and in a word, all sorts of gallantry and levity.'

He made the town sound not unattractive.

I can still enjoy a good tunnel, the sudden onset of an eclipse that turns all windows into dull reflecting mirrors and makes small children exclaim with wonder. The Rev Kilvert recorded in his diary the moment in the Box tunnel near Bath when 'people began to strike foul brimstone matches and hand them to each other all down the carriage ...' I waited patiently as a sulphurous spitting wand was passed to me by a clergyman whose face was lit in a satanic glow. The young lady to whom I passed the errant firework winced as if her bonnet might catch fire. She squealed and dropped the match. Complete darkness.

Swindon itself brought back odd memories of being forced when I was twelve into unscrewing all the light bulbs in our compartment and throwing them out of the window. The bully can't have been the brightest of older boys as a single blacked-out compartment in an otherwise well-lit train must have attracted at least some attention.

John pointed out that I was not the only light bulb criminal to have disgraced the rail network. In the mid-20th century, bulbs were regularly harvested in huge numbers for resale. Likewise, crockery and cutlery from restaurant cars. There were instances of horsehair thieves gutting the upholstery in earlier times. If I were so inclined what fittings and fixtures could I steal from the Bath to Swindon CrossCountry? Not a great deal, truth be told: a few safety notices, and perhaps the odd antimacassar from First Class.

'Had I seen you, I would have taken my flail to you and beaten you soundly. I remember at the time of the Papal Plot, when murthering men in the dark was pretty much in fashion, and every honest man walked the street in danger of his life, a very pretty invention was found; the Protestant flail, loaded with lead.'

'We only removed a few light bulbs, for goodness sake, we weren't killing people.'

'So you say.'

I have better memories of those days: of cycling the round trip of 68 miles from my home to the Swindon locomotive works to join a huge snaking line of other small boys waiting for a tour. Presumably these were organised in response to official recognition that small boys, obsessed with steam locomotives, would find a way to trespass and risk injury. In the intervening half century, I have never been averse to a good queue. It occurs to me that I first experienced the thrill of anticipation outside the walls of the Great Western Railway.

Now used as one of the biggest outlet stores in Europe, the buildings still exude both grandeur and menace. *Life in a Railway Factory* by Alfred Williams, reprinted in recent memory, provides an eviscerating account of conditions in the works. 'A jagged piece of steel, ten or twelve pounds in weight, flew from the die and struck him between the eyes, knocking out half his brains...But he was murdered all he same, done to death by the system that is responsible for the rash haste and frenzy such as is common on the night shift.'

To dispel all thoughts of near decapitation, I wandered down the train to find that all the passengers had barricaded themselves into their seats behind impenetrable barriers of luggage and were feigning sleep. Come on people, give me your stories! When I saw that the only awake passenger was watching a montage on his laptop of photos of Osama Bin Laden I decided to give up for the day.

As I walked back to my seat, quite prepared to have a second discussion with John about the dangers of knot-weed, I overheard a completely unwanted question from an adolescent boy to his pal, 'Does that mean that when you fried it, it was still alive?'

DAY TWO
Cheltenham – Exeter – Exmouth –
Paignton – Torquay

The woman in the opposite seat transformed her square metre into a travelling beauty salon. Carefully arrayed on the upholstery were curling tongs, waxing equipment, exfoliants, straighteners, manicure sets, lip brushes – in short an entire cabinet of curiosities. I never for a moment thought that I could dredge lines from Pope's *Rape of the Lock* from some cranial archive but here they come...

'*And now unveil'd, the toilet stands display'd Each silver vase in mystic order laid ... Here files of pins extend their shining rows, Puffs, powders, patches, Bibles, billet-doux...*'

I never did understand how the Bibles fitted in. Anyway, the woman on the 10.00 Cheltenham to Exeter train proceeded to apply her tools and implements to every pore, blemish and orifice. She plucked, puckered, buffed, mascaraed, highlighted, lowlighted, preened and polished until, after several minutes, I realised that it was no longer necessary to peer discreetly and so I unashamedly gawked. She held several brushes simultaneously which she dabbed and feinted at her personal palette which disappeared beneath a thick veil of make-up. Expecting her to rise from her seat like a peacock in full plumage, or a camp diva *en route* to the Notting Hill carnival, I suffered disappointment when she left the train as what she was, a business woman who now felt that she could face her day.

I had to restrain Defoe from following to remonstrate. He had a profound hatred for all 'painted women' whom he castigated in both *Moll Flanders* and *Roxana*. 'I concur with St Jerome,' he said by way of explanation. 'How can she weep for her sins, when fearing her tears should make furrows in her face.'

The crowd at Stapleton Station seemed to have been waiting for over a hundred years: W G Grace jostled with Raja ram Mohan Roy, the founder of a Bengali reform movement, and Ben Tillett, the trade union leader. This journey was proving sufficiently bizarre without Network Rail feeling obliged to contribute full-sized murals.

I had previously noticed a young man in a blue striped blazer and massive music hall moustache that he twiddled incessantly. Having left the train, he returned seconds before its departure to retrieve his umbrella, which he waved melo-dramatically in the air.

John, as always a font of largely unwanted knowledge, sagely drew my attention to Taunton Rugby Club and reminded me of the controversy surrounding its firework display. Seven motorists were killed on the M5 in thick fog which some claimed was accentuated by smoke from the pyrotechnics. A train driver said he could barely see two feet beyond his cab.

'Beggars chased me on the road to Taunton,' said Defoe.

'Tell me,' I said, as his tales tended to be more interesting than John's.

'We were surrounded to such a degree, that we had some difficulty to keep them from under our horse heels. It was our misfortune at first, that we threw some farthings, and halfpence, such as we had, among them, for thinking by this to be rid of them, on the contrary, it brought out such a crowd of them, as if the whole town was come out into the street, and they ran in this manner after us through the whole street, and a great way after we were quite out of the town; so that we had to ride as fast as we could to get clear of them.'

I left him alone with his thoughts while I interrogated an ancient but gleeful couple with a dog, both wearing shorts and silly hats. They were holidaymakers from Nottingham, there used to be four of them but ... Her voice trailed away.

Her mother was in a home. He had worked as a crane driver, a lorry driver, a forklift driver and probably a screwdriver. Each year they parked their caravan in a different part of the country and explored by train. They were revelling in each other's company and that of the dog, plus the sheer pleasurable shock of still being alive.

The man on his own in the next seat declared his own passion, which was for Ladybird books. Having come late to the seductive innocence of the series, I could echo his pleasure and we competed to see who could name the most illustrators. He won with a list that included Charles Tunnicliffe, Robert Ayton and John Berry. I didn't know that the first book to be published in the standard fifty-six-page format was *Bunnikin's Picnic Party* or that a Charles and Diana book produced in five days in 1981 sold one and a half million copies.

He was a retired teacher who now aspired to be a writer. I told him this scenario was familiar. He said that he was writing a children's book but was reluctant to tell me more in case I stole the story line. Eventually, he foolishly decided that he could trust me. It was about a king who set his children the task of collecting sunbeams. I assured him his secret was safe with me.

When I returned to John I found him in animated mode. 'Did you see that?'

'What?'

'Grown men giving other men piggy backs in a field!' I felt aggrieved to have missed this manifestation of homoerotic love in a Devon idyll.

'I think they were soldiers. We had just passed through Lympstone Commando station.'

Were they fully clothed? Did they think they were back in school? Were they preparing to enact the Battle of Wounded Knee by taking it in turns to be the horse? So many questions.

The train stopped opposite a sign on Exmouth station making it clear that THESE TOILETS ARE CLEANED TWICE A DAY BY STREETSCENE STAFF AND ARE REGULARLY PATROLLED BY POLICE OFFICERS. ANY INCIDENT OF PUBLIC INDECENCY WILL BE DEALT WITH ROBUSTLY. The threat of robust dealings must have worked as the line of men entering the toilet, piggyback style, had declined to a trickle.

'Stop this, I beg you, Sir!'

'What's the matter now?'

'This talk, this rank humour, ill behoves you. Sodomites should be tried and executed in secret. And that an end on't!'

'Oh for goodness' sake! Lighten up.'

'Half an hour, no longer,' instructed John as I set off to enjoy the forgotten sensation of pavements. Half an hour in Exmouth was ample time to gut and fillet the contents of at least eight charity shops. I was tempted by an early copy of *Alice in Wonderland* but the condition was poor. Outside the final shop a dog was tied to a substantial bookshelf positioned to channel customers inside. In response to an unheard signal it set off down the street with bookshelf and contents dragging behind, spilling books with every laboured step.

Murals featured again, this time on Exeter station. Their subject matter must please the camp piggyback commandos every time they slip back into civvy street. Dartington Hall student Bridget Hall ostensibly took various figures and poses from Michelangelo's ceiling and adapted them as travelling scenes involving contemporary travellers.

Defoe looked puzzled as he stared out of the window at the passing acres of agricultural land.

'Where are the people? Where are the towns? Devonshire was the largest and most populous in England, Yorkshire excepted. It was so full of great towns, and those towns so full of people, and those people so universally employed

123

in trade, and manufacturing, that not only could it not be equalled in England, but perhaps not in Europe.'

I decided not to embark on an explanation of post-industrial decline, shrugged and glanced at the parked lines of freight wagons. This idyllic route also carried nuclear trains from Devonport Dockyard to Sellafield. These are short but very scary trains often consisting of no more than three flatbed wagons, each carrying a fifty-ton lead-lined, water-filled flask, each flask holding approximately two tons of used uranium and plutonium rods. According to the nucleartrains website, this is the equivalent of 37,000 million million Becquerels, one Becquerel being sufficient to generate one click on a Geiger counter.

This mood of catastrophising was not alleviated by John pointing out that we were travelling on the Dawlish sea wall. The Great Storm of 2014 gouged out chunks of its masonry and left sections of the track dangling above thin air.

'You know but little of storms,' muttered Defoe dismissively. 'Read my account published in 1704 *The Storm: or, a Collection of the most remarkable Casualties and Disasters Which happened in the Late Dreadful Tempest Both by Sea and Land*. Let me quote...'

'Must you?'

'At Plymouth, the lighthouse had not long been down when the Winchelsea was split upon the rock where the building stood, and most of her Men drowned; at Portsmouth several of the Ships were blown out to sea, whereof some were never heard of more; most of our sea Port Towns look'd as if they had been bombarded, and the Damage of them is not easily computed.'

'You've made your point.'

A young couple took the seats on the opposite side of the table. She was in despair because of her age and outlined the awfulness of being seventeen to her marginally older companion.

'I can't get ID, God, I've tried. Nowhere will let me in. The bouncers are bastards! You don't know what it's like.' But I did, remembering all too well that awful time spent ticking the days off the calendar waiting for the magical moment when I could apply for my bus pass, and the ultimate Holy Grail, the Senior Rail Card. I felt her pain.

John pointed out a line of nondescript carriages in a siding. 'Camping coaches,' he declared pompously. In the 1950s British Rail parked redundant rolling stock up and down the country at 150 different locations, offering them as holiday accommodation. Publicity material urged campers to 'Make a friend of the stationmaster who will be glad to help you in any way he can to make your holiday a success. He knows the locality and can advise on outings, fishing, golf, and in many other ways. Drinking water and toilet facilities are available on nearby stations.'

Above the coaches, the cliff was constrained by a matrix of hairnets to prevent holidaymakers being crushed as they slept by crumbling red sandstone rocks. The man on the opposite side of the aisle was staring at his tongue and making strange clicking noises.

Still in crusading mode after contemplating disaster by nuclear fallout and a collapsed sea wall, I asked John if we passed near to Buckfastleigh. I looked forward to shouting abuse as we passed close to the abbey where the bastard monks make the tonic wine that is arguably a greater contribution to Scotland's ruin than the Tory party. Known variously North of the border as 'Wreck the Hoose Juice' and 'Cumbernauld Rocket Fuel', it has been demonised as a significant cause of crime, disorder and social deprivation. When the justice minister suggested that retailers should stop selling the wine, she was met by armies of drunken neds waving *Don't Ban Buckie* banners. John told me that the abbey is situated on a heritage railway line on which we would not be travelling. No monk abuse then.

Defoe grew suddenly attentive. It must have been the implied connection between members of the Catholic clergy and irresponsible behaviour. He rose from his seat, assumed a prominent position in the carriage and addressed the startled passengers:

'For God's sake, Britons, what are you doing? And whither are you going? To what dreadful precipices are ye hurrying yourselves? What! Are you selling yourselves for slaves to the French, who you have conquered; to Popery!'

This unexpected sectarian rant left me speechless, a deficit that Defoe interpreted as awe and approval, until I told him to 'Sit down you fool!'

'You don't understand,' he said, shaking his head ruefully.

'Are you talking to yourself again?' asked John.

My image of Torquay had been formed by Basil Fawlty, and first impressions of the station were not auspicious. Not only was pampas grass growing between the tracks but tumbleweed was meandering down the deserted platform. Deserted that is, apart from two blind men walking slowly, the one behind with his hand on his companion's shoulder.

We spent the evening in the lounge bar of the posh hotel next to our decidedly humble abode. A dinner dance was being held in the next room. The singer, a youngster in his seventies, elicited not a shadow of acknowledgement from his profoundly indifferent and probably deaf audience. To complete the disturbing cameo, the two blind men were sitting at the table next to ours, playing cards in silence.

I have no wish to make cheap jibes at the elderly, it is after all a status I have begun to embrace. I was disturbed though, by the *danse macabre* being enacted in slow motion by those couples still capable of movement and thought. The sight should have been life-affirming, a raging against the dying of the light, but it was Chaucer who came to mind and not Dylan Thomas. What sins had they, along

126

with the Pardoner, committed that they were condemned to stay alive? The evening was affording them no pleasure. One couple made it to the lift but they were still there every time the doors opened. They had no idea how to press the button. None of the other guests spoke and their faces were no longer capable of expression. People came to Torquay to die.

The room was suddenly flooded with light and laughter as I recalled the day, several years back, when I visited a cremation site on the banks of the Bagmati River in Kathmandu. Ancient buses that had transported dead granny and her relatives several hundred miles, blocked the car park. Smoke from the various pyres ambled upwards as friends chatted amiably. Most memorably, the doors of the hospices that lined the river were thrown open so that the dying could gaze on the river where soon their ashes would be strewn. Come on Torquay! Throw your doors open, light the fires, let the dying look with content on the soothing waters of the Bristol Channel.

I had little sleep that night, kept awake by the gurgling death rattles of the other residents. It was either that or the plumbing.

DAY THREE
Torquay – Newton Abbot – Penzance – St Erth –
St Ives – St Erth – Truro – Falmouth Dockyard –
Truro – Liskeard – Looe – Liskeard – Par – Newquay

The woman on the Newton Abbot train greeted me like a long-lost friend. This, after all, was very much the first day of the rest of her life and she wanted to share her joy. She had resigned from her boring job, and had possibly turned her back on her long-term partner, though this detail was less clear.

Having thrown over the traces, she was about to enrol at an outreach campus of Exeter University to study Sustainable Development, Climate Change and Risk Management. Such was her enthusiasm, I resisted the comment that her previous job must have been very boring indeed. She dissected each component phrase of her course with messianic zeal and soon the carriage was awash with statistics, models of global warming, environmental disasters and strategies for avoiding man-made apocalypses. Converts from all corners of the carriage rose from their seats to hurl their polystyrene cups in the air. 'Amen!' they shouted. 'Amen!'

'You do realise,' she said, ignoring the acclaim, 'that this is the route of Isambard Kingdom Brunel's atmospheric railway?' I muttered a vague denial but was rescued by the Great Man himself who sat in the vacant seat. He placed his stovepipe hat on the table and lit a huge cigar.

'I don't think you are allowed to ... And anyway, that seat's taken by Daniel Defoe.' Despite realising that this narrative was becoming overcrowded with imaginary people, I let him have his say. In any case, Defoe had slunk back into his book.

'It was the rats. Little buggers. They insisted on eating the tallow that was necessary to re-lubricate the leather that was being sucked dry, literally, by the vacuum. Why didn't I think of that?' In obvious despair, he smacked his hand across his head causing several inches of ash to fall into my lap. 'I'm just a failure. A pity that I didn't drown when the Thames Tunnel collapsed. I should have thrown myself off the Clifton Suspension Bridge when the work stopped. And now this. All because of rats.'

'Don't be hard on yourself,' urged the mature student, taking his hand. 'Don't listen to that critical inner voice. You are being led astray by your super ego.'

'You're probably right,' said Isambard. 'After all I was responsible for the Regulation of the Gauge for Railways Act.'

'Exactly,' said the student.

Although his comforter left the train at Plymouth, Isambard insisted on providing a commentary as we crossed the Royal Albert bridge.

'See,' he said, as the criss-cross of girders interrupted the view of the Tamar, 'I built this too...' Bored with him now, I looked instead at the shipping on the river.

I could just make out HMS *Beagle* transporting Charles Darwin on its second survey voyage. The crowds on the far bank were dispersing back into the town, disappointed at not having caught a glimpse of Napoleon on board HMS *Bellerophon*. Upstream, RAF personnel were trying to salvage the remains of a Lancaster bomber which, having returned from a raid on the U-boat pen at Lorient, became tangled with the cable tethering a barrage balloon. Placards had been prepared to welcome the *Titanic* into Plymouth Sound after its maiden voyage.

Relieved when IKB left to find the buffet car, I settled into my seat only to realise that Defoe was back. He looked thoughtful.

'One thing, which I was a witness to in this place, I cannot omit. About midnight the noise was very dreadful, what with the roaring of the wind, intermixed with the firing of guns for help from the ships, the cries of the seamen and people on shore, and, which was worse, the cries of those, which were driven on shore by the tempest, and dashed to pieces. In a word, all the fleet except three, were dashed against the rocks and sunk in the sea, most of the men being drowned... This was a melancholy morning indeed; nothing was to be seen but wrecks of the ships and a foaming furious sea in the very place where they rode all in joy and triumph, but the evening before.'

As we crossed Bodmin Moor, the sounds of drowning seamen were replaced by the unearthly wailing of the legendary Beast. I looked at John. I wouldn't be surprised

129

if it had been him all along. To avoid being torn limb from limb, like many of the sheep he had savaged over the last twenty years, I sought out a new companion.

He was in his nineties and travelling alone. When I told him he was without doubt the most interesting person in the carriage, he gripped my arm, looked me in the eye and embarked unprompted on his story.

'I'll tell you about a rail journey that had consequences. It was 1943, I was nineteen. The war was on, I wanted to enlist. I lived in Keighley Yorkshire with my parents. I took a train down to Portsmouth harbour and signed on for the Navy. That night the barracks was bombed. I crawled out of the wreckage and found the Master at Arms. "Get me out of here," I said, "I want to be safe on a ship somewhere."

'Three days later I got off the train in Thurso and sailed to Scapa Flow where I joined my ship, HMS *Grenville*. I was told to get a shave before the second front opened. I remember Action Stations being piped as we approached the French coast. We were leading the convoy, see. Escorting the landing craft. Our gunfire was returned from the cliffs. The men had to get out of the landing craft and hold their guns over their heads. I was down in the hull with the 4.7 millimetre shells when Action Stations sounded. We ran aground, there was a screen of smoke. Back in Portsmouth we had to account for every shell on the quayside.

'I was coming back to Devonport after seventy-two hours leave in Keighley. I was on Paddington station when the air raid sounded. There were two girls, they were frightened, see, so I offered to escort them back to their digs. I was a bit of a jack-the-lad then. I went back with them...'

I have never seen such a practical illustration of the phrase 'his eyes lit up'. The old man's eyes lit up, sparkled for good measure, twinkled and then settled back into their sockets.

'I got back to Devonport at three minutes past midnight. I was late, see. So I had to be punished. I was roped to the funnel and made to scrape off the paint for five days. They gave me a hammer. After that we became part of the British Pacific fleet. We went to Sydney. I couldn't tell my mum and dad where I was going. Secret, see. So I told them there was a good chance I would get to visit mother's twin brother. They knew he lived in Australia. I crossed the line on my twentieth birthday, October 11th. I saw action. We were escorting the battleship HMS *George V*, the destroyers formed an outer circle. I saw the Kamikaze planes coming in ...

'I kept thinking all the time about that ship carrying the children evacuees, City of Benares, wasn't it? Torpedoed it was. Seventy-seven kids drowned. They stopped sending kids to America after that.

'We went to Australia to protect them against the Japanese. I remember loading pineapples onto the destroyers. One or two always fell out of the crates. Lovely! There were celebrations in Sydney when the Japanese were defeated. I didn't want to join in though. We had to protect the prisoners from the Australians.

'Then they put me on a strange ship. We were testing aircraft engines out at sea. Fremantle pubs only opened for two hours in the afternoon, between four and six. Didn't stop me getting so drunk I passed out. They locked me up. I spent the whole journey back to Aden in the crow's nest. I was demobbed on September 4th 1946.

'I went back to Keighley but my parents had moved to Bournemouth ... but I managed to find them. I went to Loughborough and trained as a teacher but soon got bored with teaching and wrote to the colonial office asking for a job. They said I could be in charge of all PE teachers in Nyasaland if I wanted but I went to Cyprus instead ... They made me carry a pistol all the time ...'

The atmosphere in the carriage was one of tangible awe and respect. I think that several passengers forgot to get off at their stop.

I asked him where he was going today. He said that three times a week he travels to Penzance where he sits on his favourite seat and stares at the sea for three hours at a time. Because of his impressive contribution to this narrative I asked him for his name. As he gave it to me reluctantly, I shan't include it here.

'I too loved to talk to seamen and soldiers about the war,' chipped in Defoe who, to his credit had also been listening to every word. 'I knew the names of every ship in the Navy, and who commanded them too, and all this before I was fourteen years old.'

The announcement 'Mind the Gap' takes on added significance at Penzance station. It is more of a chasm than a gap, a geological fault capable of swallowing prams and toddlers.

Having visited Cornwall only once in my life, I was intrigued by the knobbly landscape disfigured by mine workings. Like a skin recovering from illness, the land had worked hard to hide the pitheads and winding buildings. Vegetation had clawed its way over the remaining structures but failed to obscure the brick obelisks that still poked upwards. St Michael's Mount was visible from the window, dragging itself across the horizon like a grey sea slug.

The rolling stock on the route to St Erth consisted of carriages, the windows of which could be lowered, enabling me to sample a long-forgotten delusion that I was driving the train, straining to see the signals ahead through the smoke and smuts. The fourteen-minute journey from St Erth to St Ives felt like a tour through an exhibition of Railway Posters from the 1950s showing idyllic glimpses of families picnicking on sun-kissed beaches. Mum, Dad and two children, a boy and a girl. I did though, see the distant figures of a man and a young girl flying a kite against a backcloth of waves piling up like white-tipped platelets.

My only previous visit to Cornwall was in the early 1960s.

It was unusual for my parents to take a holiday at all, but they took me, my brother and a school friend to self-catering accommodation. My memory is blurred but we watched as a man in his early twenties was dragged out to sea by the undertow and drowned. His friends waded into the water but couldn't reach him. I have a vague memory of running along the beach to raise the alarm, and the bleak atmosphere when we returned to the chalet.

A poster on Falmouth station urged me to be mindful that a million older people eat every meal on their own every day, and asked if I would be willing to keep them company. We wandered past the Falmouth maritime museum and the mini cruise ship, the *Astor*, moored in the harbour. According to Trip Advisor, the handles in the shower alcoves on board the *Astor* are particularly inconvenient, which I will bear in mind when booking my next cruise.

Meanwhile John was expounding his view that Falmouth would be the ideal place to relocate the Trident missile system when Scotland becomes independent. By some sort of Zeitgeist, an air raid siren sounded at that precise moment. Subsequent research revealed that it is part of Falmouth Docks fire alarm system, but it is an actual air raid siren.

John pointed out that I naturally tend to gravitate towards the older passengers on trains, as if they are likely to be more tolerant of one of their own. I suppose he had a point but how many young women wouldn't be upset by a man in his mid-sixties sidling into the seat alongside them? Nevertheless, and with a degree of trepidation, I consciously sought out single young women on the train to Truro. I located two, neither of whom screamed or pulled the communication chord.

My first victim was a student of creative writing. I was quite overwhelmed by her delight when she realised I was a writer. I attempted in vain to dampen her enthusiasm by pointing out that, unless she was careful, she might find herself in her dotage, travelling the rail network and pestering people. She seemed undaunted, and I urged her to persevere.

'A writer's lot is a thankless task. You could end up impoverished and imprisoned,' Defoe interrupted.

'Don't put her off!'

The second woman in her mid-twenties had trained and worked as a journalist but, disillusioned with a hack's life, was currently volunteering as a care assistant in an old folks' home. She had applied to Kings College London to become a nurse. Her experience of staying with her boyfriend's parents had made her realise how much she missed her own, and we talked about the common phenomenon of taking parents for granted and then missing them when it was too late.

Defoe was upset. 'Both my father and my youngest child died when I was in Newgate prison. I never got a chance to ... I wanted to say ...'

I smiled sympathetically and turned my attention back to the woman who told me that she was in the process of buying a houseboat. Consumed with envy, I grudgingly and hypocritically wished her well and decided to stick to older people.

I found one sitting on her own, contentedly it must be said, before I disturbed her. She and her husband, both in their seventies, had been doctors before relocating to Cornwall. Within a short space of time all their children had uprooted themselves and followed their parents to a new life. My septuagenarian sage smiled contentedly and pronounced, 'And we have all lived happily ever after.'

Meanwhile Defoe was staring at John as if appraising him for some unspecified activity. All became clear. 'The wrestling in Cornwall is indeed a manly and generous exercise,' he mused. It was true, John's arms were the size of small pigs. 'And that closure, which they call the Cornish

Hug, has made them eminent in wrestling rings all over England, and for their dexterity at throwing up the heels of their adversary, without taking hold of him.'

While still in the grip of a fantasy during which I had John in a Cornish headlock, the conductor on the Truro to Liskeard train offered the view that the people she meets are 'all nice ... sometimes they're grumpy but there's always an explanation which may have to do with the reason they are travelling in the first place.'

She had a point, but it is probably easier to maintain an optimistic view of humanity when you spend your working day passing through tumbling valleys with cottages smothered in ivy, and fields lightly sprinkled with sheep, and a dark green wood above which black crows hover.

John had been especially eager that we travel on the eight and a quarter mile single-track community railway that links Liskeard to Looe. As with the Settle to Carlisle route, locals had become 'friends' of the line.

Coombe station could benefit from a few more friends, as it currently welcomes an average of just under one passenger a week. More popular is St Keyne Wishing Well Halt (a request stop) where travellers, hoping for better times and a win on the lottery, drop their secret wishes written on tiny pieces of paper through the metal grid.

They can then seek further consolation by visiting the adjacent 'Magnificent Music Machines' museum of fairground organs. If this too fails to lift their spirits, they are recommended to hop aboard the Looe Valley Line Rail Ale Trail Train to visit the eleven pubs within falling distance of the track. They are only allowed to travel on the return journey if they can correctly pronounce the full title of the excursion without slurring or repetition.

John was right to comment on the startling beauty of this route. However, the idyllic scene assumed a more menacing aspect when the undergrowth attempted to kidnap the shambling carriage masquerading as a scheduled train. Vicious tendrils and green fronds slapped at the windows and snared the wheels.

The train lurched to a halt whereupon a passenger, presumably chosen for his biceps, muscled his way down the carriage, climbed onto the track and manually altered the points. What happens, I wondered, when all the passengers are of ordinary build? Are old ladies roped together and urged to apply their dwindling but collective strength to the lever? John, tiring of my nonsense, pointed out that the man was a railway employee and had boarded the train for this very purpose at the previous station.

I sidled alongside a young woman who was visiting her sister before starting her shift at a Premier Travel Inn. To this lonely traveller she seemed utterly lovely, her smile revealing a gap tooth of which the Wife of Bath would have been proud. 'Take me, take me to the nearest Travel Inn,' said my lost inner voice while my much better behaved outer voice thanked her and wished her a safe onward journey.

'I too am lonely, and would welcome spiritual consolation.'

Ignoring Defoe and choosing a morally more correct path, I spoke to a youngish couple who were passionate advocates, not of this route but of the closed Aberystwyth to Carmarthen line in Wales. They were part of a cultural/political movement called *Singing the Line into Existence*. Having secured funding from the Arts Council of Wales, a group of artists undertook to walk sections of the old railway line singing, dancing, recording, drawing and making site-specific art: a wonderful naïve idea that might, just might work.

The conductor on the Looe train, when asked what she thought of her job, echoed the exact words spoken by her counterpart on the Liskeard route. 'All people are basically nice,' she intoned with the conviction of a North Korean diplomat. How long did this indoctrination process take? How many thought police were employed by South West Trains before all their staff spoke as one when interrogated by geriatric writers masquerading as innocent passengers? I tried one last gambit. 'You must have seen some strange sights in your time...'

The floodgates opened. 'Well, there was the flitting ...' Our perseverance was rewarded with a tale of dismantled beds and wardrobes being dragged onto the train. Rolls of carpet being crammed into overhead racks, white goods blocking the toilet door...

The hour and a half spent in the hotel bar overlooking Par Station impacted when we eventually boarded the Newquay train. The local beer made the passing scenery appear beautiful beyond description, certainly well beyond my capacity to describe. My just decipherable note to myself said enigmatically, Widow Wadman.

In his wandering novel, *The Life and Opinions of Tristram Shandy*, Laurence Sterne, unable to summon the words to describe the unsurpassed beauty of the Widow Wadman, invites the reader to fill a blank page with his own description.

'To conceive this right, – call for pen and ink; here's a paper ready to your hand. – Sit down, Sir, paint her to your own mind; – as like your mistress as you can, – as unlike your wife as your conscience will let you, – 'tis all one to me, – please but your own fancy in it.'

If these words are not followed by a blank space then my editor must have decided that asking you to write your own paragraph describing the late afternoon beauty of the scenery on the outskirts of Newquay was a stupid idea:

*

137

Half of the carriage lights went out and the reduced illumination softened the outlines of a massive man lurking in the doorway. I duly approached. Despite my expectations, he turned out to be a softly spoken gentle giant, a rugby player with St Austell, recovering from an ankle injury who had spent the last fortnight at the Edinburgh Festival Fringe. He had worked in a holiday camp for six years, and happily shared horror tales of the annual invasion by school-leavers hell bent on getting pissed. Prior to the camp, he had worked in various hostels in Newquay. 'Hostels are bad,' he said. 'October is the worst when the Zombies emerge to rob the houses for drug money.'

My dreams that night were populated by zombies slithering their way through the streets of Newquay, mutating into salamanders and navigating the gutters with their tongues. Surely Newquay couldn't be that bad.

It wasn't.

DAY FOUR
Newquay – Par – Plymouth – Gunnislake – Plymouth
– Exeter – Salisbury – Portsmouth Harbour

Although it was early morning, each café was guarded by a tramp. On closer inspection (but not too close), these men were less gentlemen of the road than superannuated crusties; remnants of the generation of hippies who discovered Newquay in the 1960s. Now wearing bird's nest beards, and still rolling their own, these grizzled custodians of happier times stared unfocussed at yet another day.

A man in a parked van waved and smiled at me. While he had obviously mistaken me for someone else, I was more than happy to return the gesture.

When I met up with John, he was resplendent in his new XXXXL t-shirt which carried a none too subtle message to middle England. WELCOME ALL ASYLUM SEEKERS AND IMMIGRANTS. THE DAILY MAIL F*** OFF. My instincts told me there could be trouble ahead.

The landscape on the journey to Par was lightly coated in flour. It could have been icing sugar. It could have been clay dust. The wagons parked in sidings were all shrouded in white. A phrase came into my head. 'Christ in the Clay-pit.' What did it mean? Where had it come from?

Back in the sixties I would wait expectantly for the next edition of the Penguin Modern Poets series and devour it avidly, luxuriating in the delusion that I was going to be a poet at least as good as Shelley, but more interesting, and certainly an unacknowledged legislator of the world. Jack Clemo, the Cornish poet, featured in Volume 6 along with Edward Lucie-Smith and George MacBeth.

Not only was Clemo deaf but, according to his obituary, he experienced at the age of six an attack of blindness which 'induced the mental nightmare of inarticulate terrors and panics, changing him from a plump, jolly pink-faced little fellow to a thin, pasty-faced brat, dull-eyed, silent and morbid. Then, at thirteen, after a reprieve, he was, as he put it, thrust afresh, with ripening apprehension, into the struggle with primeval darkness.' He claimed that he found Christ not in church but in the blood stained mud of the quarry.

The lingering hint of primeval darkness on Par station was alleviated by a genial conversation between a man and his dog.

'The dog may be descended from the one I heard of in these parts,' said Defoe.

I braced myself.

'Yes. It was said of this dog that if they gave him any large bone or piece of meat, he immediately went out of doors with it, and after having disappeared for some time, would return again, upon which after some time they watched him, when to their great surprise they found that the poor charitable creature carried what he so got to an old decrepit mastiff, which lay in a nest a little way out of town, and was blind; so that he could not help himself, and there this creature fed him.'

I glanced at the adjacent platform where two elderly male railway workers were chasing each other, playing peek-a-boo around a pillar. The winner celebrated by slapping his colleague on the head. The Fat Controller at Par station is to be congratulated for having the foresight to combine staff motivation with gay bonding.

The conductor on the Plymouth service gloomily announced that all trains were currently obliged to progress at a snail's pace as one of their number had hit a bridge. This seemed beyond explanation unless there remained the fear that vibrations from another train, within a radius of fifty miles, could cause the bridge to tumble. To confound the situation, ours attempted an incline for which it was ill-suited. Ramblers walking on an adjacent path stared into our windows. At one point the conductor stepped off the technically still moving train to make a phone call at one of the stations before climbing back on board.

The Gunnislake train on the Tamar Valley line was also in no great rush. I caught sight of JMW Turner knocking out a quick sketch of the area. Lowering the window, I shouted, 'What do you think of the area, John?' After placing his brush carefully on his easel, he cupped his hand to his mouth and shouted back, 'I have never seen so many beauties in such a limited spot as I have seen here.'

There was plenty of time to talk to everyone in the carriage. The middle-aged woman on a shopping expedition shook her head in disbelief when I explained our mission; the Art and Design student reacted in a similar manner and sought refuge in her portfolio; the pub landlady told me that her husband had been stationmaster at Plymouth, while her father had been a guard for forty-five years. The elderly couple were self-confessed railway buffs. (An odd expression that gave me unwanted images of them standing in the nude on a railway crossing.) He smiled in a self-deprecatory way when his wife informed me that he was the owner of the Bristol Society of Model and Experimental Engineers.

I approached a young woman sitting on her own. Horrified at my inexorable progress through the carriage, she told me that she was German and did not want to be 'interrogated.' I repressed the instinctive, and probably racist, retort 'We have vays of making you talk', apologised and slunk away. On reflection, I had seen her standing forlorn and lost on Plymouth station and should have let her be.

My unease stayed with me. For the first time on any of the journeys I felt that I had intruded where I wasn't welcome. I had to leave her in a better place even if it was only in my imagination...

The young woman wept tears of relief as she played with the stem of her wine glass. 'I had such doubts, such worries. Perhaps you are not the man you seem on-line. Perhaps this is all a dupe. I am leaving my mother and father for a madman I never meet. I travel for three days and the fear comes with me. But...' She held his hand and fought for her words. 'You are same kind man who say nice things to me... You are more beautiful than your picture. I tell you funny thing; on last train when I worry most, an old, old man with no hair, he approach and ask to speak to me. And I think it is you!'

On our return to Plymouth, John opened his jacket, revealing the provocative logo on his chest and, with menace aforethought, approached a man reading the *Daily Mail*. Violence was avoided on this occasion, but it was only a matter of time.

He soon made amends by adopting an old lady with several suitcases at least as big as she was. She was staring forlornly at the train as it drew in, daunted by the challenge of boarding. In gracious mode, John safely installed her and her bags. She wanted to talk.

'What do you do for a living?'

'Nothing,' said John.

'And what do you think of young people today?'

'I think they are the finest generation this country has produced.'

'You see, I left my handbag in the house. I had fallen out with the person who is at home, who can be most unreasonable. I left without the bag. It had my tickets and reservations. I got a taxi but I couldn't pay, my purse was in the bag, I had to go back and missed the train. I'm going to Lake Garda don't you see. It's good for my rheumatism ...'

We found ourselves squashed opposite two middle-aged businessmen *en route* to London. One was senior to the other and spoke most. Defoe muscled his way between them, desperate to talk as trade and commerce were his meat and drink.

'Gentlemen,' he cleared his throat. 'Permit me to read to you some informative and pertinent extracts from my celebrated publication, *Being a Compleat Prospect of the Trade of this Nation, As Well the Home Trade As the Foreign*. In a nutshell, I advocate that the expansion of England's domestic produce, particularly wool, would be the path to true prosperity ...'

He was starting to annoy me now. 'Shut up! They're not interested.' He faded away.

Mercifully the two men remained oblivious of this gratuitous intrusion. After coded references to colleagues, deadlines, specifications, and having convincingly played being important people, they abruptly dropped all pretence and regressed to the schoolboys they in fact were. Where would they drink tonight? Which bar should they visit first? Would they go on somewhere after?

142

The excitement was too much for the less important businessman who left for the buffet car, returning with a huge carry out. To their credit, they offered cans to both of us, but we nobly declined. Their conversation grew more animated and incoherent and I was reminded of a TV documentary when, in the interests of science, the presenters consumed alcohol in front of the cameras to demonstrate its insidious and pernicious effects. The boss man confided in his new best friend that he was in possession of a full-size Paddington Bear suit...

The improvised cairn of Tennent's lager cans nearly toppled as an enormous man squeezed past the table. The conductor's physical presence expanded into the carriage like a human sealant.

'He must be a Hungarian border guard,' suggested one of the businessmen. While I was trying to fathom the significance of the allusion, a woman sitting opposite poked a finger into the giant forearms of her male companion and commented, bizarrely, in an Eastern (possibly Hungarian) accent, '...and I thought HE was big!'

Not to be outdone in this spontaneous descent into the surreal, the other businessman suggested, 'He must have a water cannon up his vest!'

Southampton came and kept coming with acre upon acre of cranes and gantries. At any moment, a Lego-obsessed giant, bored now that he had built a wall one hundred feet high, would pluck the reddest of the shipping containers and place it across the tracks for fun. The carriages would arch into the air and land in the Itchen. Some of us would survive by holding on to the bows of the kayaks swarming in the bubbling water.

I caught myself staring obsessively at the passing houses, intent on becoming the only person (John was too frequently asleep to qualify) who had seen each and every habitation in the United Kingdom that could be glimpsed from a railway carriage. Struck by the essential sadness of this ambition, I was forced to admit that the urge was part of my motivation for travelling. The realisation depressed me but I had to see it through. What percentage of Britain's homes was visible from the railway? Including distant glimpses of housing estates, back-to-backs, tenements and posh houses in the suburbs, the answer would have been a significant number. More importantly, what was to be gained by collecting the nation's homes in this way? Did I think that I would somehow own the kingdom, having seen more of it than anyone else alive? Was this megalomania masquerading as completism?

I turned my attention to what could be seen in the patchwork quilt of single rooms on the dense outskirts of Portsmouth; a chequerboard with squares illuminated at random; slices of domestic life; figures frozen in poses at the sink; a family meal; an empty space at the table. I was stealing photographs of other people's lives.

Henry Miller wrote in a letter to Anais Nin, 'Going home by train, I had a tremendous surge of ideas, caused by seeing the houses lit up in early evening; their bleak barren ugly qualities impressed me, and yet the soft light, often in a red-papered room, with people quietly sitting at the table, and coming in such quick succession – window after window – like souls exposed, affected me greatly.'

The dockside pubs lining Portsmouth harbour, mock Tudor and brash, seemed welcoming from afar, although I was anxious about John's T shirt. Instinct told me that the natives of Portsmouth probably treated the *Daily Mail* with the reverence bestowed by fanatics on the Bible and the Koran.

'At least do your jacket up,' I suggested in a tone of voice I hadn't used since I last chided my adolescent children about their dress code several decades ago.

'It won't do up,' he replied.

'Well I don't fancy being chased through the streets of Portsmouth before being tarred and feathered while tied to a lamppost, even if you do.'

He grunted and sullenly pulled his coat together.

My worst fears were soon realised. As we strode through the door, John's coat opened and a table of very large women put their pint pots down with a synchronised noise that was more ominous that an All Blacks haka. Two of them rose and pointed. We turned and fled, having inadvertently walked in on a KEEP BRITAIN WHITE AND PURE branch meeting. While hiding in an alleyway I googled the BNP and Portsmouth, only to read that local members, fearing that the Party was lurching to the left, had formed a splinter group called *Pro Patria* which I suspected was not a Wilfred Owen appreciation society.

Keeping to the shadows, we made our way to our lodgings in the Royal Maritime Club. At Reception we were asked if we 'were Navy'.

Flattered to be mistaken for a swaggering young salt who was giving a barnacled Poseidon a taste of shore life, I said, 'Sadly no.' The same question was repeated at the bar. Had we answered in the affirmative every drink would have cost us a pound less. 'Retired,' I muttered. The barmaid smirked and charged us full price.

In the lounge, we had no alternative but to eavesdrop on a conversation about the evils of immigration. Well into her cups, and to the approval of her peers, a loud Welsh woman embarked on a surreal diatribe about Aborigines. Perhaps she had a point. It was quite possible that I had missed the news item about the douce residents of Hampshire complaining about the intrusive noise of didgeridoos. There again, she may have been confusing her aborigines with her immigrants.

Seeing the shocked expression on Defoe's face I couldn't resist reminding him that his hero, Robinson Crusoe, was in fact a slave trader. He chose to say nothing. It was time for bed.

DAY FIVE
Portsmouth harbour – Ryde – Shanklin –
Portsmouth Harbour – Southampton – Brockenhurst –
Lymington – Weymouth – Bristol – Severn Beach –
Bristol – Cheltenham

En route to the Isle of Wight ferry we leaned over the rails at the harbour's edge. I made a mistake and told John that the large ship was SS *Great Britain*, one of Isambard Kingdom's achievements. The great man himself emerged from the shadows. 'No,' he said. 'That's HMS *Warrior*, built in 1860. My ship, the *Great Britain*, was far superior. Launched in 1843 she was the most advanced ship of her time. This is an upstart, hardly worth looking at. You see, I wasn't a complete failure after the vacuum railway, I still had talent, I just wanted a chance to prove myself…'

The next figures to emerge from the mist were part of a statue of the Portsea mudlarks, small scallywags who for many years entertained passers-by by diving into the harbour mud flats to retrieve pennies. I lived briefly in Portsmouth in the mid-fifties and remember being taken to watch the leaping urchins. My parents' reaction was a mixture of curiosity and embarrassment that I should be exposed to such poverty-driven exploits.

A record of slightly earlier times describes how the mudlarks would continue to bellyflop into the mud even when German planes were bombing the dockyard. Sailors would empty their pockets when on their way to war and throw their money to the children for luck. I wondered if the old sailor who had shared his life story on the train to Penzance had been one of them.

146

Another memory. I was four, of that I am certain as my brother was in the process of being born in a Portsmouth hospital. As a treat my dad had taken me to Southsea beach for a picnic. It was a glorious day and, in my tottering enthusiasm, I fell into the sea. Dad stripped me and dried my clothes on the hot pebbles, leaving me to joyfully flaunt my nakedness. I can still taste the salt water and the sense of freedom.

We duly purchased our tickets to Ryde which to a paperback writer seemed appropriate. Until recently a season ticket to travel the 2234 feet along the wooden pier would entitle the purchaser to a significant discount on all other lines in the Kingdom.

Defoe, in lively mood, told me that he was looking forward to the trip as he had never visited the Isle of Wight. He said he would take notes and publish his thoughts on his return.

The brooding mystery of the Napoleonic forts rising from the Solent was dissipated by learning that they now function as luxury hideaways for the rich. When not staring at the sea, residents can learn the ancient art of *sabrage*, the art of removing the cork from a champagne bottle using a sabre.

It seemed unlikely that any of the few passengers on the Shanklin train frittered away the hours perfecting their skills in *sabrage*. A slightly melancholic businessman told me that he had been widowed for fifteen years, and still struggled. He loved the island and found it very friendly but might soon have to move to be closer to his son.

A man in his thirties was a carer whose partner owned horses, and he too felt immensely fond of the island, '…even in the winter, I love the lanes, the woods, the sea.' He was taking his washing to his mother who lived at the other end of the line.

All further conversation was precluded by the noise and alarming rocking motion of the carriage. The rolling stock

147

had been recycled from the London Underground several decades previously, giving the impression that the entire Isle of Wight was a time capsule waiting to be opened by curious visitors from the twenty first century. It must be the only eight-mile stretch of railway that incorporates sleeping policemen to ensure that the trains never exceed the statutory 45mph speed limit. Even this sedate pace was insufficient to prevent the repositioning of several vital organs.

Thoroughly shaken and not a little stirred, we boarded the ferry for the return trip.

The lounge was busier, now occupied by escapees from Parkhurst and Albany prisons. I recognised Peter Sutcliffe, Ian Brady and the Kray Twins, all of whom had taken this short trip across the water. There was no sign though of Keith Rose, the qualified pilot who escaped in 1995 and lived rough in a garden shed in Ryde. The prisoners did their utmost to pass themselves off as a collection of bored businessmen with meetings on the mainland.

As we re-entered Portsmouth harbour, I scoured the skyline but failed to spot Nelson's flagship, the *Victory*. I knew it was there somewhere but couldn't for the life of me find it. I could only assume that it had finally slipped beneath the waves under the weight of tourists.

Defoe was jumping up and down, excited at the scale of Portsmouth's fortifications.

'Look, besides the battery at the Point, there is a large hornwork on the south-side, running out towards South-Sea Castle; there is also a good counterscarp, and double moat, with ravelins in the ditch, and double pallisadoes, and advanced works to cover the place from any approach...'

'Please, Daniel! Enough! What with John bending my ear about bizarre non-existent junctions and single token workings, and you with your pallisadoes, I've had it up to here!'

He seemed shocked at my outburst and muttered something inaudible.

On the Portsmouth to Southampton train, I experienced an odd perceptual blip. Once again I was discreetly eying up my fellow passengers, trying to spot those who would let me harvest their stories and sweep leaves from their lives into my bag. While speculating about these strangers, I gradually became one, and, for a moment, had no separate existence. I was looking for myself in the carriage wondering which of these people I was. Perhaps this was proving to be one train too many.

This existential crisis was nipped in the bud when a smart young woman asked if she could sit next to me. I dropped down from the luggage rack or wherever my soul had taken temporary refuge and engaged again with the world.

A recent graduate in forensic psychology, she was waiting for her police check before taking up a post in a women's refuge. Ultimately she wanted to work in the prison service. She had been working with a sex offender for a year and clearly expected a response from me along the lines of How-could-you-work-with-these people. She waited but it didn't come. She thanked me for not being judgemental, and said that the most challenging aspect was spending time with someone who probably wished he was dead and knew that view was shared by a significant number of people. Before she left the train, she smiled and told me that the offender she had mentioned was now working delivering pizzas. She was simply one of the nicest people I had met on my journeys so far.

Meanwhile an altercation was taking place across the aisle where a large woman insisted on sharing her seat with both her equally large husband and their suitcase. Eventually, unable to cope with the amount of squirming that this arrangement necessitated, she expelled her large husband whereupon he relocated next to me. He was a retired postman who had worked all his days in the countryside where he befriended the farmers and the old people for whom he brought messages and carried out chores.

The large woman was squirming again. She was desperate to join in but, unable to talk over the suitcase, had to confine herself to staring daggers at her husband. Eventually he capitulated under the weight of her unspoken warnings and lapsed into a moody silence.

I left him and John to grunt at each other while I stretched my legs. This involved passing through First Class where the privileged occupants looked up from their *Daily Telegraph*s to scowl at the intruder violating their space.

Once safely through to the other side, I saw a middle-aged man whose t-shirt declared I AM NOT NORMAL. A provocation if ever I saw one.

'Why are you not normal?'

'I'm getting off in twenty seconds.'

'Fine. You have fifteen of them to answer my question.'

'I ... um ... I don't feel I have anything in common with people who think they are normal ... I'm not normal ...'

'Nor am I,' said his wife.

The lad was dressed completely in blue, ensconced in a gargantuan Portsmouth FC shirt that could have doubled as a marquee outside of Fratton Park. At his side was a huge bag with the logo PORTSMOUTH FOR LIFE. He was beaming happily, and beamed even more, if that was possible, when I approached him. I told him I had watched Portsmouth play at least twice. He nodded when I said they were having a good season. He nodded when I asked him if he had followed them since he was young. He thought about his answer and told me, very slowly, after struggling to form his words, that his father had been a Liverpool fan but that he supported Portsmouth. I wished him good luck for the remaining games and returned to my seat.

In my absence, all available space had been commandeered by a posse of tweed-jacketed braying men, presumably *en route* to watch the rugby international at Twickenham. All my non-judgementalism, all my determination to extend a benevolent empathy towards all passengers recruited for selfish narrative purposes, went out of the window. They were boors communicating in innuendo-laden code, an unlikeable phalanx of moneyed misogynists who, mercifully, got off (or 'alighted' in railspeak) at the next station.

Bizarrely, their places were taken by a party of women, equally determined to conform to stereotype. I was perhaps developing an unhealthy interest in hen parties, but this group more than satisfied my prurience. They all were dressed in pink, and each was armed with a personal champagne bottle. One of them pointed at an obese passenger struggling through the carriage, 'It's the Hulk!' she shrieked. The incident passed without retaliation.

The next beckoned at two innocent young men passing through the carriage. 'Don't be shy, little boys,' she urged in a voice half Cruella De Vil, half an inebriated Marlene Dietrich. Horrified, the lads fled beyond the door of the next carriage. Gleefully, Cruella got to her knees and mimed a sex act against the glass.

The competition was now well under way. The third member of the troupe rose unsteadily to her feet and surveyed the carriage for a victim. John and I shrunk into our seats. A man, evidently called James, failed to take avoiding action and was approached by the woman hellbent on mischief. 'Time for a dare!' she announced before squashing herself onto his lap to the raucous approval of her peers. What happened next is not for inclusion in the pages of a respectable travelogue.

They poured themselves onto the platform at Bournemouth before the least inebriated was despatched to rescue their two friends who had fallen asleep on the train. Reunited, they swayed in an undulating circle and drained the bottles.

Delighted that they had left his train, the conductor

greeted his new passengers with a powerful impersonation of Robin Williams' 'Good morning Vietnam!' suitably adapted to reflect the geographic realities.

I felt cheated as no New Forest ponies were visible from the train. Apparently, between fifty and sixty are killed each year in road accidents. It must be a sort of *rite de passage* for aspiring boy racers. Equally disappointing was the absence of tanks on the army range as most of them are now deployed in various Taliban fun parks. Defoe peered into the wall of trees and seemed thoughtful.

'I cannot omit to mention a proposal I made a few years ago for re-peopling this forest.' He opened my account of his journey and pointed to the diagram on p203.

'This contains four thousand acres of land and two large highways ...I proposed to single out twenty men and their families. To each of these should be parcelled out in equal distributions, two hundred acres of this land. To each of these families, who I would now call farmers, it was proposed to advance £200 in ready money, as a stock to set them to work, to furnish them with cattle, horses, cows, hogs etc. and to hire and pay labourers, to enclose, clear and cure the land ...'

'What went wrong?'

His brows grew dark, 'Where the mistake lay, is none of my business to enquire.'

I left him to his thoughts and, as the train approached Dorchester, paid a visit to the toilet. Although not locked, the door wouldn't open. Someone was pushing from the other side. I persevered until I saw a very small, obviously frightened, man staring at me through the crack. He wasn't alone. Several small people were taking it in turns to keep a foot against the door. I told them to relax, assured them I wished them no harm and showed them how to operate the lock. Their leader thanked me and introduced himself as George Loveless. He explained how he and the other Tolpuddle Martyrs had escaped from the assizes but were now having second thoughts. They had decided to surrender to the authorities at the next station as conditions in the toilet were immeasurably worse than prison.

Defoe was far from impressed. 'Pure fabrication,' he said disapprovingly. 'There is no place for invention in a serious account.'

'You've changed your tune,' I countered. 'You never even visited half of the places you describe.'

Dorchester station should of course be renamed Casterbridge in acknowledgment of Thomas Hardy's legacy. The association reconnected me with the first time I read *Jude the Obscure* and turned the page to discover that two children had been hanged by their older half-sibling who placed a sign around their necks 'Done because we are too menny', and then hanged himself. Probably one of the most shocking moments in literature. Hardy also wrote about train journeys.

Faintheart in A Railway Train

And then, on a platform, she:
A radiant stranger, who saw not me.
I queried, 'Get out to her do I dare?'
But I kept my seat in my search for a plea,
And the wheels moved on. Oh could it but be
That I had alighted there!

I have mentioned this poem to several friends, all of whom could identify similar moments in their own lives. One described making eye contact with a woman travelling in the opposite direction on a station escalator. They both turned to watch the other disappear for ever. Another remembered a similar experience, also railway related. He and a woman on the opposite platform of a London station saw each other. His heart lurched and he suspected the reaction was mutual. Predictably a train passed between them and she had gone when the platform was next in view.

The incidents occurred decades previously but both had total recall. Is this a universal experience? At times in our lives, does our instinctive yearning for a soul mate lead us to project impossible expectations onto transient encounters? Is there something emotionally unsettling about train journeys?

As if reading my mind, a station poster gently urged me not 'to get too carried away. Please wave your loved ones off from the platform. If you're not travelling and board the train you might end up travelling with them.' How terrible would that be?

Dorchester has other associations with hangings and this perhaps explained why Judge Jeffries plonked himself down next to John and ordered one of us to place his portmanteau in the space at the end of the carriage.

Defoe instantly hauled himself into the luggage rack and pulled several coats over his head.

'Hard day?' asked John.

'Three hundred of the treacherous bastards. All sent to the gallows. Another 1300 transported.' He rubbed his hands with glee. 'Some cry me an egregious courtroom bully,' he confided. 'Just doing my duty. A large port,' he demanded of the passing trolley man.

'So, rumours of your alcoholism are well founded,' said John.

'It's for my kidneys, they trouble me a lot,' he muttered, unscrewing the miniature and pouring the contents down his throat.

'And what about the seventy-year-old woman you ordered to be burned at the stake for harbouring those two fugitives from Sedgemoor, eh?'

154

'I commuted her sentence to beheading. I'm a man of compassion but as I find your attitude less than convivial I will convey myself to first class.' With that he left.

It was a while before Defoe clambered down from the luggage rack. Even then he seemed unnaturally anxious. 'Has he gone?' he asked.

'Yes,' I said.

'I suppose I was the lucky one. I escaped his retribution. Unlike poor Tutchin...'

'Who?'

'A poet friend of mine. He was flogged through every market town in Dorset, the flailed flesh hanging from his body... I saw men digging their own graves, I saw men in gibbets...' He covered his face and sobbed.

There were still three hours before we reached Gloucester. John was doing his best to keep me awake with enthralling details about forgotten branch lines and the complexity of signalling procedures.

I enjoyed a brief conversation with an old man who had known the writer Fred Archer but my concentration was waning. Through the window, I watched a burglar climb over a fence into someone's garden on the outskirts of Weymouth. I saw a naked fisherman on the banks of the Avon. I watched in a desultory manner as three Asian men in full jungle combat wear wandered down the train.

JOURNEY FIVE

West Midlands/South Wales

DAY ONE

Glasgow Central – Birmingham New Street –
Northampton – Coventry – Leamington Spa –
Moor Street – Worcester Shrub Hill – Worcester
Foregate Street – University of Birmingham –
Redditch

It's a mistake to stare closely at railway tracks from the platform edge, despite Network Rail's best attempts to introduce retention tanks. Prohibitions against flushing toilets in stations still fall on deaf ears, and much worse is still falling onto the tracks. Petitions have been organised at Liverpool Street Station in London and questions have been asked in the House.

As the 5.50 emerged from Glasgow there were more edifying sights. Dawn was slowly dragged across the sky. Lights showed in the cabs of lorries parked for the night. Above Lancaster a hot air balloon hovered. John thought it was a weather balloon but I disagreed, preferring the thought of hardy, if frozen aeronauts, on a pioneering voyage over the uncharted hills of Northern England.

'If any passengers fancy a cooler journey I suggest you

make your way to Carriage B where the heating has failed.' We braced ourselves for subsequent announcements: 'There is a small fire in Carriage D, so if any passengers fancy an impromptu BBQ ... There is a leak in Carriage E so if you missed your shower this morning...'

We were joined by an avuncular middle-aged man who sighed as he tapped his laptop. He blushed and hesitated when asked what he did for a living. I was intrigued and waited for a confession that he ran a chain of money laundering businesses in the Midlands, or moonlighted as a people trafficker.

'Employee relations, pensions, that sort of thing,' he confessed, assuming we would despise him for the dullness of his profession. I reflected instead on the multitudes of people worried about their future who had been reassured by his comforting presence and gentle advice.

He told us that his daughter was a writer currently backpacking with her boyfriend in South America. He missed her but at least he could read her blog, 'follow her on apps, that sort of thing.' Yes, he missed her. Realising he had nothing to lose, he told us that he had a small obsession with the fortunes of Luton Town Football Club. Even this darkest of secrets could not diminish him in my eyes.

It was apparent from his questions that the man sitting across the aisle, with shaven head and powerful arms, no longer lived with the daughter cuddling into him. He inhaled every detail of her day-to-day routine and, when she left to go to the toilet, became agitated at the amount of time she was taking. As he rose to rescue her from unthinkable horrors, she emerged from the end of the carriage with a wedge of paper towels, a present for her dad.

As we crawled through a 1930s housing scheme on the outskirts of Preston an elderly woman in a large pink housecoat stared forlornly at us from her window.

On Preston station a man was struggling with a suitcase

157

the size of a Mini Cooper. Rather than buying tickets for his extensive family, he had engaged the services of a contortionist who had taught his wife, three children and family dog how to fold themselves into a tiny space. He dropped his burden into the gap between a young girl holding a filigreed wire hamster cage, and a group of Muslim clerics.

The young worker in the buffet car was bored and keen to talk. Evidently shoplifting on trains is not unheard of. She had recently confronted a thief who had dived into the chill cabinet under the cover of a large poacher's overcoat, and helped himself to several bottles of Prosecco. She should at least have a locomotive named after her.

She hinted darkly at some of the things she had seen perpetrated by stag parties but I could not persuade her to divulge what had occurred. Before leaving the buffet car I took mental note of the fact that Tilting Ale was produced in Macclesfield for Virgin Trains. Perhaps they also sold an Overflowing-Toilet IPA and a The-Seat-Reservations-Have-Crashed vintage cider.

John was still talking to himself about the rise of the Scottish Fascist Party in the 1930s when I got back, only pausing when interrupted by the train conductor announcing that it was Bernadette's 6th birthday and exhorting all passengers to join him in singing Happy Birthday.

UNCLE JOES MINTBALLS KEEP YOU ALL AGLOW declared the sign near Wigan.

According to Neil Armstrong, the marshalling yards at Crewe are visible from the moon. Burnt out and graffiti-daubed carriages and long obsolescent track testing vehicles stretch to a vanishing point with, in their midst, a poignant clutch of Pullman carriages, relics from a time when train travel could be glamorous. Painted in fading chocolate and cream, these ancient dowagers all have names stencilled on their sides. Sheila is coupled to Meredith who is coupled to Alison who is coupled to Jayne in a sort of genealogical roll call. Sadly, individual names are no longer bestowed on modern carriages. ('Jesus, I was crammed into Maud again this morning!') but the quaint habit of naming locomotives persists, albeit in more surreal and utilitarian forms.

Avid collectors of trivia can still extract pleasure from watching Sir John Betjeman barrelling through the night. Virgin's Voyager trains variously commemorate Christopher Columbus, Sir Walter Raleigh and Michael Palin. There can be little excuse for Top of the Pops, Lady Penelope, Bolton Wanderers or indeed Aisteddffordd Genedlaethol. However, the winner in this category is between the pithily named 'London Borough of Havering Celebrating 40 Years', and 'London Borough of Newham Host Borough 2012 Olympic Bid'.

By way of welcome respite, the conductor took to the airwaves with the ominous warning that we could expect 'shuddering' in Wolverhampton. This news came as no surprise. Shuddering is a wholly understandable reaction to the ugliness of that conurbation. John spoiled things by pointing out that part of the train was due to be decoupled and attached to another, hence a small shuddering. I preferred my own hypothesis.

There was just time to eavesdrop on two of the oldest businessmen in the United Kingdom. Besuited, befuddled and deaf, they were shouting phrases borrowed from younger colleagues that made no sense. Bottom lines were yoked to blue sky thinking. I've got you on my radar sat oddly with need to get all my ducks in a row. The phrase that did resonate with me was 'You must capture the conversation!' I'm doing my best, I thought.

'It's not going well, is it?'

I wasn't certain that I had granted Defoe permission to instigate conversations. He was my creature, and accordingly could only respond when I chose. 'What?'

'This epistle, this itinerary. Whatever you call it.'

'What do you mean?'

'Where is the life? The joy of existence?'

'I'm doing my best, for goodness sake. It's bleak out there. This is the Midlands. The people on this train would sooner be somewhere else. Anywhere.'

'Call yourself a writer!'

'There's no need to be insulting.'

'How many books have you written?'

'This will be my fifth, what's that got to do with anything? Sometimes you're more irritating than John.'

'Not wishing to seem a braggart but I have 314 periodicals to my name, including several fictional histories. What do you call them? Yes, novels. A strange name. There is little that is novel or new in the behaviour of our fellow citizens. You must engage with your subjects more robustly. You are, it must be said, inclined to endow the trivial with spurious significance.'

'You're one to talk. What did Jonathan Swift say about you? "One of these authors (I have forgot his name), is indeed so grave, sententious, dogmatical a Rogue, that there is no enduring him."'

'It is the green-eyed monster which doth mock,' retorted Defoe with undisguised bitterness.

Topol got on at Wolverhampton, resplendent in his greasy hair and overcoat. Despite his considerable girth, he hauled himself out of the carriage window and proceeded to play his fiddle on the roof. When he returned, to the applause of his fellow passengers, he milked them for donations claiming that he was not a rich man.

On the outskirts of Birmingham a group of men convened a meeting in a swing park. There were no children in sight. The men were all wearing long black coats. As had happened before on an earlier journey, the image disturbed me and was reluctant to fade. With sinking heart I looked more carefully at it...

160

Big Man sneered as he counted out the notes that Micky had given him. 'Fifteen fucking pounds. You're taking the piss.'

'I want out, Big Man, hands up, I'm no good at it. Debt collection or whatever you call it, it's not my thing.'

Big man put his right hand into his overcoat pocket and slotted his fingers into the five brass rings of the knuckle duster. The other men stood, leaving the swings to rock emptily.

Since our last visit here, the revamped New Street complex had opened. Gushing in praise for the soulless atrium into which light now streamed, John was agog. Part Ice Station Zebra, part Dubai shopping mall, part air terminus, I felt underwhelmed. When I pointed out that the platforms were still dark and cramped John took it as a personal insult.

Word quickly spread through the Northampton train that none of the toilets were working. 'It's the buttons,' explained a young lad before punching the door panel in an elaborate tattoo that led to the door sliding open to reveal horrors beyond description.

Needing to talk to human beings uncontaminated by these sights, I foisted myself on two students standing in the passageway between carriages. I was learning that it is much easier to talk to strangers who are standing on trains than those on the airline seats next to the window. A related thought is that passengers who avoid sitting down at all, even when there is space, have something of the non-conformist about them.

These two were students at the University of North-ampton. One was studying journalism and the other acting. The journalist knew that he didn't ever want an office job and was volunteering part-time with a local radio company. Defoe muscled his way into the conversation.

'I have been rightly clep'd the Father of Modern

161

Journalism. A dangerous trade which might well land you in prison.'

Meanwhile the wannabe actor said that all he had achieved so far was as an extra in a recent blockbuster, the title of which I had never heard. I agreed that it was a start.

Defoe, who was still there, tapped the lad on the chest and told him to 'Only choose those plays where the Moral of the Tale is duly announced, enforcing sound Truths; making just and solid impressions on the mind; recommending good and great Actions, raising sentiments of Virtue in the Soul, and filling the Mind with just resentments against wicked Actions...'

As I listened to the boys I felt instantly old, an elderly man in the final quarter (fifth? less?) of his life remembering with a painful and poignant envy what it was like to be that age. I must have learned something in the intervening decades, but for the life of me I couldn't think what.

I cheered up a little when I returned to John and saw that he was being plagued by the sun. Squinting angrily and playing with the blind he was being teased from on high, where I noticed the second balloon of the day. I defy anyone to feel anything but reassured by the sight of a balloon floating serenely.

The man sitting opposite was slumped forward, resting his head on a book called, ironically, *Broken Brains*. 'Drawing on real life examples and anecdotes from neurosurgery and neurobiology, this engaging introduction to brain function and dysfunction is ideal for those interested in learning more about the brain in an accessible way.'

With half an hour to spend in Coventry, I left John in the company of his own inertia. The pavement next to the car park was blocked by the body of a man, presumably drunk, possibly down-and-out but not necessarily either. People were stepping over him as if he were a puddle of something unpleasant. It reminded me of India where people lying

162

in the street were quite likely to be dead, and hence best stepped over as they were beyond help. This man might not have been beyond help, but like everyone else I didn't want to get involved. This moment of self-disappointment was ameliorated by the sight of two policemen ambling forwards, relieving me of a decision.

I crossed the small park separating the station from Coventry city centre. Intrigued by a large green man sculpture, I played the tourist and tried to learn more about his significance, not having thought of Coventry as the centre of the pagan world. My phone search revealed nothing, but a link took me to the recent case of a local man charged with committing an indecent act by rubbing himself against a playground slide in a park. Apparently he was in love with the slide but has been banned from attending any location including parks, leisure centres, swimming baths, lidos or recreation grounds where there is a slide. Deciding that there was something fundamentally pagan about Coventry after all, I returned to the station where the man was now sitting in an upright position against a wall.

Eager to exorcise the demons of Coventry, and to recover from having been roasted in an overheated carriage at gas mark ten, I took advantage of a fifteen-minute wait in Leamington Spa to put my nose out of the station. The concourse lulled me into a sense that all was well with the world; lovers, about to be separated, were kissing as if this shared breath was their last; a small boy was chasing pigeons. Then things went wrong again.

As I stepped into the car park I heard the scream of a terrified woman. I looked behind cars but there was no sign of her. Sure that I had not imagined it, I looked again for the source of the wail and saw a man with a flame thrower eradicating weeds that were intruding onto Network Rail property. Had he burned the poor woman to death? The West Midlands was an odder place than I had imagined.

Much of the fifty-five-minute journey from Moor Street to Worcester Shrub Hill was spent talking with a dishevelled young man slumped against the window, an astrophysics graduate from Aberystwyth University who was working as a cashier in a branch of the TSB.

'It's all numbers,' he said in a self-deprecatory tone, implying that three years' immersion in dark matter, black holes, stellar dynamics and galaxy formation was the ideal preparation for helping Mrs Miggins understand the complexities of her current account.

'What keeps you sane?' I asked.

'Medication and sleep,' he replied.

Other institutions that had benefitted from his mathematical skills included a Travelodge where he worked as manager, and a charity bookshop.

I asked him what his ideal job would be and he said anything at Jodrell Bank. We agreed that one bank was probably like any other, and that the TSB would soon make a breakthrough in the field of astroparticle physics.

When he asked about my previous publications, I explained that my last novel, *The Aeronaut's Guide to Rapture*, was an attempt to reinterpret the fall of Icarus. His eyes lit up, he dived into his bag and emerged with the Little Black Penguin Classic that retold Ovid's tale. 'You must keep it,' he said. 'A souvenir.'

The massive moon leading the train into the University of Birmingham station shed its light on a poster urging me to make my will. Was our onward journey likely to be unsafe? Was John harbouring murderous instincts? As the commuters probably possessed the highest collective IQ in the kingdom, I thought it might be wise to heed the warning.

The chocolate painted station at Bournville reminded me of a visit to the factory when my children were young. They had hoped to meet Willy Wonka and his politically incorrect staff of Oompa-Loompas. They had anticipated dipping their fingers into steaming vats of molten chocolate, but instead had to be content with a tour of old advertising materials. I knew from that visit that George Cadbury had made Robert Owen look like a novice when it came to model villages for his workforce. In addition to introducing a pension scheme, he built a school, a museum, a hospital and a reading room. He bought land for football and hockey pitches, bowling greens, a boating lake, a cricket pitch and an outdoor swimming lido.

It was the end of the day and every occupant of the carriage wanted to get home. The middle-aged cyclist was now regretting having brought his bike as he still had miles to go once he left the train; the bald businessman was wondering why he had agreed to talk at the Rotary that evening and was completely unprepared. The youth still twitching with school-induced agitation just wanted to get back to his bedroom, his Xbox and the Star Wars Battlefront.

'We'll find some joy tomorrow,' I told Defoe.

'Doubtful,' he said.

DAY TWO

Redditch – Aston – Walsall – Birmingham New Street –
Gobowen – Shrewsbury – Smethwick Galton Bridge –
Stratford-upon-Avon – Smethwick Galton Bridge –
Birmingham New Street – Cheltenham

In the booking hall of Redditch Station a young man enquired about the cost of a single ticket to Llanelli. 'F***s Sake, Jesus wept!' he exclaimed, on realising that for the same price he could buy a medium-sized family car. The cost of tickets on this route possibly explained why the carriage was void of passengers.

Eventually we were joined by a solitary commuter going

into Birmingham to buy his daughter a present. She was a train driver earning much more than her graduate siblings and, before that, had been a guard for seven years. Was I aware that, in the event of a fire on a train, the guard is obliged to leave it burning while he/she sprints a mile down the track to place a detonator on the rails? No, I wasn't aware, but the implications were massive. How were the fitness levels of guards maintained so that they could sprint a mile? Did competitive running form part of the selection process?

A graffiti-emblazoned wall distracted me: HOLD TIGHT NANNY. Perhaps Nanny was losing her grip on reality and one of her grateful charges was exhorting her to show resilience in the face of adversity. Perhaps the artist used to wake from hideous nightmares and ask Nanny to hold him tight less the horrors returned. I recalled too that the security services had resorted to recruiting by using graffiti which only true nerds and techies would understand.

The Afro-Caribbean man with several briefcases, who specialised in leadership and management training, declared he had the perfect job as he loved people and travel. His clients included further education colleges and various charities. Without him saying so in as many words, it was obvious that he also specialised in making strangers feel they had known him all their days; he had clearly graduated with a degree in welcoming smiles, general beaming and unbounded charisma.

Now feeling that everyone on the planet, and certainly on this train, truly loved me, and that the day would indeed be characterised by joy in all forms, I approached my next stranger, confident that he too would warm to my mission and tell me astonishing things about his life. He certainly looked interesting with a ponytail and what I assumed was an instrument in a case. A travelling minstrel with plentiful stories to tell.

'Can I talk to you for a while?'

'Why?'

'I'm writing a book about train travel ...'

He stared at me as if he had been approached by a free-booting geriatric madman, which was not a hundred miles from the truth. 'No,' he said. My crest fell, my bottom lip trembled. 'I've a lot on my mind ...' I mumbled something and returned to John.

The outskirts of Birmingham reinforced my sense of loss. Absurdly, and although it was summer, I caught myself humming lines from *In the Bleak midwinter* (The Darke setting): 'Earth stood hard as iron, water like a stone/Snow had fallen, snow on snow, snow on snow'.

Everything in Birmingham was piled on top of everything else. Tyres were heaped on tyres, scrapped cars were piled on top of other scrapped cars. Tyres on tyres, cars on cars, and everywhere as hard as iron. In one factory yard, corrugated sheds were piled on each other in a rusting tower. The whole was bisected by flyovers and flyunders and fly-where-you-likes. The foreground opened onto marshalling yards and lines of derelict railway carriages. Eventually the skyline reasserted itself, flaunting its mosques, monuments and football stadia in a crenelated architectural frieze.

Passing through Walsall, I knew I had to get back on my horse and talk to people again. The analogy was suggested by the sculpture of a black metal horse parked in a field. Its eleven companions had bolted to adorn canal banks and the edges of platforms throughout the Black Country. Designed by Kevin Atherton they have a following on the internet: 'One day I noticed that one of them (I think the one near Dudley) had been embellished with an appendage in the form of a long, thin, sand-filled sock ...' 'Additionally, you can see a real horse roped to the ground on the canal path adjacent to Dudley Port Station ...'

The old man slumped in the corner by the window didn't

look as if he had the energy to shoo me away. I parked my horse next to him.

'I'm eighty-seven, an ex-stonemason. I take every day as it comes. Never underestimate people. The quiet man in the pub might turn out to be a wonderful karaoke singer if you ask him onto the stage. I worked on the Royal Observatory and most of the churches in Birmingham. What about the original builders of those churches? No safety harnesses then. No sir. I'll tell you something, there's not enough stone in that New Street station since they done it up. It's all glass and metal, not the same. No, I never had an accident, least not a serious one. I was lucky see, perhaps God was looking after me as I was looking after his churches.'

'Some fine churches in Birmingham,' said Defoe.

'I know for a fact that you never visited, so don't start making things up.'

'I've been supporting Villa since I was fifty, different then mind. I was born outside of the Birmingham ground, St Andrews, but I was a bit of a rebel so I went to support the other lot. Never looked back. What's that you're asking me? Do I notice days more than I used to? Yes, son. In the olden days, they just slipped past. Now you've got to notice each one or they will soon all be gone...'

'Do you see that old building up there on the hill? Aston Hall it is. Well, I'll tell you something strange. One day I took my missis up there, for a treat like, and this man, the guide, was showing us round. And there was this old desk in one of the rooms, really old it was. Anyway, I says to the man, the guide, "There's a secret compartment in that desk". Don't ask me how I knew, I just did. I went up to the desk and touched it in a certain place, and it opened, the secret compartment...'

During the journey, John developed his own system for rating the quality of the countryside. His criteria were unclear, but I suspect that his gold standard was the

168

landscape as depicted in Constable's Hay Wain. I didn't want to engage him in a discussion of the Augustan landscape and the subsequent influence of the Romantic Poets. If he decided to award Shropshire a six, I wasn't going to argue.

The tallest man I had yet spoken to blocked the passageway between carriages. I had sympathy with his plight as he could not have folded his legs into the space between the seats without unscrewing them. He was a bowling alley security guard and happily expounded the many joys of ten pin bowling, admitting that he was not often called on to evict errant bowlers unless, inebriated, they vomited down the lanes.

He had worked for twenty years as a bouncer in a nightclub, but in all that time had never appeared in court to refute charges of excessive manhandling. He far preferred the bowling alley. His wife had always wanted to visit Scotland.

Shrewsbury provided yet another example of man's inhumanity to man when it comes to locating penal establishments.

> They hang us now in Shrewsbury jail:
> The whistles blow forlorn,
> And trains all night groan on the rail
> To men that die at morn.

This must be the fourth time that we have visited stations overlooked by prisons. Victorian architects were obliged to build both institutions in the least fashionable parts of town, thereby ensuring that belching smoke and raucous noise would seep into the cells of the condemned. Defoe had much to say about Shrewsbury.

'This is really a town of mirth and gallantry ... Here is the greatest market, the greatest plenty of good provisions ...

it should not be forgotten here, one blot lies upon the town of Shrewsbury, namely that here broke out first that unaccountable plague, called the sweating sickness, which spread itself through the whole kingdom of England. The disease begins very suddenly, with a sense of apprehension, followed by cold shivers, giddiness, headache and severe pains in the neck, shoulders and limbs. Accompanying the sweat is a sense of heat, delirium, rapid pulse and intense thirst. In the final stages there will be either general exhaustion or collapse, or an irresistible urge to sleep, followed by death.'

I was feeling a bit warm, Birmingham had given me the shivers, and John was spending an inordinate amount of time asleep. As we left for Smethwick Galton Bridge, he woke and pointed out what he claimed was one of the biggest signal boxes in the world. I was more interested in the woman who was holding a large tissue to her face. Either she was fearful of contagion or her teeth were falling out.

I soon lost sight of her, as the entire population of the West Midlands was syphoned into this one carriage. This was a situation conducive to plague, but distraction was provided by four very large girls cramming themselves into two airline seats. Presumably some Darwinian principle was at work as the top layer seemed oblivious to the pain and discomfort of their less important friends. Peer pressure assumed a new meaning.

Equally overwhelmed, the conductor took to the airwaves to plead for calm, begging passengers not to colonise available seats with their strategically placed belongings.

In the middle of all this a young woman sat quietly, exuding an unworldly serenity. Her face belonged in the 15th century. She had slipped from her ornate Renaissance frame in a Midlands municipal museum and, for some reason, chosen to travel by train. Gazing on her features made the hubbub still. Her pony tail plaited in ribbons placed her in the court of the Duke of Milan in the 1490s rather than coach C of the 13.34 cross country to Stratford-upon-Avon.

A cloudburst momentarily transformed the train into a bathysphere as rain streaked across the window. An indistinct mermaid floated past trailing fronds of emerald green. 'We are now cruising at a depth of three thousand feet,' intoned the conductor.

I naively assumed that the Bard's own station might be peppered with quotes from his works just as the bridge across Waverley Station, in Edinburgh, is decorated with *mots justes* from Walter Scott. The word 'train' features at least four times in the *Merchant of Venice*, as does the term 'rail'. Instead, the station was drab and dispiriting.

Four men, similarly dressed in grey overcoats, sat equidistant from each other on a bench with their hands crossed and their heads bowed in a tableau of melancholy. They could have been travelling salesmen from the 1950s, their identical suitcases holding cloth samples that would be inspected between finger and thumb by sceptical haberdashers up and down the country.

My low mood stayed with me as we joined the train back to Galton Bridge. I knew I had to locate a stranger whose story would elevate my spirits and enervate my soul. I found him sitting on his own in the last carriage. Late forties with long lanky black hair.

'Do you mind if I talk to you?'

'Yes, I do.'

'Sorry.'

'I don't want to talk. Go away.' He rose slightly with clenched fists.

It was a relief to be back in John's comfortable presence. Defoe too made welcoming noises. We discussed whether I was right to dismiss an entire region of the United Kingdom as unfriendly and miserable on the evidence of two rejections and, on balance, decided that henceforth the West Midlands deserved to be cut adrift.

This impression found further justification in the behaviour of a woman who rushed down the carriage to claim a double seat for herself and her friend, who was struggling with their luggage. To deter anyone else from sitting next to her, she placed her hand on the empty seat. Understandable behaviour perhaps, except that she placed her hand pointing upwards in a rigid claw, soon claiming a victim as an innocent passenger lowered herself onto the trap.

The train stopped at a station in the middle of nowhere and for some reason the lights failed.

'Everybody out!' shouted a large woman in a South African accent. Bemused, John and I watched as several passengers reached for their bags and began shuffling through the gloom. 'I didn't mean it,' said the woman. 'It was only a joke.'

Muttering, the passengers returned to their seats.

The woman said that she was a full-time carer for a lady in her nineties and was embarking on a week's leave which, she suggested, explained her high spirits and spontaneous impulse to evacuate the carriage. John asked her where she lived in South Africa and, with the skill of an inquisitor, elicited declarations of Boerish, if not boorish, tendencies. Rhodesia and Ian Smith were mentioned with degrees of reverence, but bombastic Nationalism gave way to maudlin digression as she detailed the appalling acts perpetrated on her neighbours by marauding savages.

'They would lop off the ears.' She mimed the act, holding an imaginary ear between thumb and forefinger while slashing the air with her free hand. 'They cut out your tongue.' This mime was more difficult to achieve without slurring. 'They chop off your limbs!' She cleverly reduced herself to a writhing torso.

Soon she and John were trading atrocities. John claimed

that the Selous Scouts were positively inhuman, while she countered that the Frelimo mercenaries were more unscrupulous than the worst devils imaginable. Soon the carriage was awash with body parts, blood swished under the seats and victims howled. Above the mayhem she roared that the current President of the Republic was no more than a cattle trader.

'That is nothing,' declared Defoe. 'In the year 1556, a maid was set in the pillory for giving her mistress and her household poison. Besides the shame of the pillory, one of her ears was cut and she was burnt on the brow. Two days after, she was set again on the pillory and her other ear cut...'

By now John had become alarmed at the passions he had unleashed and steered their discussion into the calmer waters of the UK and South African postal systems. Mercifully she left at the next stop, remembering to take all her luggage, personal possessions and prejudices with her.

Day Three
Cheltenham – Newport – Hereford – Cardiff –
Merthyr Tydfil – Abercynon South – Aberdare –
Pontypridd – Treherbert – Radyr – Cardiff –
Ebbw Vale Town – Cardiff – Penarth

John was unable to give the countryside a rating as there wasn't any countryside to rate. Wiping the window with an arm of my jacket revealed that the condensation was three-dimensional. The landscape had lost consciousness under an anaesthetic of mist.

All details were in abeyance; all sharp edges blurred. The far bank of the estuary had been air-brushed and merged with the sky. By peering with my hand between forehead and brow, I could make out the silhouette of Turner's

Fighting Temeraire. Defoe asked if we could pay a quick visit to see the 'monstrous fat woman of Ross who was more than three yards about her waist; that when she sat down, she was obliged to have a small stool before her, to rest her belly on and the like.'

I told him that it was no longer acceptable to ogle fat people, and anyway, Ross station had been closed for forty-odd years and... 'Three yards? Are you sure?'

'Most certain.'

Defoe shook his head as we waited in Hereford station. 'It is truly an old, mean built, and very dirty city.' He muttered something about two standing stones that had been moved by the devil, but I was losing interest.

Enthusiasm was restored to the day by David Williams who beckoned John and me to join him at his table *en route* to Cardiff. No sooner had we settled than he began his life story. It was almost as if someone was playing a horrible joke on us; a small goblin had preceded us onto the train and sought out a volunteer willing to tell massive porkies for the benefit of an old fraud whose mission was to disturb innocent passengers.

He introduced himself, shook our hands, declared that he was seventy-six and pretended that he was Manchester United's main scout in Italy. I was transported back to a hideous TV show that I watched in the early sixties called *What's My Line*. Gilbert Harding and Isobel Somebody would guess the occupation of contestants who could only mime the answers. It would have taken them ages to even get close.

David had played school rugby for Wales before taking on a coaching role for a team on tour to Italy where he met Sir Alex Ferguson who was performing a similar function with a Scottish football team. They bonded instantly and Ferguson offered David Williams a job scouting for football talent. I may have missed out some important details as my

174

note taking couldn't keep pace with the animated narrative.

Other passengers sat spellbound by the household names David conjured from the ether: Gareth Williams, Clive Rowling, Denis Law, George Best, as if he was presenting a Sports Personality of the Last-Three-Decades-Award ceremony.

Graciously acknowledging their applause, he introduced his next guest, a certain Ryan Giggs, who, through designer stubble, explained how much he owed David Williams. Next was the Welsh International Aaron Ramsey, who agreed with the scout that he had in fact wanted to sign for Manchester United and not Arsenal, but not even David Williams could make Ferguson listen to reason.

A posse of suave young Italians clutching lattes ambled from the buffet car to pay tribute to the man who discovered them. Federico Macheda, Davide Petrucci and Michele Fornasier paused to sign autographs for the swooning conductor, while Guiseppe Rossi tore off his shirt and tossed it down the carriage. The conductor decided not to issue a yellow card.

John, refusing to be overawed, interrogated Williams about the detail of ever more obscure Serie B games as if to test the man's veracity. He passed the test, although the effort of memory drained him of all energy.

'I love Wales,' he said. 'But the longer I stays away, the less I wants to return home. I've lived in Parma for forty-six years now. My mother always used to warn me not to trust people from North Wales. And whenever I meet Sir Alex he greets me with *Twill dyn pob Saes* which I will not translate for fear of upsetting any English people who might be listening to our conversation.'

Subsequent research turned up an article in *The Independent* that described Williams' uncanny ability to enter Italian football grounds in disguise, hiding the fact that he was spying on potential signings. It was even suggested that, at smaller grounds, he might dress up as a tree. Had I known this before, we could have enjoyed an even more interesting conversation.

Before he got off the train, presumably having spotted a wood, small forest or copse that he fancied the look of, he took down his bag from the luggage rack and produced a creased picture of himself with the Welsh youth rugby team, which was what he wanted to be remembered for. On leaving, he gave me his business card that I have since shown to several strangers, having now assumed the identity of an Italian scout for Manchester United.

Perhaps Arriva Trains Wales deserve credit for this latest marketing ploy; they have successfully recruited a small army of Train Anecdotalists whose duty is to regale unsuspecting passengers with implausible tales to while away the long hours of journeying.

It was difficult to decide which of the biblical plagues had recently visited Cwmbran. Possibly boils and lice, judging by the appearance of the first escapees. Rumours of hail, locusts and darkness may also have played a part in the mass exodus of the population to the railway station and the next train to Cardiff Central.

Our first sight in the capital was of a woman dropping her bag at the top of an escalator. Her week's shopping cascaded towards the level below. She could only watch, her face even bleaker than Munch's screamer, while tins of dog food, washing powder, treats for the children and a steak for the old man, tumbled against the legs of surprised commuters.

John was eager that I experience the Welsh valleys, spreading out his fingers to explain that if Cardiff was his palm then his fingertips represented Coryton, Merthyr Tydfil, Pontypridd and Ebbw Vale.

Hyperventilating at the prospect of this itinerary, I concentrated on the configuration of a dead pigeon and a

176

pram wheel on the tracks. On the platform, a young lad in full Welsh rugby kit ran on the spot with a ball under his arm. Again, impressive marketing by the local tourist board, determined to breathe new life into the hoariest of national clichés.

As we embarked on our first valley ascent, I challenged Defoe who seemed to be intentionally avoiding the view from the window.

'What did you write about this part of Wales? Didn't you make some ridiculous comparison? Hang on, I've got it here: "...the Andes and the Alps, though immensely high, yet they stand together, and they are as mountains piled on mountains, and hills upon hills; whereas we see these mountains rising up at once, from the lowest valley, to the highest summits which makes the height look horrid and frightful."'

'Journalistic licence. In any case, you yourself are inclined to fabrication and exaggeration.'

The single carriage to Coryton was on loan from the local fairground, the proprietors having agreed to lease their House of Horrors in exchange for an unlimited travel card. The floor shook at the merest hint of a gradient, of which there were many. The gradual but unrelenting ascent caused oxygen masks to fall from the roof of the carriage. Up, up and more up. The tiny stations were so close to each other that passengers could have passed on gossip by shouting up the line. On those occasions when the climb becomes too difficult for the clapped-out diesels, they can still be called on to haul the train by rope, hand over hand, while singing *Bread of Heaven.*

John conjured the 1950s, when dirty overloaded coal wagons would propel locomotives down the valleys at reckless speeds, a flash of red fire from the footplate illuminating the crew as they wrestled with the brakes.

This mystical mood persisted as we explored the second finger of valley. *En route* to Merthyr Tydfil John stared

177

out of the window and mentally stripped back layers of landscape, erasing rows of modern bungalows, demolishing intrusive supermarkets, cutting down trees and reinstating a black industrial past. He sketched in pit heads, wash houses, winding gear and slag heaps, pointed out overgrown railway sidings and breathed new life into crumbling buildings. We were brought back to the present by a small boy who, taking advantage of the slope on the return journey, skateboarded effortlessly down the carriage.

The highlight of the third finger to Pontypridd was the old woman, talking to herself, whose purpose in life was to keep the carriage clean. She *tut-tutted* at abandoned coffee cups; gathered up used newspapers; wiped the tables. Only then did she sit back and glower at any passengers who might have been thinking of opening a packet of sandwiches. Her familiarity with the guard, and staying on the train at its destination to perform the same function on the return journey, showed her commitment.

On Pontypridd station, a menacing drunk stood in the rain, ranting against architects who designed platform shelters that offered no protection from the elements.

'They think they're wizard with their computers ...' He assumed a supercilious expression and mimed tapping at a keyboard. 'They drive their big cars ...' He gripped his steering wheel. 'But they don't stand in the rain!'

The fourth finger could wait for another day.

DAY FOUR
Penarth – Cardiff – Barry Island – Barry –
Maesteg – Bridgend – Swansea – Pembroke Dock –
Whitland – Milford Haven

I was still half asleep on the train to Cardiff; it may have been the onset of the sweating plague. In Penarth the previous evening, I forsook John for forty minutes or so to see if my legs still worked, only to find myself in the pitch dark holding onto a wall. Swallowed by a Black Hole, I half expected to be spewed out in Guatemala or some such place. Either that, or my eyesight had failed completely. After fending off several muggers and some unpleasant poltergeists, a man with a dog led me to a street with sufficient light to silhouette the charred beams of a former hotel.

Had John and I decided to hunker down among the charred beams, we would have been spared the Brian Blessed booming competition over breakfast as two Englishmen, sitting at opposite ends of the room, roared at each other.

'I once drove for forty-eight hours without a break,' shouted one, in a voice so loud that the cruets shook. 'I live in such a remote area,' countered the other, 'I was quoted twenty-three thousand pounds to have a landline installed.' Their voices were still echoing in my head as we arrived in Cardiff where a seagull the size of a small dog made an emergency landing on Platform 7, snatched a toddler from its pram and languidly flapped towards the docks. The parents reacted with commendable stoicism.

A two-carriage train arrived ten minutes late, driven by a schoolgirl who had opted for work experience on the railway as an alternative to detention. Arms folded on the lowered window, she chewed gum and surveyed the waiting passengers.

The duty stationmaster's office which faced the staircase was covered in glass on three sides. After pulling down my eyelids and noting how travelling was visibly aging me, I noticed something odd about the reflections. By tilting my head at an angle, it was possible to make out the dim shapes of figures inside the office. This was no ordinary glass; this was a one-way mirror. Astounded by this flagrant violation of civil liberties, I watched aghast as a woman approached the glass and applied her lipstick. I distinctly heard laughter

179

coming for the other side. The same happened when two young lovers leant against the deceptive surface and kissed. Presumably video recordings were available on the dark web. GCHQ have much to learn.

As we approached Barry station I placed a hand inside my jacket. My heart was beating faster and, being of a hypochondriacal disposition I found myself wondering how, if my death was imminent, I would be transported back to Glasgow. John would continue the journey on his own, I was certain of that.

In fact, my heart was beating like a lover's as we approached what had been, over fifty years previously, my personal Shangri-La. Fourteen years old and wearing shorts, I rushed with notebook and pencil between the lines of rusting steam locomotives, almost three hundred of them, bought for scrap by the Woodham Brothers. Unable to believe my good fortune I was experiencing a heightened pleasure that I would never know again.

Somewhere I still have the square black and white photos, taken with my Brownie, of weeds reaching up towards the decaying regiment. Before the preserved-locomotive societies blossomed, and more stringent vigilance was applied, the yard was visited by looters equipped with oxyacetylene cutters to remove nameplates and other potentially lucrative mementoes. I stood on the station bridge and looked towards the deserted waste land. Deserted, that is, apart from a single footplate cowling from a class 2-10-0 9F now serving as a small hut.

As we crossed the estuary, the theme of industrial decay reprised in the half-submerged hulks of wooden ships whose ribs protruded from the mud flats. The sense of reconnecting with a time, and a feeling I didn't fully understand, stayed with me once we arrived in Barry Island.

Directly opposite the station is a mothballed fun fair where gales had dislodged the tarpaulins from a gaudy carousel and a surreal teapot. Strings of dead fairy lights hung from girders and an incongruous mechanical clown stood paralysed. Pressing my face to the railings I stared at the tumbling innards of broken slot machines. I have no idea why the sight of unravelling reels of oranges and lemons could so move me. I am not aware of any nostalgic hankerings for fun fairs, and yet I felt a degree of emotional engagement that made no sense.

I said little to John when I rejoined him at the station. He was leaning against the closed booking office writing in a book I had not seen before, a record of complaints that he would, in due course, present to the railway authorities. He was currently exercised by the huge swathes of uncovered platform that obliged passengers to wait in a grubby, rain swept bivouac. I tried to make sense of what I had felt, but made little headway.

Our timetable meant that I had only twenty minutes to explore the cosmopolitan delights of Bridgend. It was more than enough. Initially assuming that several streets had been closed prior to demolition, on closer scrutiny it became apparent that most of the shops were open, although heavily disguised by poverty.

Wandering into a charity shop dedicated to the Welsh Air Ambulance, I thought the obese young assistant was demon-strating the flight path favoured by one of the ambulances until I realised that he was pursuing me with an aerosol of air freshener. Deeply offended, I returned to the station.

As I stared at a Gilbert rugby ball lying between the tracks I once again paid mental homage to the Welsh Rugby Union marketing department and their subliminal advertising campaign. Their decision to randomly locate hundreds of balls across the principality was inspired.

The IT specialist straddling the plates between two carriages had found the perfect metaphor for his dilemma. Does he stay in a job where he feels exploited and bullied or

181

should he get out? He had had a bad day; the systems had gone down and he was the scapegoat. Hovering between Carriages B and C, he seemed pleased to talk to someone who was not blaming him for every ill in the universe.

It was with some reluctance that I approached the man leaning against the door of Carriage C. He seemed to be in a world of his own and I wasn't certain I would be welcome there. 'I'm a writer too,' he said. 'I'm a poet, I'm just back from a workshop. My work received a commendation in the Bard of the Year Competition at Leicester University fifteen years ago, Dylan Thomas' daughter was judge.'

By now his smile was illuminating this dark corner of the train. 'That was before I had my breakdown at the age of twenty-one. You see everyone in my family was a doctor, parents, brothers, everyone. I was a bit different though. And then I found poetry! Once I had poetry I didn't need to see my psychiatrist again.'

He offered to show me some of his work and was happy for me to transcribe words from a recent epithalamium he had been asked to write.

No need for tears, except those of joy. The son has his wife, the girl has her boy. No need to go chasing after other girl's charms. Now you are married with clenching of palms, A lifetime together is now what awaits ...

'I've got a home in Worcestershire, and a few friends. It's enough.'

The impact of that last phrase resonated. How many of us ever feel we have enough? Here was a man who seemed genuinely fulfilled; who had enough.

As John had taken to pointing out that I tended to gravitate towards those passengers who looked most likely not to respond with abuse, I decided on a bold course and sat opposite a young and very smart woman. Rather than summoning the conductor, she welcomed my intrusion and told me that she too was a writer. That made three of us. Or four of us counting Defoe. This seemed beyond a coincidence. I glanced down the carriage to see if the trolley attendant was urging the passengers to pretend that they were writers if approached. Some of them had embraced the idea with alacrity and were loudly declaiming soliloquys to each other.

I gave the young woman the benefit of the doubt. She claimed to be Carly Holmes whose novel *Scrapbook* had just been published by Parthian. She behaved and spoke more like a writer than I could ever manage. I listened in awe, and not a little in love, as she described her penchant for magic, and her love of the Gower Peninsula now passing on our left. With her long languid locks tumbling over her face (Mills and Boon, are you interested?) she described how she had almost fallen foul of the DH Lawrence estate over a copyright issue. (Shimmering with a black passion she reflected on the quasi-mystical nature of sex.) She had also been nominated for a Dylan Thomas award, that man again. (Beware the cockstarved mantles of myrtle, rancid and bleak as the broken gulls.)

Carly's website introduces her thus, 'The village I call home is on an estuary, haunted night and day by the call of birds whose names I never remember but whose cries I wouldn't be without.'

'I'm a writer too,' said Defoe, equally intent on flirting with Carly. Ignoring him, I promised to read her book and returned to John, but my conversation with Carly had been overheard by a young couple whose shared body language was inviting me to approach them. I explained my mission.

'Yes, we heard,' said the man. 'Well, I can tell you, you've struck gold with us.'

'Pure gold,' echoed his partner.

Now convinced that I was the victim of an elaborate hoax, I let my disbelief show.

'No, it's true,' said the man again. 'I'm a prolific

183

songwriter. Prolific.' He gave an impressive emphasis to the middle syllable of the word as only a Welsh person could.

'Prolific,' echoed his partner.

'And my girlfriend here is a prolific landscape painter. She does commissions.'

He was clutching his guitar as if eager to demonstrate his true prolificacy, while she gazed on him fondly from beneath her fedora. They were so proud of each other, I regretted my initial cynical thoughts.

He was James Smiles, singer with the Telekinetics who can be seen at the open mic night at Cromwells in Pembroke. According to one admirer on Facebook, James is f*****g quality. According to his girlfriend he has written a very good song 'about a boy and a girl'. She was Rebecca Alexandra Fleetwood Wooldridge, painter of land and seascapes. Not gold perhaps but a valuable alloy nonetheless, compounded of mutual support and a commitment to the dream.

To escape the travelling artists' colony, I resumed my sightseeing from the carriage window. Scouring the skies as we stopped at Gowerton, I hoped to glimpse the world's rarest goose *en route* to the Wetlands where it would be feted and photographed, but had to settle for a few languid herring gulls.

Llanelli proved much more interesting. The train doors flew open and the entire rugby team of 1972 poured into the carriage, turning it into a sea of celebratory scarlet. The players had forsaken the male joys of the communal bath and were still stinking of Felinfoel beer, embrocation, sweat, amateurism and the reek of satisfaction from thrashing the All Blacks 9 - 3. John tried to snatch a word with Carwyn James but the coach stared straight through him. The same happened with Ray Gravell who faded away to ever-fainter strains of *Sospan Fach*.

Rather than dwell on the psychic implications of their brief appearance, I gazed at the Bristol Channel as we approached Pembrey and Burry Port station, and was rewarded with the sight of Gwyr-y-Bwelli or Men of Little Hatchets. A small tribe of trolls was at work in the estuary dismantling a large wooden ship that had foundered on the dunes. This activity was lucrative in the early nineteenth century and, judging by the level of activity and the sound of a hundred tiny hammers, still was. A glowing beacon may, allegedly, have been lit to lure the ships in the direction of the small people waiting expectantly during the night with their hammers poised.

There was also a lot happening in the estuary close to Ferryside. There must have been a fresh outbreak of the Cockle Wars that bedevilled the area in the 1990s. Gangs of poachers from as far away as Glasgow had descended, in the words of *The Independent,* 'to plunder the molluscs from under the noses of the Fish Protection Officers'. Groups of men faced each other across the sands with baseball bats while their pit bull terriers strained at the leash.

Defoe, who had been mercifully quiet, couldn't resist commenting on the rolling countryside, 'This part is so very pleasant, and fertile, and is so well cultivated, that 'tis called by distinction, Little England, beyond Wales.'

'I wouldn't say that out loud if I were you.'

Wandering through Pembroke Dock proved to be a desolate experience. Its saving grace was its unqualified commitment to Halloween. White spray-on cobwebs and splatterings of false blood served to disguise the fact that the shops had no goods to sell. A retailer run by Herod and Sons was churning out a line of howling, face-painted children, and the uncharitable thought occurred that Pembroke Dock was not gearing up to celebrate the feast of All Saints. The truth was that the town was entirely inhabited by the Undead with open coffins stacked in every alley, and local zombies lurching down the middle of the street.

Leaving the town, I wandered towards a bleak stretch of

mud where I found the Martello gun tower. Not wishing to attract the attention of whichever legal firm is retained by the local tourist board, I must also state that if the sun had been shining and the tide had been in, and the museum open, and if I had been in a better frame of mind, then the stumpy tower with its sumptuous vista could well have been the highlight of my entire journey.

Meanwhile John had retreated to a pub yards from the station, a move he came to regret. Still shaking from his ordeal, and clutching at my arm, he described the hellish scene within.

While the completely drunken patrons slurred their way through their individual *danses macabres*, the pub decorations detached themselves from the ceiling and collapsed on John, festooning him in a hijab of paper spiders and miniature witches. The barmaid ordered the least drunk customer to rescue him, which he did by hauling on one end of the frieze, compounding John's distress with an undeserved garrotting. As he fought for breath, the obliging patron placed the decorations in the middle of the floor and stamped on them as if they were on fire.

'Excellent description; puts me in mind of sections from *Moll Flanders* ...'

'Thank you,' I said modestly.

Our train arrived fifteen minutes prior to its timetabled departure and the reluctant conductor allowed us on board to recover our equilibrium. When it was finally allowed to escape, caution was thrown to the wind and we took a short cut across several fields. Bouncing its way through a farm and a small river, it got back on track and delivered us to Whitland where it was soon apparent that the station had been transformed into a disco by an odd knot of dysfunctional youths with a ghetto blaster. The token girl in their midst decided to provoke her boyfriend by leaving him to dance with her dog. 'Here's metal more attractive, Rover!'

186

The animal, accustomed to being a pawn in their relationship, let itself be steered on its hind legs across the platform.

John, meanwhile, was staring upwards, not for divine guidance, but at the station roof. 'Look at all the shit up there,' he observed, before making a new entry in the *Great Ledger of Observations and Complaints*.

Our final destination for the day was Milford Haven, where John's innate stubbornness and his inadequate map took us on a more extensive tour of the docks than either of us wanted. As we circumnavigated the posh marina, I entertained the slight hope that perhaps tonight would offer some respite from the usual Dickensian bed and breakfast accommodation. The thought of a reading light that worked and a shower that emitted actual hot water was a sustaining one. However, having retraced our steps at least three times, and thrown ourselves at the mercy of several passing strangers, we found ourselves on the threshold of the Heart of Oak.

To our astonishment we were greeted by the embodiment of the Living Christ. Majestic, bearded, and with a soulful demeanour, the barman acknowledged our presence with a slight incline of the head.

'I know, I know,' he said, 'It's a curse.' With that he took out a faded picture of the Turin Shroud and held it next to his face. The likeness was uncanny. 'I've got used to it,' he said. There were four other customers and a large black dog. John grunted some greeting which was reciprocated by the one member of the group still sufficiently sober.

'Where are you from?' asked John.

'Chepstow.'

'That's not Wales!' shouted John. I cringed. The expression on the face of the insulted customer suggested that he was undecided between lynching or keelhauling. 'What are you drinking?' asked John, roaring with laughter, and the atmosphere changed in an instant. We were their new best friends.

187

I looked at my friend in a new light. He was quite capable of conjuring a hail-fellow-well-met persona that was startling in its inclusivity. We were soon swept up in a miasma of anecdote, confession and Anglophobia.

I listened in awe as John regaled us with thoughts on fishing quotas, natural gas, the government, and rugby matches between Wales and Scotland. He then asked permission to sing. His audience grew silent and respectful and even the barman paused as John launched into *Sosban Fach*.

'F*** me,' said a man in the corner. The barman nodded a silent reminder that he should moderate his language, but the sinner's tongue, bitten by Satan, was no longer capable of untrammelled speech. Every sentence on which he embarked was left hanging in the air after a few incoherent words that floated aimlessly into the ether. He beamed approval and mimed undying friendship for us both.

'One of our regulars died recently,' said the barman. 'He had no money see, so we all chipped in and got him a headstone but the local vicar wanted rent for the plot in the graveyard. I phoned him up. "Is that My Lord from The Heart of Oak?" asked the vicar. Yes, I said. "There will be no fee, Dear Jesus," said the vicar.'

The silence that fell over the bar was broken by a large black dog who had taken an extreme dislike of the customer in a green anorak.

'He's jealous,' explained a woman.

'I've been working away from home for the last eight weeks,' slurred her partner, 'and I think the dog's taken my place.' He cupped his hands over his genitals like a footballer in a defensive wall.

'It was my accent, you understand,' said the Lord Jesus, for no apparent reason. 'Because I sounded posh every school I went to assumed I was bright and put me in the top stream. I couldn't cope...'

Unabashed by his wistful lament, the punters moved up a

188

gear and engaged John in discussion best summarised as The Joy of Crabs which may, or may not, have been the title of a sex manual rejected by publishers in the 1960s. John, for his part, struck terror into their innocent hearts by conjuring apoplectic visions of Milford Haven being incinerated by an explosion in the vast gas storage tanks situated a few miles inland. The pub sound system burst into life and saved the locals from the full impact of his vision. When the music died and returned from whence it had come, one of the locals embarked on a quasi-maudlin anecdote about the time his Belgian son-in-law arranged to meet him in the middle of the night to pass over £1000 worth of cod and monkfish. The happy beneficiary would drag the crate into the pub and dispense his fish like

'Loaves and fishes,' suggested the barman in reverential tones.

'You know,' said one of the company, 'I've travelled all over the world but I've only ever visited England once, I went to Blackpool one year.'

That night John and I slept like dead people in the upper reaches of the Heart of Oak. We agreed in the morning that it was the best night we had spent on our travels, and furthermore that the pub itself was probably the friendliest and most welcoming we had encountered across the length and breadth of the kingdom. I made a mental note to send a copy of whatever book might emerge from the journey to the Holy Barman, with the description of his pub underlined.

DAY FIVE

Milford Haven – Llanelli – Cardiff – Ebbw Vale –
Cardiff – Shrewsbury – Birmingham New Street –
Glasgow

Carriages have character. Some are mournful, functional and quiet. Others are animated and full of excitement. Ours fell into the latter category.

Chatter, gossip and laughter propelled the train towards Llanelli. Companionable and inclusive, the travellers embarked on another day of routines, small surprises and innumerable interactions with colleagues, friends and family. The ambience impacted too on our mood and I decided that John was, after all, not a bad person to spend time with. He, for his part, decided that he could live with my irritating deafness and disinterest in the minutiae of rail workings and wagon deployment.

He was however, disconcerted by a change to our itinerary.

'The next train will terminate in the station as the driver has been taken ill.'

Mercifully the driver had managed his way into the station without careering through the buffers. I glanced towards the cab and was reminded of a moment, over half a century in the past, when I watched as the driver of a steam locomotive was lowered on a stretcher onto the platform at Crewe from his fiery footplate. Was it a heart attack, heat exhaustion? Had the fireman wrestled heroically with the controls while simultaneously tending to his fallen companion and the voracious maul of the firebox? In childish dreams, I frequently became that heroic fireman frantically shovelling coal as the locomotive hurtled through the night.

The announcement continued. 'Is there a doctor on the station? And would anyone welcome a shot at driving the train? We have a copy of *Driving for Duffers* and several relevant Ladybird Books.'

Recovered from his disappointment of not being able to travel on the scenic Mid Wales line, John suggested we should attempt the final finger of the valley lines and make a pilgrimage to Ebbw Vale. I chose not to provoke him by admitting I was increasingly indifferent to our destination. Instead I concentrated on the cameo unfolding on Neath station where a smartly dressed young man dived to the platform floor to retrieve a twenty-pound note.

I could tell it was a twenty-pound note as he held it between thumb and forefinger and proffered it at passing strangers. I practised my lip reading: 'Anyone drop this?' I could also read his thoughts as he stuffed the note into his pocket. 'Did anyone see me? No. It's all mine!' Why is it always the least deserving who have all the luck? Why did this young financier or insurance broker find the money and not the shabby woman struggling to keep her children under control?

I was pondering this and other great mysteries when we started the slow journey to Ebbw Vale. A sullen youth, exuding aggression and facial pus, threw his headphones onto the table and played his appalling music as loudly as he could, thereby punishing the cruel world that had visited him with boils.

Defoe moved his hand up to the side of his face and fingered the unsightly mole of which he was so conscious throughout his life.

Towards the head of the valley the collective mood changed. The youth turned off his music and a hungry baby stopped in mid wail. The hills became greener and I'm sure that the woman in the car park blew kisses at me. I reciprocated in a moment of seraphic content. The journey was developing a distinctly spiritual dimension.

I admired the isolated temples on the hillside and the incense rising from the valley, and was confident that the Sherpas of Ebbw Vale would protect me from all boil-faced trolls. When we arrived in Nirvana, I noticed that the pilgrim reception centre was masquerading as a high school but I wasn't fooled. I knew also that the crows flying over the valley were the souls of the dead, recently liberated from their bodies.

The dream only partly faded with the return journey. Six female venal spirits, expelled from the monastery, sought solace in a carry-out as they braced themselves for the Sodom that was Cardiff. Leather-booted, thick-thighed and old enough to know better, they caroused discordantly. To my horror one of them embarked on an excruciating rendition of *Queen of the Night*, shattering one of their wine glasses, and with it the last semblance of pleasure that I was deriving from the journey. My bottom lip trembled. I wanted to be home.

'You lack commitment,' said Defoe. 'No fortitude or stamina. Your book will never be finished. In my opinion...' but I snapped shut my Penguin Classic, cutting him off in mid-sentence.

JOURNEY SIX

Essex, Sussex, Mid and North Wales

DAY ONE

Glasgow Central – Euston – Kings Cross –
Finsbury Park – Hertford North – Hitchin –
Cambridge – Broxbourne – Hertford East –
Hackney Downs – Chingford – Liverpool Street –
Manningtree – Harwich Town – Manningtree –
Colchester Town – Wivenhoe – Clacton

An itinerary that combines part of the South East with bits of Wales needs some explanation.

For arcane reasons that John and no one else understands, the counties of Essex and Sussex are not covered by a regional Rail Rover ticket. So instead of the usual cheeky £70, we had no alternative but to re-mortgage both of our houses and invest in an all-UK ticket. Having committed to such a preposterous sum, it made sense to hoover up those sections of the Welsh network not covered by our earlier expedition. An unfortunate consequence was the requirement to travel on seventy-eight trains in six days. There are no words to describe my sense of dread as we boarded the 5.40 Virgin Cross Country from Glasgow.

The entire carriage was soon asleep. Edgar Allan Poe

characterised sleep as so many little slices of death, while for Jules Verne it was the friend who keeps us waiting. The aisle was knee-deep in strange abandoned dreams; falling dreams that fade before impact, unsettling lustful dreams, anxiety-driven dreams about tasks unfinished.

En route to the toilet, I felt like matron inspecting the dormitories. No snoring or grunting please; no accidental touching. The only passenger not in Lethe's embrace was an elderly puritan simultaneously reading the Bible and a book about heaven. Perhaps he was a devil watcher, sniffing the air for tell-tale hints of sulphur.

Soon I too fell asleep. When I jolted awake I saw, in my peripheral vision, the shadow of a man who disappeared the moment he saw that I had noticed him. I was not expecting a psychic visitation but felt that whomever my subconscious had summoned, that person was sympathetic towards me somehow: my *alter ego*, an *id* perhaps.

The first overheard phone call of the day dispelled any possibility of spiritual encounters. '…dodgy dealings if you ask me. People grow up, don't they? Haven't seen him since the tribunal in Fleet Street. Twenty-five years ago … he did apologise, fair play to him. He tried to kill himself…'

A quick Google search of Fleet Street and tribunals revealed a firm of Criminal and Regulatory Barristers who specialise in fraud and have appeared in some of the highest profile trials involving organised crime, terrorism and murder. No wonder my guardian angel had appeared. Defoe was tugging at my sleeve. His expression was desperate.

'What's the matter?'

'That man, don't tell him I'm here.' Like a child, he put his hands over his face so that he might not be seen. 'That lawyer! He's pursuing me for the debts I can't pay. I can't go back to prison. I can't!'

I moved to comfort him. There was not a hint of the old pomposity. Just the vulnerability of a man in despair.

'Write this down,' he begged. 'Write these words. It's a letter to my son-in-law, Henry Baker, the only man who won't betray my whereabouts...'

'Is this your last letter? The one you wrote before you died?'

'Just write ... I am near my journey's end, and am hastening to that place where the weary are at rest. Give my little grandson my blessing. Kiss my dear Sophie once more for me; and if I must see her no more, tell her this from a Father that has loved her above all his comforts, to his last breath.'

The day had not started well. Deciding that little good comes from intrusive eavesdropping on complete strangers, I focussed instead on the physical appearance of my fellow passengers. I was expecting most to be of the well-heeled, healthy-living middle classes, who can afford the luxury of travelling on trains. Instead, I was struck by the over representation of fat people in the carriage, and this is not necessarily a slight on John. In truth, there is nothing slight about John.

I have no wish to be judgemental or sizeist, and I respect individuals' right to court early death if they wish, but the train was full of monsters. Most of the armrests were embedded in someone's flesh. Thin passengers moved sideways to avoid accidental contact with overhanging buttocks. To their credit, Virgin Trains have made efforts to acknowledge the obesity crisis. The rack at the end of the carriage, normally reserved for the safety notices that no one reads, was stuffed with leaflets urging participation in the Weight Watchers classes held in Carriage C (especially reinforced). Furthermore, the conductor would be happy to recommend liposuction clinics. Was the Fat Woman of Ross on the train?

Determined to qualify for the next class, the man who

joined at Wigan sat next to John, and proceeded to stuff himself with crisps. Judging by the noise, these were no ordinary crisps, but made from rodent bones and clinker. Conversation was impossible, drowned by a sound that brought Matthew Arnold's *Dover Beach* to mind.

'Listen! *You hear the grating roar / of pebbles which the waves draw back and fling, / At their return, up the high strand.'*

Eventually he stuffed the last crisp in his mouth, made even more noise by crunching up the packet, belched loudly, and sat back a contented man.

At Crewe, the seat next to me was taken by a man who, having organised his office on his quarter of the shared table, took out his laptop and started redesigning someone's garden. His body language made clear that he would not welcome idle chat. At first I thought he was playing a computer game as tiny objects hurtled across an unnaturally green screen. Gradually these objects revealed themselves as fence posts, duck ponds and gazebos. At one point, he subtly expanded the perimeters of these gardens.

Now feeling trapped and bored, I wandered down the carriage with all heads turning to observe my progress like flowers tilting towards the sun. I wanted to bless them, give words of encouragement or indeed absolution. I wanted to reassure them that all their worries, like this journey, would pass.

The sliding doors at the end of the next carriage had developed their own malicious intelligence and were providing amusement to a table of leery youths. Whenever an innocent passenger attempted to pass through, the doors would snap together and break his ribs. The adjacent toilet had been requisitioned and turned into a temporary field hospital where the maimed were treated by Virgin Trains staff.

'Beware the Watford Gap if you are leaving the train. Please remember to take with you all your prejudices against the North of England and Scotland and drop them gently next to the train.'

Euston Station, 'one of the ugliest concrete boxes in England', had not improved since our last visit. Viewed in this light, the brief walk to Kings Cross was especially welcome. A smiling Buddhist monk approached and offered me a trinket. Despite decades of avoiding all tabloid newspapers, my cynical soul reminded me that there is a global infestation of false, begging Buddhists. I declined his bracelet but was then stricken with doubt. What if his smile was genuine? What horrible karmic revenge would the day inflict on me?

As we left Kings Cross station for Finsbury Park, a tramp emerged from the toilet. An archetypal tramp with stiff, stained gabardine trousers held up with string. To be fair, he had left the toilet in good shape. What does that last comment reveal about my attitude to down and outs, hobos, and gentlemen of the road generally? Buddhism first, then tramps. Had I absorbed a *Daily Mail* view of the world through some sort of osmosis? Anyway, the toilet was clean. The tramp was sitting in an aisle seat. He was wearing very smart shoes with his tramp footwear in a bag at his side. Surely not another imposter. There had to be a more charitable explanation. Was he on a psychological journey from businessman to dosser, hankering for a life more pure? I winked and told him his secret was safe with me

At Finsbury Park, John, for some reason, tried to leave the train from the wrong side. I caught him pulling at the locked door while muttering about the absence of a platform. This journey was proving difficult for both of us.

Looking up at Alexandra Palace, the former home of the BBC, I noted that, at least on this occasion, it wasn't on fire. And then, bizarrely, the train intercom started to broadcast a live transmission from the 1953 coronation. Richard Dimbleby's fruity clipped vowels struck awe and patriotism into the hearts of every passenger: 'So to that stirring music majesty, splendour and beauty pass from our sight as the Queen goes in her lovely robe out of the nave of the abbey. History has been written and sung here today...' The heralds heralded and the trumpeters trumpeted. Pomp and circumstance floated regally down the aisle. The trolley dispensed cups of char and spam fritters and I waved at the departing train as it left Hertford North.

My patriotic reverie was interrupted by a station announcement warning against tissue beggars. This was a phenomenon with which I was completely unacquainted. The station assistant was unctuousness personified when we asked for an explanation. Evidently, innocent – and very generous – passengers are giving as much as £10 to beggars who leave packets of tissues on the seat next to them before telling tales of personal hardship.

While waiting for the train to Hitchin, I conducted some research on my phone and discovered whole forums are devoted to the phenomenon. I even discovered an agonised disclaimer from British Transport Police acknowledging that 'some people who beg are indeed vulnerable.' Now there's a surprise.

The following journeys presented few opportunities for either tissue beggars or myself, as the trains were largely empty. Instead we crept through sleepy towns and pleasant countryside (John unhesitatingly allocated a seven) without being disturbed or being able to disturb anyone else.

This changed after Cambridge where two Stormtroopers boarded the train to Broxbourne. Dressed in black with chiselled jaws they swept down the aisle, presumably searching for Jews, homosexuals and the disabled. I had no idea if they were security guards or genuine members of a neo-Nazi re-enactment society. A middle-aged couple protested their innocence, 'We are only going to buy a bed for our son.' Grudgingly the Stormtroopers moved to the next carriage.

Relieved, the couple were soon lost in a reverie about the Japanese rail system.

'The queues on the stations are outside of the gents, not the ladies...there are many more men employed than women you see?' I didn't really, but there was no stopping them. 'All ticket collectors wear white gloves, and bow respectfully at the end of the corridor. Staff become visibly distressed if the train is late ...' As my attention waned, I looked out of the window at the heaps of intestines lining the tracks after the ritual disembowelments prompted by the announcement of a bus replacement service.

They left the train at Ware. This of course made great sense. They were going to Ware to buy a bed, where else would they go? The most famous bed in the world is The Great Bed of Ware. Originally built for a local inn in 1590, it now slumbers in Room 57 of the V & A. It gets a mention in *Twelfth Night*. At three metres wide, it can accommodate at least four couples.

An elderly woman cocked her head sideways, popped a tomato in her mouth and stared at me. To avoid any further eye contact, I feigned interest in Ponders End station. By an association, not difficult to detect, I found myself pondering my own end. This was becoming something of an ongoing preoccupation. Too late now to die a young man's death, a clean and in-between the sheets holy-water-death was probably the best I could hope for. Though I wasn't certain about the holy water bit. Pursuing this line of thought for a moment longer, it occurred to me that, if my grandchildren should ever read this book, they will know by then how I, eventually, met my end. Excuse this brief aside: 'Hi Kids!'

To compound this gloomy speculation, the former premises of Grout, Baylis and Co., manufacturers of crepe used for widow's weeds, was visible from the station.

It was difficult to dispel intimations of death as the train embarked on its slow descent into North London where drab, nondescript scrubland gradually morphed into Hackney Downs before surrendering to urban dereliction. The train paused for breath on a bridge outside Bethnal Green. In the High Street, an abandoned shop entrance had been curtained off with bedding. Who was living behind the makeshift screen?

Soon we creaked and inched our way towards Liverpool Street, passing so close to the tenements that, had it been possible to open the carriage window, I could have scooped up the tired geraniums from an adjacent sill.

Down below was a matrix of tiny domestic backyards piled high with the detritus of living: bikes, mattresses, a mangle which had presumably been there since the late 1950s. Looking upwards, I saw a tiny SOLD notice on a window on the fifteenth floor of a block of flats. It was either for the benefit of passing angels or visiting neighbours who would have to read it backwards. A cat stretched on a wall decorated with a stubble of broken glass.

At Liverpool Street Station the crowd stared upwards at the departure boards, patiently waiting for the face of the Messiah to appear between the lists of destinations. A man walked slowly, holding a copy of a Wilbur Smith book in front of him as if it were a sacred object. A woman swaddled a baby which, on closer inspection, turned out to be a tiny dog festooned with pink bows. A dwarf couple, rocking their way down the concourse, pushed a large pram between them.

The train to Manningtree was crowded. The large woman sitting opposite us rested her bosoms on the table. 'I hate this world. It's horrible! I fear for my daughter.' Neither of us knew how to respond although John treated her to one of his more forbidding stares. 'It's happened again,' she said pointing to the TEENAGE RAPPER KNIFED TO DEATH headline in the *Evening Standard*. In the absence of any meaningful comment from either of us, she ripped off the ring pull from a can of Strongbow and emptied the contents down her neck.

'You needed that,' said her partner.

'You're not joking. I nearly died!' I decided, on balance, that the last phrase had not been offered as an ironic reference to Philip Larkin's *Whitsun Weddings*. She moved her hand to her partner's crotch. He remained emotionless, unless the veins standing out on his bald head were a subliminal clue.

She too was undergoing a transformation, her face becoming redder and redder and causing her nose ring to glow. To release steam, she embarked on a monologue built on comments gleaned from the paper, which reached a crescendo as she read out Donald Trump's views on abortion. At this moment her comatose partner rallied and whispered something in her ear which, judging by her not unfavourable reaction, was of a lewd and libidinous nature.

'Stupid crutch!' she shouted. I initially assumed that she was making a derogatory reference to her partner's anatomy but then I noticed the elbow crutch at her side. Eventually she manoeuvred herself out of the seat and made her way to the toilet, while the train continued its way to Hades via Sodom and Gomorrah.

Mercifully, it took a detour (engineering works on the Gomorrah line) and loitered alongside the Stour Estuary. After the last encounter, I wanted to throw myself into the restorative waters, fall back on the mud flats and listen to the gulls. Instead, we passed through Mistley. The name resonated uncomfortably. It came to me: Manningtree and Mistley were in the Witchfinder General's fiefdom.

During the Civil War, Mathew Hopkins and his sidekick, Witchpricker Sterne, established themselves as the Pol Pots of Essex. The latter derived his name from his special witch-detection method involving poking pins, needles and bodkins into the skin of lonely, eccentric old women to see if they bled. It was Mathew though, the main man, who persuaded the one-legged Elizabeth Clarke to confess after stripping her naked and depriving her of sleep for three nights.

This was grist to Defoe's mill. He joyously produced a large pin from his wig and made to bury it in the calf of a woman sitting on the other side of the aisle.

'Let me prick you, Mistress Witch!'

'Don't even think of it!'

With a degree of petulance, he reinserted the offending item into his artificial locks.

As we waited on the platform a young woman approached John to ask if this was the Colchester train. He assumed his most avuncular persona and, without resorting to sleep deprivation, extracted a confession of sorts. She was excited. She had finished her first day in a new job with an energy company. Everyone had been friendly and welcoming. She had previously worked in events management but had been unemployed for a long time. She had been brought up in New York. John missed the 'New' bit of that sentence and embarked on a confusing paean to the beauty of the Minster and the instability of the Ouse. She recovered well and changed topic to her new partner and new baby, waving at us as she got on the train.

Any sense that God was in His/Her heaven and all was well with the world was dispelled by John's insistence that we wait for a small eternity to travel the half mile from Colchester Central to Colchester North and back. He had taken far too literally my requirement that he organise routes that covered every single mile of railway track in the kingdom. This was beyond stupidity.

I looked at the sky, idly recalling how H G Wells' refugees from *The War of the Worlds* escape from the Martian-plagued capital and make their way to Colchester. Mercifully there were no green flashes, and no sounds of falling canisters. Perhaps we would be safe after all. Defoe heard the plague reference and sprang awake.

'The town of Colchester has been supposed to contain about 40,000 people. One sad testimony of the town being so populous is, that they buried upwards of 5258 people in the plague year, 1665. There were signs. There were the dreams of old women, some heard voices warning them to be gone, for that there would be such a plague in London, so that the living would not be able to bury the dead. They told us they saw a flaming sword held in a hand coming out of a cloud, with a point hanging directly over the city; there they saw hearses and coffins in the air carrying bodies to be buried; and there heaps of bodies lying unburied...'

After this tiniest of journeys, John approached the driver as he was about to climb into his cab. 'Excuse me,' he asked, 'does this train stop at Wivenhoe?'

'Don't ask me, I just drive the thing.'

Pitched somewhere between the surreal and the ignorant, the elliptical and the dangerous, this reply raised the possibility that the subsequent journey would be serendipitous for the driver, and a magical mystery tour for ourselves.

Defoe stared at the Essex coastline.

'On this shore are taken the best and nicest, though not the largest oysters in England ... The chief sort of other fish which they carry from this part of the shore to London, are soles, which they take sometimes exceeding large, and yield a very good price at London market. Also sometimes middling turbot, with whitings, codling, and large flounders...'

DAY TWO

Clacton – Thorpe-le-Soken – Walton-on-Naze –
Thorpe-le-Soken – Colchester – Marks Tey –
Sudbury (Suffolk) – Marks Tey – Witham – Braintree –
Shenfield – Wickford – Southminster – Wickford –
Southend Victoria – (walk) Southend Central –
Shoeburyness – Fenchurch St. – West Ham –
Stratford International – Ashford International

There was little magical or mysterious about Clacton unless it was that everything I touched in the B & B fell apart: towel rail, toilet roll holder, shower curtain and several light switches. Puzzled to discover these new powers, I stepped over the detritus and walked along the Esplanade.

A pier, palm trees and a calm sea almost erased the memory of the previous evening's pub quiz, but not quite. 'The next round, ladies and gentlemen, is about aircraft – things that fly in the sky. OK, first question, what does RAF stand for? I know, some of these are tricky but stick with it. OK, second question ... what colour is Donald Duck's bow tie?'* The pause that followed was an intellectual black hole that sucked in the pub's pork scratchings, tepid beer, customers and fittings.

During this cosmic hiatus, we were joined by the epony-mous caretaker from Pinter's play who alternated ferocious eye contact with a repertoire of facial expressions. When he screwed up his face after the second question, I thought he was treating us to his Donald Duck impersonation. I nodded at him and said, 'Very good, I like that.' We left soon after.

The morning had started well but deteriorated rapidly. Rarely had I seen John so outraged. The innocent woman earning a pittance in the coffee shop on Thorpe-le-Soken station timidly broke the news that she was not allowed to accept Scottish pound notes. While making clear that his incandescence was not aimed specifically at her, but at her boss who was, by this time, hiding in a small cupboard, he banged his fist on the counter and launched accusations of racism, cultural imperialism and general badness.

Marginally embarrassed, I walked along the platform to enjoy the idyllic surroundings of rural Essex. Across the track I could see down the length of a garden into a conservatory where a harassed mother was trying to get her kids ready for school in a flurry of lunch boxes, satchels, gym kit, unfinished homework, inhalers and something for show and tell. The same scene was no doubt being enacted concurrently up and down the country.

Frinton station is famous not only for its huge mural of Winston Churchill but also for the part it plays in dividing the community. In its own way, it is the Berlin Wall of Essex. Residents who live on the far side of the station are perceived as a threat and a menace to the law-abiding pensioners who live nearest the sea. The good folk, approximately 300 of them, each pay £100 a year to security guards who patrol their streets. The good pensioners, in true blitz spirit, also get their sleeves rolled up and aim speed guns at slowly passing milk floats. Winston would have been proud.

Realising that one of these vigilantes had joined the train, I told John to take his feet off the seats and sit up straight. The man in question was wearing military camouflage with 'Army Commando' embroidered on his epaulettes. He was the size of a small tank, a Challenger perhaps, and was waging his own private war with the conductor. 'Ridiculous price for a ticket! It's never cost me that in the past.'

'That must have been the Super Off Peak Saver Sir.'

'No, it wasn't!'

'I know my job Sir. I think you may have been lucky in the past and got away with it.' The courageous conductor escaped with his life while his antagonist spent the rest of the journey stuffing photographs into small see-through bags. I feigned sleep rather than talk to him about the killing fields of Bosnia and the strange compulsion he had since developed.

Equally menacing was the tall passenger with a dotted line tattooed across his neck with the words CUT HERE. It was a bold statement that would give pause to any jihadist beheaders in the next carriage. He was approached by a man who asked him for a roll-up. Initially failing to cadge a smoke, the man upped his offer, 'I'll swap you a bottle of Yazoo.' The deal was done. In Essex this exotic currency would always be preferable to Scottish pound notes.

Only as we stepped off the train at Colchester did I see the tiny, anxious woman sitting close to the door, with Miss Havisham layers of make-up and an enormous shopping trolley containing a Pekinese.

Another small drama was being acted out on Colchester station Platform 1.

'I'm so sorry about last night ... I was such a bitch,' a female rail employee said to her male counterpart. He looked embarrassed, trying to suppress the memory of how she turned to him at the bar and told him he was a boring lover, and she knew he would never leave his sad little wife.

I thought about them as we followed numerous dead ends through the maze of the Essex rail network. This was new territory for John who took mental notes of every track that joined ours, of every small station, of every cutting and embankment. Our carriage drew up alongside its 1950s predecessor parked at a railway heritage centre, affording an unobstructed view of faded upholstery and doors with hanging leather straps. I confess to nostalgia and am forced to admit, that, in my own way, I am at least as sad as John. Above the seats were framed prints of Weston-Super-Mare and Windsor Castle, tantalising holiday destinations for excited passengers.

John took pleasure in informing me that the viaduct over which we were crossing was constructed of seven million bricks. Although I was indifferent to this statistic, Defoe embarked on a hymn of praise to the brick which for reasons of extreme dullness is not reproduced here. He then told me that he knew of nothing for which Sudbury was remarkable, 'Except for being very populous and very poor. Indeed, the number of the poor is almost ready to eat up the rich.'

Of more interest was his observation that there were few women in our carriage. He had an explanation ready at hand, which mercifully was not because the women had been eaten. Instead he blamed the damp.

'All along this county it was very frequent to meet with men that had had from five to six, to fourteen wives; nay, and some more. And I was informed that in the marshes on the other side near Canvey Island, there was a farmer, who was then living with the five and twentieth wife, and that his son who was but about thirty-five years old, had already had about fourteen. The reason, as a merry fellow told me, who said that he had had about a dozen and a half wives (though I found afterwards he fibbed a little) was this; that they always went up into the hilly country for a wife: that when they took the young lasses out of the wholesome and fresh air, they were healthy, fresh and clear; but when they came out of their native air into the marshes among the fogs and damps, there they changed their complexion, got an ague or two, and died.'

We had to wait at Witham station and it was here that I caught sight of one of the most astonishing sights of the journey so far: a petite middle-aged woman trainspotter. It is difficult to think of any other occupation or pastime that is so exclusively male as train spotting. Hunting, fishing, shooting, burglary, all fail the test. Here was a phenomenon.

She was taking photos of a large freight locomotive. 'I love spotting,' she said. 'My husband can't get out as much now so I do the spotting for him. I send him photos on WhatsApp... That's a class 66 by the way, owned by the Mediterranean Shipping Company, probably come from Felixstowe Docks ... We went on the *Mayflower* last weekend, we are desperate to go on the *Flying Scotsman*.'

I nodded and reflected on the strange things that love can do to people. Meanwhile John was idly watching the progress of a large rat through the undergrowth.

The driver stopped at White Notley out of a sense of nostalgia for one day, decades before, when a passenger actually got on the train. It was quite possible that John spotted his remains on the seat across the aisle. It was undeniably a bone. It may have been dropped by a stray dog, or possibly a magpie nesting in the overhead locker.

Cannibalism in Essex is a frequently researched topic on Google, and not just because of Defoe's belief that the poor eat the rich. Disappointingly, the *Essex* referred to in the search engine is the ship of the same name which foundered in 1820 having been struck by a monster whale. Two survivors were found gnawing on the bones of their former shipmates. Although the link with John's discovery is tenuous, it helped pass the time until we reached Shenfield.

Here we watched awestruck as a pensioner completed a lap of the station car park on a mobility scooter modelled on a Harley Davidson. A bespoke vehicle of this nature will set you back the best part of £6000, and may attract the attention of the police although its maximum pavement speed is 4 mph. Meanwhile *Born to Be Wild, The Pusher, It's Alright, Ma (I'm only bleeding)* and *The Ballad of Easy Rider* played on an endless loop.

I asked John what he thought of Essex in general. Pulling himself up to his full height, and breadth, he issued one of his finer pontifications. 'Indescribably mundane, aspiring to mediocrity, unambitious, content with its own insipidity, whose inhabitants have deserved reputations for wearing hoodies and the lowest hanging tracksuit bottoms.' For all the world like Dictionary Johnson impressing a gullible Boswell, he continued, 'Its sole redeeming feature is a proliferation of geans.'

'Proliferation of what?'

'Geans.'

Thinking he had said 'gangs' I connected with recent injunctions taken out by the Bluewater shopping complex against bands of marauding youths, wearing the aforementioned hoodies and falling-down trousers.

'No,' he said angrily. 'Geans. Wild cherry, a white flowered rosaceous tree, *prunius avium* to you. You see them especially alongside the railway. According to legend, the only way to stop a cuckoo singing is to make it eat three meals of geans.'

'How could you make a cuckoo eat anything?' I asked.

John added one more damning epithet to his earlier litany. 'Indifferent,' he said.

Defoe, enjoying this game of Essex bashing, chipped in with, 'This flat country is justly said to be both unhealthy and unpleasant.'

The plentiful supply of leaflets on the Crouch Valley Line make clear that the residents are fighting back, determined to rescue the county's reputation. Henceforth any utilitarian function that the local rail network may previously have fulfilled, will be abandoned in favour of luxury and entertainment.

'From April 3rd, the experience starts the moment you step onto the platform at Wickford where you will be greeted with musicians playing whilst you enjoy the food and cultural workshops on the platforms...'

I asked John if he could benefit from a cultural workshop. He growled. There was more:

'Three carriages will be decorated with a world theme of batik, saree cloths and colourful bunting on the train. Enjoy a Bhaji on the train with Indian food from samosas to chickpea curry. There will be an opportunity for Henna hand painting.' If John were to derive any benefit from having his hands henna painted, he would first have to unclench his fists.

As the train from Wickford to Southend was empty, we surmised that all potential travellers had decided to defer until April 3rd. Still, there was something odd about having all three carriages to ourselves. Our own personal train. A ghost train.

Eventually our isolation was compromised by a young woman with mobile phone who slunk aboard at South Woodham Ferrers. 'I was very pleased with my answer,' she declared proudly. Eavesdropping is an activity not without frustrations. Even I couldn't ask her what question she had answered, and what was it about the reply that she had found so gratifying.

While I speculated on this and similar nonsense, I noticed that John was having some sort of crisis. He had risen to his feet and was waving his fist (non-hennaed) at the vent from which the conductor's exhortations to take all belongings when we left the train, had emanated. 'Please also desist from kicking out the windows and remember not to defecate on the toilet floors!' he shouted. The woman with the skilful answer looked shocked. 'I can't take these announcements any more,' he offered. I was surprised that he was the first to crack as this was only the thirty-third train we had been on over two days. Our journey was only just beginning.

It continued briefly on the Docklands Light Railway. I still derive a childish pleasure from the DLR. It swoops and weaves between futuristic buildings and seems to duck its head when challenged by low bridges. The connections between carriages stretch to breaking point before the train recovers from an unforeseen lurch.

More than anything the experience is reminiscent of the early forays into 3D cinema. Strapped into an open cab the innocent viewer is hurled through the galaxy on a roller-coaster. Despite the small hyperbole here, I did find myself squeezing into the front seat, which should be surrendered, should the need arise, to a Train Service Operator…

The smell and sheer quality of the rolling stock on the train for Ashford International provided me with a Madeleine moment. This must be the Eurostar. In the twinkling of an eye, my wife would produce champagne and two glasses from her hand luggage. We would toast each other like young lovers and sit back waiting to be whisked to Paris. But no, I was sitting opposite John who still seemed grumpy.

*Answer to pub question number 2 – Red.

DAY THREE

Ashford International – Eastbourne – Lewes –
Seaford – Brighton – Ford – Littlehampton – Ford –
Bognor Regis – Barnham – Portsmouth Harbour –
Havant – Guildford – Aldershot – Alton –
Clapham Junction – East Grinstead

I spent much of the night dissecting the furious row I had had with John about absolutely nothing while drinking insipid beer. Possibly he had slunk off later and travelled back to Scotland, leaving me to find my way around an increasingly complex rail system. It wouldn't be the same. Who would explain the inner workings of the signalling systems?

When a large man burst into my room in the middle of the night it occurred to me that I had upset John more than I had realised. Being dragged from a dream in which wizened Pekinese stealers and OAP riders on Harley Davidsons featured large, I braced myself for a beating. The large man waved a screwdriver and informed me that he was trying to hunt down a faulty smoke detector and, with that, left. I wasn't convinced that John hadn't put him up to it, but he was already at the breakfast table when I arrived and I was pleased to see him.

Three Japanese travellers on the train to Eastbourne were wearing face masks. It had been curry night in Wetherspoons but their reaction seemed excessive. Was it a fear of germs, or contamination from contact with foreigners? Apparently, sales figures for face masks have tripled in the last decade. This is partly attributed to worries over 'micro particulate matter' following the earthquake and nuclear accident of 2011. Bizarrely, masks are also seen as fashion accessories, and an increasing number of companies are offering masks with floral, polka dot and even hound's tooth patterns. There's even a mask whose seller claims it will help you lose

211

weight. It is infused with the scent of raspberry which will, apparently, boost your metabolism.

Meanwhile, the rapid sucking in of gauze gave the wearers the look of startled blowfish. The cause of their excitement was a field of sheep. Until then I had not realised that sheep were an endangered species in Japan.

To prevent myself thinking about germ-ridden oriental sheep-fanciers, I sat next to a young History of Art student who was on her way to a museum in Hastings to study Inca artefacts. This last phrase resonated in an unwanted way as I was transported back three decades to a school for disturbed adolescents. I was part of an inspection regime and the teacher under scrutiny had spared no efforts to prepare his model lesson. He had brought into the class some Peruvian artefacts that he had purchased from a thief in South America. As he held them and, it must be said, the whole class, in the palm of his hand, the door burst in and a lad, stripped to the waist, strode to the front, beat his chest, picked up the aforementioned artefacts and swallowed them ...

The young girl opposite was looking at me strangely, as well she might, so I instigated a conversation about train travel. She responded by telling me that since the Trans-Siberian Railway, all journeys had been an anti-climax. She paused to enjoy a moment's reverie of her own. I tried to empathise and, in her dark irises, saw her staring lustfully at a young Cossack squat-dancing around a samovar as the train sped across the darkening steppes.

Defoe was pleased to see Lewes again, 'A pleasant town, well built, agreeably situated and full of gentlemen of good families and fortunes.'

I thought of engaging him in a discussion as to the definition of a good family, but thought better of it.

'You've been a loyal servant. You always kept your end up.' The conversation was being conducted by a large man who accompanied each encouragement with inclusive hand gestures. 'Let's get the disciplinary out of the way. Yes, I know there are issues. A slap on the hand is the worst you can expect but the next time ... I agree, that's the trouble with women ...' He went back to his copy *of The Sun*.

As the train loitered in Hastings station, a tree surgeon sliced his chainsaw through a branch overhanging Platform 3. Where were Health and Safety when you needed them? Several innocent commuters were about to be knocked senseless by a large bough. As the train moved out, I felt cheated that I wouldn't witness the mayhem. There was some compensation in seeing that the tunnel we were entering was called the Bo Peep Tunnel (1309 metres long), which explained why the Japanese tourists were excitedly running towards it, bleating as they went.

The tedium of the journey was partially alleviated by the multi-coloured beach huts at Bexhill. I had long been susceptible to beach hut envy, similar to the yearnings I felt for canal boats. Some part of my psyche wants to live in a small empty space near to water.

According to *A Short History of Beach Huts*, 'the first huts were horse drawn and featured an enclosed room with a collapsible hood at the seaward end to shield patients as they were submitted naked to the waves by burly attendants called dippers,' a concept whose time has surely come again.

This not unpleasant thought was rudely interrupted by John who, on realising that we had passed through a hamlet called Hampden Park, was indulging in a rant about cultural appropriation.

His mood had changed for the worse. 'A thoroughly shitey place!' he declared after crawling through Newhaven. Ignoring him, I looked at the line of lorries waiting to board the Seven Sisters Ferry. Drivers chatted idly in knots or slumped in their cabs with heavily tanned right arms resting on the open window. It was a life that I had often fancied.

Again, it was the small sleeping quarters built into the roof of the cab that held the appeal. The attraction of waking up in a foreign layby is probably not understood by most people.

For the next part of the journey, I was stared at by Andre from the safety of a poster. 'I WORK AT THE STATION. I LOVE SEEING THE SMILE ON A CUSTOMER'S FACE … IN MY SPARE TIME I MOONLIGHT AS A GIGOLO AND A CAT BURGLAR.' Andre had several chums equally eager to declaim their loyalty to the rail network. John having travelled in North Korea, would recognise this sort of propaganda.

Better to engage with a real human being, and in truth there was no one better than Thomas, a sixty-eight-year-old retired house painter. 'I still do the odd job. I'm going to see a client today. I'll make him happy. He'll see me alright.'

Thomas was a man completely at ease with himself, pleased to have got through most of his life unscathed.

'I'm the black sheep of the family.' Don't tell the Japanese, I thought. 'My sister is high up in a bank in Manhattan. My other sister, she's a head teacher, and married a judge. Could still turn out to be a useful contact. I've been to prison five times …' Thomas paused for effect before delivering the punch line ' …but only to paint them. I come from good stock. My mum's ninety-six, hale and hearty and in good health. My dad died at sixty-six. A hard death. Leukaemia was more difficult then. Eight pints of blood a day. I miss him.' I nodded. 'I've lived all my days in London but I don't miss getting up at six every morning. I use my hands to make people happy. Perhaps I've a few years left. I used to chase the sun but I'm over that now. I like the Scots, good sense of humour, rugged. The thing about culture is to think first, then decide. Some people just jump in and get it all wrong. Live and let live, that's what I say.'

The train slowed as we neared Brighton. I was looking

forward to spending at least a small amount of time in the iconic English town. Perhaps long enough to see the pier, and rub shoulders with Graham Greene's Pinkie Brown. We could go for a beer in the Four Feathers and share some thoughts on how Catholicism views sex and violence. I could counsel him on the wisdom of marrying Rose and warn him about placing too much trust in Cubitt, his mobster ally.

Defoe was relieved that we had insufficient time to explore Brighton further. 'A poor fishing town, old built and on the very edge of the sea. The sea is very unkind to this town, and has by its continual encroachments, so gained upon them, that in a little time more they might reasonably expect it would eat up the whole town, above 100 houses having been devoured by the water in the few years past.'

I was sure the place had not changed in the intervening 210 years and was pleased when John told me that we had to leave immediately for Ford.

There were many frustrations associated with this whole adventure, not the least of which was the transient glimpse of places in which I would have liked to linger. It was unlikely that I would get the chance again. I was that child always being dragged away from the toyshop window to be incarcerated once more in my carriage prison. As Hastings and Worthing had passed in a blur, I was feeling sorry for myself. All these small opportunities denied. Eventually John told me that, if I behaved, I could spend half an hour in Littlehampton. Nelson Mandela's release from Robben Island paled into insignificance as I seized the day. What had Mandela said? 'I went for a long holiday for twenty-seven years.' My imprisonment felt much longer.

I embraced Littlehampton with an enthusiasm that was first cousin to ecstasy. Who could do other than marvel at the wooden tower clock masquerading as an ancient monument? Or indeed, at the plethora of stonemasons, or the five charity shops, or a pub called the Contented Pig? The pub was beyond exciting, plastered as it was with lurid accounts of smugglers and murderers.

The key turned in the lock once more. Littlehampton had been but a dream. 'Is this your 'at?' The bin liner wallah who joined us at Barnham station brandished a fetching straw boater. John winced. 'You wouldn't believe what people leave behind on trains.' I asked him to elaborate. 'I've found babies, dogs, pushchairs ...' He was through to the next carriage before I could pursue this line of enquiry. Did Network Rail run orphanages? Oscar Wilde's Ernest had been found in a handbag on Victoria station. Perhaps there was a baby farm at Swindon. The infants' natural language would be that of train announcements. Their destiny would be to adorn publicity posters declaring their undying pleasure in seeing smiles on customers' faces. Those unfortunates who failed to thrive would be forced to join the nocturnal army of grey men who wander the tracks at night tapping the rails, listening for imperfections.

'Your narrative is endangered by these ludicrous digressions, and empty speculation.'

My next victim was himself a train driver, enjoying a variant of the busman's holiday. He only drove freight trains, and only at night. A former colleague's taxi driver husband suffered from anxiety attacks and could only work when it was dark, but this was different again. He described with mounting passion the secret joy of driving 200,000 tons of containers from Southampton to Crewe into the cone of orange light that illuminated the track ahead. My envy of people who only live or work in small spaces was returning. I mentally added locomotive footplates to beach huts, canal boats and lorry cabs. 'You have to enjoy lone working; enjoy your own company. Your only contact through a long night might be a single phone call.'

I had never received good news at three in the morning. Usually a child had been arrested or taken to A&E, paralytic with drink, or someone was dead. Obviously, night shift was different. Perhaps the phone calls from Signalling Control were preceded by a dog whistle to ensure he hadn't fallen asleep over his dead man's handle. Then again, perhaps his wife would miss him and phone in erotic endearments.

I asked him if concentration was an issue. 'Not for 99.5% of the time,' he said and I saw the fleeting shadow of a frown. There was history here, but I didn't want to intrude. He told me that someone had thrown themselves under his train soon after he started on nights. 'At least they wanted to die,' he explained. 'It was not like a young girl chasing her dog across the line...'

I nodded sympathetically while disagreeing fundamentally with him in my head. Most people who kill themselves do so, not because they necessarily want to be dead, but because they want the pain to be over. This was not the time to have that discussion. He had found a way to deal with his trauma, and who was I to unpick his thought process?

To distract myself I scoured the skyline of Chichester for its cathedral and forced Leonard Bernstein's arrangement of the Psalms into my head.

Yea, though I walk through the valley of the shadow of death, I will fear no evil.

Ever the gent, John offered his seat to three ancient women on Havant station. All of them were in their nineties. Beryl, clearly the troublemaker in the group, whose parchment face bore witness to the life-span enhancing qualities of Woodbines, announced for no apparent reason, and at no one in particular, 'The world's changing.' Recognising that this was usually the prelude to a *Daily Mail* style rant, her friends shushed her. Muttering, she settled back into her novel, moving her head as she devoured pages of steamy scenes. The youngest of the trio explained that twice a week they travel to Farnham 'to shop, go to the bingo, and

217

misbehave. We've never won anything. We just go for the chat.'

The third of them smiled benignly as she wandered alarmingly close to the platform edge.

As we approached Guildford, John gave the countryside an eight. Ignoring him and his gratuitous assessments, I spoke to a young student of Criminology and Society at Portsmouth University. He told me that the subject of his dissertation had been Militant Islam and Multiculturalism.

At that moment three SAS soldiers with blackened faces lobbed a stun grenade into the aisle and frog-marched the young lad away to be tortured. Before he disappeared, he shouted to me that he had joined several Islamic Societies at University to better understand cultural issues. He said that the two main preoccupations of young Muslims seemed to be anger with the media and annoyance with their parents whose rigidity was alienating.

A formidably large conductor, accompanied by his appraiser whom he was clearly trying to impress, negotiated the student's release. Now flustered, and facing an even more formidable adversary, the young man confessed that his railcard had expired. The appraiser nodded approvingly as his minion found the appropriate penalty notice. The large official declared that he didn't often get to meet such intelligent people and left.

'There was a man lived near this place,' said Defoe who had finally worked out where we were. 'Sir Thomas Bludworth, once Lord Mayor of London, a person famous for the implacable passion he put the people of London to at the time of the Great Fire: "That is nothing," he said. "They could piss it out."'

'He got that one wrong then.'

We were delayed on account of an earlier incident – 'a man under the train' – on the Alton–Aldershot line. This sombre announcement found its perfect echo in the huge

Brookwood Cemetery stretching like a small country into the distance. John became especially animated as he pressed his face against the window, searching in the adjacent undergrowth. Although it is difficult to hear someone whose face is squashed flat against glass, he did communicate something.

In the 1840s the demand for funeral plots in the capital outstretched the availability of sanctified ground. Graves were reopened and the newly dead forced to share with long forgotten relatives. Churchyards became hazardous and stank, appropriately, to high heaven on account of the bones cluttering the footpaths. Drinking wells became polluted with the liquid detritus of death.

The solution was to build a cemetery 25 miles out of London and utilise the existing railway to carry both coffins and mourners. The plan was not without challenges. The Bishop of London had grave reservations, fearful that respectable mourners might find themselves in proximity to dead people from lower social strata. So much for death as The Great Leveller. In the Bishop's own delicate words to a Commons Select Committee, 'It may sometimes happen that persons of opposite character might be carried in the same conveyance. For instance, the body of some profligate spendthrift might be placed in a conveyance with the body of some respectable member of the church, which would shock the feelings of his friend.'

This nonsense led to the introduction of six distinct categories of accommodation on the Necropolis trains, and to two additional stations being built at Brookwood: one for those of a conformist disposition, the other for their non-conformist brethren. The Luftwaffe put these debates to rest by obliterating all Necropolis carriages during a particularly accurate bombing raid.

We passed Aldershot barracks but there was not a soldier in sight, not even a bullied squaddie sucking his thumb by a perimeter fence. This may of course have been their camouflage day. Perhaps the parade ground was teeming with commandos, armed to the teeth, but we couldn't see them. Maybe the entire army was fighting a series of wars, so illegal the public could never be told.

The fact that the landscape on the other side of the track had been well and truly blasted suggested that Our Boys had been practising. There were further clues as to their likely destination: the pontoon bridge slung across a canal hinted at a second invasion of North Germany. Alarming evidence suggested that a gypsy traveller encampment had been used for bazooka practice.

The canal had a peculiar effect on John. He became animated and showed more enthusiasm than at any previous point on our many journeys. 'That's Webster's canal!' he shouted, claiming that forty years earlier he had helped a university friend renovate a building close to this very spot. Evidently this friend was looking after a dog called Webster who went missing and was subsequently found wandering alongside this particular stretch of canal. This tale seemed so dull that I made a small mental note not to include it in any subsequent narrative.

DAY FOUR
East Grinstead – Victoria – Paddington (tube) –
Swansea – Llanelli – Shrewsbury

I had done my research and been intrigued by East Grinstead's many eclectic claims to fame. *Good King Wenceslas* was written here. It is the headquarters (UK and Ireland) of the Caravan Club and has connections to Winnie the Pooh. During the war, having destroyed the Necropolis Railway, the Luftwaffe dropped bombs on the Whitehall Theatre killing 108 people who were watching a Hopalong Cassidy film; one moment enthralled by Hopalong with his oversized black hat and his beautiful white horse, the next moment dead.

East Grinstead's other claim to fame is as a Pandora's box of bizarre religions. The Rosicrucians rub shoulders with Opus Dei while the London England Temple of the Church of Jesus Christ of Latter-day Saints compete with the Jehovah's Witnesses and the Scientologists for the attention of the locals.

'Step this way and learn how esoteric truths from the ancient past provide insight into the spiritual realm...'

'Ignore him! Be a true Catholic. Embrace misogyny, elitism and engage in mortification of the flesh!'

'These are false prophets. Embrace your inner Thetan...'

(If, by the way, the title of this book is not *Scientology; A Load of Old Cobblers*, my publisher has chosen not to learn from the writer whose book, critical of the cult, sold in vast numbers as the followers of Ron Hubbard removed all copies to protect Joe Public from its lies.)

The evening in East Grinstead had started inauspiciously. While negotiating a dystopian vortex of pedestrian flyovers, we heard cries from a young woman in distress as she was chased by a man. John, the hero, deployed himself across their path and prepared not only to wrap her in his protective arms, but also to punch out her assailant's lights. 'Are you all right?' he asked.

The girl slowed her pace. 'Yes, I'm fine thanks,' whereupon she skipped past and let her pursuer chase her once more. More running was going on in the town centre with several gangs of youths chasing each other. It was clearly some sort of game, a mating ritual practised by the inhabitants of East Grinstead.

The train to Victoria developed a malfunction as the doors opened to their own time scale, prompting distress among many people as their unthinking routines seemed on the point of unravelling. Evacuees who missed the last helicopter out of Saigon could not have been more upset, nor the two animals on the quayside when Noah pulled up the gangplank.

One traveller who would not have been perturbed was the tiny woman who squeezed into the seat next to John, exuding a unique quality of stillness denied to mere sleepers.

The way John strode towards the exit at Victoria suggested that he had absorbed none of her serenity. Despite my warnings, he insisted on donning his rucksack, which resembled a poorly packed barrage balloon, and proceeded to smash several innocents about the head. He remained oblivious even when one of his victims had both his spectacles and phone swept into the gap between carriage and platform.

On the Swansea train I met Peter Richards who seemed delighted to talk to me about his career as a clock and watch maker to the Great Western Railway. He was an apprentice at Swindon works from 1950. When I asked why the railways would need a dedicated clock-making department, he patiently described the huge clock that used to dominate Paddington station and explained how it was the master to which all others in the station were connected. It sent out pulses to its subservient clocks every two seconds. The cogs whirled in his head and, by dint of close physical proximity, mine as well. He then reminded me that every guard on the GWR had to carry one of the company's timepieces. Where are these watches now? Pawned, purloined, auctioned, broken, bequeathed, ticking their way into eternity.

A highlight of his career was being asked to calibrate the wear on the connecting rods of King Class locomotives. Long before sex occupied my every waking adolescent moment, it was the Kings that thundered through my dreams. They were the largest locomotives ever built by the GWR and specifically designed to win back the accolade of the most powerful express passenger steam train in Britain.

'Feel my hands,' he said, bringing me back to the present.

This was the first offer of physical contact I had received on my journeys so far. 'They're sweating.' They seemed fine to me, but he explained that this phenomenon meant that he could no longer work with watches and was henceforth condemned to tinkering with station clocks. Thereafter he joined the RAF, working with instruments, and was posted to Cyprus.

Richard told me he got a medal but denied having done anything heroic. Coincidentally, or not, he also told me about a rebel who placed a bomb in the jet pipe of an aircraft. The plane expelled the bomb and hoisted the perpetrator with his own petard.

I returned to John who was staring mesmerised at the young family across the carriage. The parents were preventing their two small children from clambering onto the table which held two triangular boxes of sandwiches, a Game Boy, a packet of dinosaur stickers, a box of crayons, crossword books, several half-eaten chocolate bars, an apple with a single bite, items of clothing, not to mention the newspapers, phones and iPads belonging to the parents. Small wars have been fought with fewer resources.

As John was now staring out of the window, vacillating between awarding the countryside a five or a six, I wandered off to see if I could capture someone else's soul. The first woman I approached was mortified at the thought of talking to a stranger, and declined before lapsing into a faint.

I had more success with my next victim, a retired anaes-thetist who referred to herself as a born-again human since she stepped away from the operating theatre. Her new passion was promoting equine therapy for young people with eating disorders. The approach has already been used to treat ADHD, anxiety, autism, cerebral palsy, dementia, depression, developmental delay, traumatic brain injuries, PTSD, behavioural and abuse issues.

'Pray, Doctor, can you assuage the pain of the palsy,

223

dropsy, gout and the stone with which I am sorely afflicted?'

I had an image in my head of timid thin girls emerging from a wood at twilight, spreading out across a field and slowly walking towards an acquiescent herd of horses, heads lowered, pawing the ground. Each girl walked slowly up to a horse and put her wraithlike arms around its neck...I wished her well with her new endeavour and instinctively looked at the passing fields for therapeutic horses, or indeed, thin girls.

On the way back to John I passed through the buffet car where one of the attendants was holding a bank note to the light. 'Look you, it's got two 'eads!' Her colleague, well used to accepting forged notes, took it from her and snapped it into the till.

This theme was continued in the next carriage where a fat clergyman was counting out a thick wad of notes. There was only one plausible explanation: he had absconded with the diocesan poverty fund and was *en route* to meet his mistress in Swansea from whence they would embark on their new life together.

Furious, Defoe produced a crumpled pamphlet from his coat and thrust it in front of the probably innocent clergyman. I snatched it back and read the title:

A Seasonal Warning and Caution Against the INSINUA-TION of Papists and Jacobites In favour of the PRETENDER

Fields of horses, eager to help distressed girls, gave way to Port Talbot's steel works which were still recovering from the Terminator's visit. He had cynically ripped the metal entrails from the corpse and thrown them casually among the escalators going nowhere and then trampled the metal chutes, just because he could. Meanwhile the angry genies of steam hissed and spat.

I spoke to the family whose children and worldly goods were still piled on the table opposite. The father told me that, when not wrestling with unruly children, he was a civil servant who advised organisations facing insolvency, and he looked rueful when recalling difficult conversations with the owners of small Welsh businesses. 'I can't walk down any street in Swansea without seeing places I closed down.'

John's enthusiasm for the delights of the Heart of Wales line proved infectious. Stretching from Llanelli to Shrewsbury, it promised some of the finest scenery in the kingdom; there was the prospect of estuaries, castles, mountains, viaducts, tumbling rivers and glimpses of numerous Victorian spa towns.

I had visited Trip Advisor to ensure that I was fully prepared for the bucolic vistas and Arcadian delights of central Wales. Several grumpy pensioners posted tales of three hours standing in a single carriage without a toilet. A surreal account by someone who claimed that the route was so crowded that it took her a week to get on a train was accompanied by invidious comparisons with the Indian railways. This thought cheered me as one of the best journeys I had ever taken involved hanging on the outside of a train from Kolkata.

The list of possible destinations extended to seven pages: Swansea, Gowerton, Llanelli, Bynea, Llangennech, Pontarddulais, Pantyffynnon, Ammanford, Llandybie, Ffairfach, Llandeilo, Llangadog, Llanwrda, Llandovery, Cynghordy, Sugar Loaf, Llanwrtyd, Llangammarch, Garth, Cilmeri, Builth Road, Llandrindod, Pen-y-Bont, Dolau, Llanbister Road, Llangynllo, Knucklas, Knighton, Bucknell, Hopton Heath, Broome, Craven Arms, Church Stretton, Shrewsbury. Yorton, Wem, Prees, Whitchurch. And not a toilet.

John glanced disdainfully at a large heap of collapsed dog blocking the aisle. 'His name's Bobby, he's got cancer. More specifically, epileptic lymphoma. Here, hold him for me.' The woman, settling into her seat, held out his lead to John who took it disdainfully. 'He was given five weeks to live six months ago. He's got his own website. Lots of followers.'

It was clear that John was not going to be the dog's friend on Facebook.

'The chemo's working. So is the anti-histamine. The drugs cost me £500 every three weeks. It's a lot.' I nodded and John took advantage of the slight pause to let go of Bobby's lead.

'It's rare in dogs, but common in hamsters. You wouldn't find me paying that money for a hamster. We've just spent a week on the Gower. Probably our last holiday together. He loved it.'

While John and I digested the emotional significance of the days spent on the Gower, the conductor explained to the woman that she was on the wrong train, and that this route to Crewe would take an extra two hours. 'I don't think he'll last that long,' she said. It was unclear whether this was a reference to Bobby's imminent demise or the state of his bowels.

She delved into her bag and produced some photographs. 'Look at the white puffy bits under his eyes, and the dandruff, that's when I knew he wasn't well.'

I assumed what I hoped was a sympathetic expression, which was more than could be said of John. Trying hard to ignore both the woman and the dog, he suggested that we would do well to avoid the fate that, on the 19th October 1987, befell the Swansea to Shrewsbury train, the first carriage of which plunged off the damaged Tywi bridge into the flooded river below. The woman was undeterred.

'I live in Crewe. Worked on the railway all my days. My husband was a fitter on the Duke of Gloucester locomotive, you know, 71000 ...' Sadly I did. 'My father was a copper-smith. It killed him. Asbestos. They tried to tempt me back. They said "I know your mum's just died but would you fill in for us?" I was tempted mind, and I knew that my mum wouldn't sit on a cloud all day, being idle, she would look after me, and so it turned out. After ordering her gravestone,

226

the funeral directors offered me a job and I've never looked back.'

Bobby was displaying unexpected signs of life. 'He needs to go,' declared his guardian, shouting down the carriage for the conductor. To my astonishment the young official agreed to stop the train so that Bobby could get off for a shit. This was customer service at its finest. I could tell that John was mentally compiling an entry in *The Great Ledger of Observations and Complaints*. At the next request stop Bobby alighted, and returned somewhat lighter.

As Bobby's owner resumed her monologue, she became more distressed as she shared with us, and the other passengers, details of recent events. 'My husband just left me. After thirty-five years. It's been a vile time ... I just cried my eyes out. There were twelve of us. Six couples. When he left, the others had nothing to do with me. He said he would come back if I promised not to be depressed again ... Anyway there's no place for him now if he comes back, the dog sleeps on his side of the bed.'

The enormity of this last statement hit me hard. I felt powerless. I wanted to make things better for her, and I hope that her life has improved, and that she has found suitable replacements for both Bobby and her husband. Sensing the embarrassed silence Defoe attempted to distract me.

'Did I tell you about the dog that lived at the Angel Inn at Yeovil?'

'I don't think so.'

'Well,' he continued, 'the mistress at the inn, strongly suspecting that a dog was stealing meat informed the innkeeper who speedily nabb'd the dog. Having found the thief, and got him into custody, the master of the house, a good humour'd fellow, and loth to disoblige the dog's master, by executing the criminal as the dog-law directs; mitigates his sentence, and handled him as follows; firstly taking out his knife, he cuts off both his ears, and then bringing him to the threshold, he chop'd off his tail; and having thus effectually dishonour'd the poor cur among the neighbours, he tyed a string about his neck, and a piece of paper to the string directed to his master, and with these witty west country verses on it ...'

'Oh spare us the witty west country verses,' I said, anxious lest Bobby's owner had heard.

John took pleasure in pointing out that Sugar Loaf Station only served two passengers per week, and the smaller peak, Ysgryd Fawr, had religious significance as, according to legend, it was partially destroyed by a mini volcano at the precise moment of the crucifixion. I retaliated by drawing his attention to the vast expanse of Mynydd Eppynt which had been used for artillery practice since World War Two, but he only grunted when I told him that 219 farmers and their families had been evacuated by the army when their land was requisitioned. Furthermore, the primary school, a church and the Drover's Inn had been sequestrated. I was certainly ahead on points and he looked none too pleased.

I needed to stretch my legs, an opportunity limited by the fact the train consisted of only two carriages. Nevertheless, I moved to the next one.

I liked to think I was getting better at approaching complete strangers; certainly, there had been fewer refusals on this trip. There was still that fleeting first moment, that tiny sliver of time during which a first impression and related reactions are formed. Is this man harmless? Wanting something? (Yes.) Mad? (Possibly, but non-threatening.)

With the old denim-clad, white-haired rocker in the next carriage the sliver was virtually non-existent. He was delighted to see me and, of course, would tell me what he was up to, describing how this line played a crucial part in helping him to manage a life happily devoted to drink.

'I travel on this train several times a week to visit my brother. We have three pints over lunchtime and then I travel back. Sometimes, mind you, it's more like eight pints, but I have to be careful like, on account of there being no toilet on the train. I'm a window cleaner, see, and I work in a pub. Well, to tell you the truth, I live there.' I thought that any occupation that involved climbing ladders might not be his best choice, but shared with him my wish that I lived closer to my own brother so that I could drink with him more often. After lurching from the train at Llandovery, he waved at me from the level crossing against which he was leaning.

I decided to accost one more innocent stranger before returning to John and the increasingly odd Defoe. A man in his late twenties seemed delighted to talk. 'What do you do for a living?' I asked.

'I'm signed off sick. I've got a diagnosis of mixed anxiety/depressive disorder.' He smiled as he told me this. I felt I had to offer him something in return and explained that my family were not strangers to mental illness.

'I've been to some dark places, it was the heroin, see. I've lost several friends that way. I've done stuff, I've been inside. I shouldn't tell you in case you're a policeman.' I assured him that he was right and that I would arrest him at the next station. His laugh seemed a little strained. Giving me the benefit of the doubt he explained, 'But I'm living better now.' I asked him what worked for him. 'I've got a psychiatrist, I'm on diazepam, I've got a support worker. I see her on a Monday. I'm laid back. I'm managing well. I go to the gym, I've got a girlfriend and I've got my dad. He's the main thing. He's not well so I travel down to see him as often as I can. I've got four brothers but I don't see much of them.'

I asked if his brothers have much contact with their father and he said no. He agreed that a positive consequence of his illness was that he could spend time with his sick dad in a way that his brothers couldn't. 'I don't understand it, but I'm at my happiest when I'm on this train.'

He liked the idea that this journey was a metaphor for his recovery. We chatted for a while and, before he left the train, he shook my hand. I ran after him and gave him my address in case he wanted to stay in touch.

John celebrated my return by singing 'The mountain sheep are Sweeter / But the valley sheep are fatter; / We therefore deemed it meeter to carry off the latter.' He explained this unexpected homage to Thomas Love Peacock's *War-song of Dinas Vawr* by pointing out of the window where a field of sheep were running towards the train.

This ovine theme was reprieved when I asked the passing conductor if he enjoyed his job. 'Let me explain it this way,' he replied, enigmatically. 'A few months back I was driving to work when my path was blocked by a flock of sheep. I asked the farmer if he would back his sheep up. "Why?" he asked.

'"If you don't I won't get to work."

'"So?"

'"Then the train won't go and the people will be disrupted."

'"So, my sheep are stopping people from getting to London."

'The farmer thought for a long moment, then moved his sheep out of the way.'

The conductor touched the side of his nose in acknowledgement of a profound parable about the nature of life.

I carried out a quick search on my phone as we paused momentarily in Llandrindod Wells and, to my small delight, found a website dedicated to disparaging all aspects of the town. Apparently, the worst aspects of life in Llandrindod are, in no particular order: there is nothing to do; there are too many old people; it is full of druggies and idiots.

By googling Bucknell I learned that the town straddles Offa's Dyke and that 'it was customary for the English to cut off the ears of every Welshman who was found to the East of the dyke and for the Welsh to hang every Englishman found to the West'.

It had been a long day and I felt sated by undeniably beautiful countryside and a panoply of interesting people. Despite trying to switch off my fatigued powers of observation, I couldn't help wondering why the architects of Shrewsbury station had chosen to build it in the style of a Tudor mansion. Furthermore, a plaque on Platform 3 commemorated the fact that in 1938, during a twenty-minute wait for his train, Arwel Hughes composed the famous hymn, *Tydi A Roddaist*.

'A minor and insignificant composition. Let me sing to you my *Hymn to Victory* in which I laud the English victory over the French at Blenheim . . .'

DAY FIVE
*Shrewsbury – Aberystwyth – Dovey Junction –
Pwllheli – Porthmadog*

In Shrewsbury John wandered into a Thai massage parlour and asked for a number 79 and a side of rice. He was obviously much better travelled than I thought.

My night was again disturbed. I woke at three convinced that the people traffickers from East Grinstead were determined to track me down, and were systematically knocking on all doors. I was also anxious about the woman and the sick dog.

Robert, travelling to Aberystwyth, was keen to reminisce about the days when stationmasters wore top hats and grateful passengers tipped their caps in the direction of the train drivers. 'Now they can't get out of their cabs quick enough.' He was eighty-two and had spent a quarter of a century running a care home for the elderly with his wife. 'I loved the old people, I loved their stories.'

He used to think his own father was a silly old fool. For his part, his dad considered him 'wet behind the ears.' Peeling back decade after decade he argued with his father once more, flicked the years forward and stopped when he came to his RAF experience. He loved it. The highlight was two weeks unexpected leave as he and his colleagues were evacuated from their barracks to make room for the hundreds of marchers who were part of the coronation celebrations.

In a delightful non-sequitur, he told me how to travel in the First Class buffet train with a Third Class ticket. The secret was to buy a coffee in Reading. I tucked away this important tip in case I found myself travelling back through time.

Another unrelated memory was rooted in his early teens. Wide-eyed and probably wet behind the ears, he was circling the mothballed and shuttered Blaenau Ffestiniog railway works when a clergyman emerged 'with a giant key' and opened the door for him. Incredulous, he stepped into an oily paradise and watched motes of dust dancing around the stored locomotive. 'A sleeping beauty.'

After Welshpool we ambled through Abermule, the site, according to John, of a particularly nasty train crash in 1921 when two trains were involved in a head-on collision. The flimsy carriages telescoped on top of each other and seventeen passengers were crushed. I turned to my phone and found confirmation in the shape of an archived film clip. Tiny black and white figures in waistcoats and caps scurried over the tangle of locomotive wheels and splintered detritus. Lewis, the relief station master, had gone to lunch leaving important procedures involving tokens to Signalman Jones, Porter Rogers, who was seventeen, and a trainee booking clerk named Thomson who was only fifteen. Driver Pritchard Jones was inconsolable, convinced he was at fault until the traffic controller, a man called George, who had been a traveller on the train, exonerated him.

All this in the shadow of the beautiful Cambrian Mountains. As I glanced again at the index page on my phone, I noticed that an adjacent site promised me 'the train crash of the week'. This was a lurid pleasure that could wait indefinitely.

The two middle-aged women, sitting across the aisle in mountaineering gear, were preparing to hike towards the ospreys whose whereabouts was a closely guarded secret. The older was reluctant to say more, fearing that I might be a spy for an osprey strangling squad.

Her companion was more forthcoming. She was Dutch and a geriatric specialist working in a care home in The Hague. She explained that the main challenge is working within a culture which enshrines the right to die in law. Apparently 3.4% of all deaths in the Netherlands are the result of euthanasia. She agreed that managing an appropriately supporting environment was challenging. There would be no collective raging against the dying of the light, instead a stoical acceptance and preparation for death. Old Robert must have had an easier time when looking after his old folk in the Midlands and listening to their stories.

Defoe was anxious on behalf of the mountaineering women.

'I must dissuade them from venturing further. The mountains are impassable ... furthermore the devil lives in the middle of Wales.'

I tried but failed to feign interest in John's latest railway statistic. However, and with sinking heart, I pass on the fact that the 120-foot deep cutting at Talerddig is the deepest in the world, and was blasted out of solid rock by gunpowder and sweat in the 1860s.

Despite my need for exercise, it was difficult to leave Aberystwyth station. Half of the available space is now a pub, while the other half has been converted into a vast charity market. I wandered towards the promenade.

After glancing at the hideous arcade on the pier, I made my way to the end, and sat on a deckchair. The water was visible through the gaps between the planks. A solitary gull wheeled away. Being the youngest inhabitant of a deckchair by several decades, I found I was thinking again about the dilemmas faced by the Dutch geriatric specialist. It certainly felt as if the pier was one of God's many waiting rooms. The sea and the clouds spoke of eternity and the lure of a painless oblivion.

Our privacy had been respected. We were separated from the irrelevant babble of the saloon by closed doors. The attendants moved respectfully among us, asking if we wanted any last comforts: small mementos of happier times, family photos, newspaper cuttings of wedding announcements to take with us. Everything had been taken care of. All bills, including the anticipated funeral costs. We were all facing the grey water. No one spoke. We were all waiting patiently.

We alighted (I have now abandoned my resistance to Rail Speak) at Dovey Junction. The station is unique in that it is only accessible on foot. Only five souls manage this feat of endurance in a typical week.

Surprisingly, we were not alone on the platform. A tall young man explained that he was a theology student from Cambridge about to join other minor members of the aristocracy for a jolly good yomp and hike across the hills. Judging by the size of his rucksack, his religious leanings meant that he couldn't leave home without a portable lectern, a church organ and a small choir stall.

To his credit, he was happy to endure a brief interrogation about these leanings. He wasn't certain that he was ready to join the ministry, although he did concede there might come a time when he becomes 'bored with God'. This was an interesting concept. I could understand anger, but boredom was a strange one … Not another miracle, not still turning the other cheek, not another gratuitous good deed from which we expect no return. And then this was replaced by a secret delicious yearning for a more demonic world, full of sex and wickedness. Yes, I could feel the first stirrings of empathy.

John became animated as we crossed the viaduct at Barmouth. 'Woodworm,' he declared. 'Or was it weevils? Either way the little buggers nearly did for this bridge.' His outburst was prompted by a *cause celebre* involving the elevated pathway that has spanned the Mawddach estuary for 148 years. Apparently fat worms of some description were feasting on the wooden supports, reducing them to the point of collapse. While it was deemed reasonable to save the rail track, there was no money for the footpath that shared the bridge. This meant that the good citizens of Barmouth had to undertake a detour of several hundred miles to buy a pint of milk.

It now seemed as if Defoe was determined to compete for my attention. No sooner had John sunk back into torpor than he took his place and pointed out of the window.

'I must tell you of the strange phenomenon which was not only seen but fatally experienced by the country round this place, namely of a livid fire, coming off from the sea; and setting on fire, houses, barns, stacks of hay and corn, and poisoning the herbage in the fields.'

I looked at him with barely disguised incredulity. 'Porkies,' I said.

'What?'

'Pure fabrication, and nonsense.'

Furious, he pulled his wig over his eyes.

A scenario on the Pwllheli train presented me with a personal challenge. Crammed round the table opposite was the fattest family I had ever seen, and I had to struggle with my urge to judge. I know about the cycles of poverty, low self-esteem, poor diet and comfort eating. I know about the impact of abuse on subsequent parenting styles. Yet I wanted to make the mother look at herself and her elephantine children. I could understand why some social services might take such children into care before they die of internal rupturing or whatever it is that happens when young bodies just give in. Food hung from their mouths. One of the children held a banana in her fat fist and squeezed it until its contents oozed over the table. The ooze at least prevented her Maltesers from rolling onto the floor. It occurred to me that she might never have seen a banana before and had no idea that it was a food. In these circumstances, to squeeze it might seem logical and fun. In her excitement she shifted her huge buttocks, grinding spilt crisps into the upholstery.

Eager to avoid eye contact with the mother, I stared out of the window at the long-deserted army camp at Tonfanau. Previously it had been home to 3000 Ugandan Asian refugees expelled by Idi Amin in the 1970s. The self-styled His Excellency President for Life, Field Marshal Al Hadji Doctor Idi Amin, VC, DSO, MC, Lord of All the Beasts of the Earth and Fishes of the Sea, and Conqueror of the British Empire in Africa in General and Uganda in Particular, had a reputation for cannibalism. I glanced uneasily once more at the fat family.

It was salutary how such idyllic vistas could resonate with unspeakable deeds. I looked at the sky over LLanbedr which was once again thick with Vulcan bombers. The nuclear sirens had sounded and all 26 bomber dispersal units had been activated. Wherever the intercontinental missiles would first fall, a massive retaliation against the evil Russian Empire was assured.

Perhaps my brain was overheating, perhaps I had witnessed one squeezed banana too many, but John was asleep and Defoe was talking to himself about the mountains of Wales,

'They are well compar'd to The Alps in the inmost provinces...and some of them, of very great extent, far exceeding the valleys so fam'd among the mountains of Savoy and Piedmont...'

'Do you really think so, Danny? Surely a small hint of hyperbole there? We have had this discussion before.' He was clearly upset by my comment and, taking out a small paring knife, sharpened his quill in a menacing manner.

The mood shifted as we passed through Penychain station, previously known as Butlins Penychain, for many years the final destination for thousands of holidaymakers anticipating the Wakey Wakey morning call to pleasures which encompassed the ballroom, the boating lake and the egg and spoon and sack races.

John pointed out to me the distant fantasy village of Portmeirion. I had grown up with *The Prisoner* in the 1960s and would have liked to visit the architectural pastiche of the Italian Riviera. I was tempted to do a Defoe and pretend that I had actually been, but kept this thought to myself rather than further provoke my imaginary friend.

I wished though, that I had brought my *I-Spy Castles* book. After passing close to Harlech and Criccieth, I would have had numerous ticks under the boxes that recorded features such as crenellated walls, archers' slots, ramparts and those long stone chutes through which you could shit on your enemy.

I spoke to a young, idyllically content young couple who were holidaying in the area. He was a music teacher, she a maths teacher. They exuded happiness but seemed surprised that anyone else could be interested in them or their trek through the marshes.

The elderly couple had no such doubts. 'Adventure before dementia!' declared the husband. This motto had inspired numerous forays across Europe in their motor home. Milan, Budapest, Venice, all had been conquered

237

in recent months. I momentarily entertained the thought that my own adventure was inspired by a similar wish to outwit Lord Alzheimer. John, entertaining no such doubts about his intellectual capacity, proceeded to make up false translations of Welsh place names and informed me that we were passing through, in no particular order: 'The-middle-of-Nowhere', 'The-hamlet-that-time-forgot', and bizarrely, 'The-tiny-station-distinguishable-from-all-the-others-by-two-milk-churns-guarding-the-now-closed-toilets.'

DAY SIX
Porthmadog – Blaenau Ffestiniog – Llandudno –
Llandudno Junction – Holyhead – Chester –
Crewe – Lancaster – Glasgow Central.

John almost delivered a fatal blow to our relationship by suggesting that I seemed at home in the Ffestiniog Railway souvenir shop surrounded by other quasi-demented folk executing slow wheelies between the tea towels.

Wandering onto the bijou platform, my heart went out to the sullen brothers being dragged against their will by gleeful parents towards the Third Class carriages. To compound the scale of their problem, the parents were wearing guards' hats. Had I the statutory powers, I would have had both adults placed on a register, and their offspring taken into an orphanage.

The surroundings were ominously reminiscent of *A Sound of Music*. At any moment Julie Andrews would lower one of the carriage windows, carefully attach the leather strap to the frame and regale us with song. Mercifully she ducked back inside as several Germans and an unseasonal flurry of snow swept down the platform. The snow, and the sight of an employee tapping each of the carriage wheels in turn, ushered in a different film. We were now watching the 1935 version *of Anna Karenina*.

Greta Garbo pouted moodily in the direction of the huge steam locomotive and the wheel tapping reached a crescendo that merged with a Prokofievan theme as she considered hurling herself onto the track. More music, more steam, and she had gone under the locomotive. I glanced round. Thankfully John was still there.

He soon misbehaved on the train by assuming a mock accusatory tone when a young, and undeniably pretty, train attendant came to offer us coffee. 'Why don't you resist these sexual stereotypes?' he boomed. 'Be your own woman, ask for a job oiling the engines or shovelling the coal.' His banter was meant to be friendly but the young girl was mortified, dropped the menus on the table and ran away.

'These mountains are indeed so like the Alps, that except the language of the people, one could hardly avoid thinking he is passing from Grenoble to Susa,' declared Defoe.

After the train crossed the Cob and fussed its way through several beautiful villages hewn from slate, I was more prepared to listen to John. The steam hung in the trees and snow settled gently on thick moss. I muttered to myself the one line of Robert Frost's poetry that I could remember ... Whose woods these are I think I know... And then, bizarrely, I realised that I did, in fact, know this very spot.

In the 1960s I worked with several school pals as a volunteer navvy on this self-same stretch of track. John pointed out that we were following a large loop towards the new Moelwyn Tunnel, built to circumvent the section that disappeared under a reservoir. There was no doubt about it, in the past I had played my part battling against the odds in a hostile environment. I was a sort of hero. Except I hadn't been a hero.

With a sense of embarrassed recall, I relived the moment when I wandered along a cliff top with the one girl in the party. Goodness knows what my intentions were, but we suddenly realised that we were not alone. We had been stalked by a particularly malevolent goat, complete with satanic horns and equally demonic intentions as the hideous creature was determined to nudge us off the cliff. I did my cause no good by panicking, and possibly crying, while my companion looked the goat in the eye and slapped it hard across its hairy face. Predictably, the heroine of this tale transferred her affections to another, more deserving and manly, member of our party.

My self-esteem had recovered by the time we left Blaenau for Llandudno. A lengthy tunnel turned the train windows into dark mirrors in which I saw the reflection of a man in his early forties patting down his hair and stroking an eyebrow. He was pleased to talk and I was more than happy to provide a focus for his memories.

He had left school with no qualifications and drifted into the Navy where he realised that he wasn't as stupid as he had thought. Various 0-levels followed, and he steadily climbed through the ranks until he was appointed Aide de Camp to the Admiral in charge of the NATO fleet. Despite his lowly origins he never felt ill at ease as the Admiral made a point of acknowledging his contribution when in the company of others.

'I really admired him for that. A good man.' I couldn't draw him on the detail of his travels and adventures. On reflection, had I persisted it was quite possible that those Special Forces with blackened faces would have boarded the train once again and I would have disappeared.

He told me about a journey on the Trans-Siberian Railway that he undertook soon after leaving the Navy. 'Because the Admiral was such an important man, he always got free tickets for shows. He couldn't go to most of them so he gave them to me. So, me and my brother got invitations to the perestroika exhibition that had been organised in London to celebrate détente. The thing was, there was a raffle. The tickets were a fortune, but the prizes were amazing. Anyway,

I fell in love with the second prize: a full-grown stuffed bear. I really wanted it, so we went mad and bought hundreds of tickets. Predictably, I won a journey on the Trans-Siberian Express and a stay in Moscow.'

'I remember that journey. It was night and the huge woman guard was getting pissed off with some English students drinking vodka and playing their ghetto blaster. She comes up, snatches the sound system and throws it out of the window. ...' He paused while we wondered if this practice might spread to our shores.

'Come on, now, hand over those mobile phones, you've been warned... I'm chucking them off the train!'

'Then life took a strange turn... I left the Navy and got a job working at a school for kids with autism. I was in a class when one of the boys lashed out at his pal, and I was in the way. He hit me and I went down like a stone and banged my head. It turned out that I had some brittle bone condition and I haven't been able to work since.' It was then that I noticed his two elbow crutches. 'Thing is, I really want to travel long distances, but it's difficult now as I'm registered disabled.'

John, in show-off mood, interrupted my reflections on the mutability of life by declaiming the full name of Llanfair P.G as we passed through the station.

'Llanfairpwllgwyngyllgogerychwyrndrobwllllantysiliog-ogogoch!' he declared loudly. I assume this was a primary school achievement, along with his other claim of being sick monitor. I should be more charitable of his oddnesses; pots and kettles... As a child I had written to the custodian of the station, enclosing a postal order, hoping for a six-inch long cardboard platform ticket in return. It duly arrived.

Distraction arrived in the elongated shape of the statue under the Britannia Bridge, raised to commemorate the Marquis of Anglesey who was fitted with a prosthetic limb after the Battle of Waterloo. History notes that, on realising that the limb had been ripped from his body by a cannon ball, our hero stoically informed the Duke of Wellington, 'By God, sir, I've lost my leg!' To which the noble Duke replied, 'By God, sir, so you have.'

An equally deserving hero was the frail, concave old woman who dragged her tiny body off the train at Ty Croes, dragging a shopping bag the size of a Land Rover towards a path leading to nowhere. Less deserving in this pantheon to potential heroes, was the woman returning from Ladies Day at Chester races. She had dispatched her family to Holyhead while she embraced the bacchanalian possibilities.

'I was somewhat less than a lady,' she muttered from behind her hangover-hiding dark glasses. My mind did wander a bit; being sick in the paddock, making rude gestures at the tic-tac man signing the odds? It didn't matter.

I was surprised at the proliferation of windmills in Anglesey, forty-nine of them, but where were the tilters? Where were the emboldened knights who took pot shots at pomposity and nonsense and who were ostracised for their pains? Where was Sancho Panza? Where was the bold Don?

'Cervantes had a profound impact on the genesis of my most celebrated production: *The Life and Strange Surprising Adventures of Robinson Crusoe of York, Mariner …*'

'It's not all about you, you know.'

He ignored me.

'Before this journey concludes I would like to make a few pertinent remarks and observations. I would like to record that the Welsh gentlemen are very civil, hospitable and kind; the people very obliging and conversable, and especially to strangers; but when we let them know, we travelled merely in curiosity to view the country, and be able to speak well of them to strangers, their civility was heightened to such a degree, that nothing could be more friendly, willing to tell

242

us about everything that belonged to their country, and to show us everything that we desired to see.'

Despite my better instincts, I had to acknowledge that, on this occasion at least, Defoe was completely right.

JOURNEY SEVEN

The North West of England

DAY ONE

*Glasgow Central – Carlisle – Bus replacement to
Appleby – Hellifield – Heysham Port – Lancaster –
Wigan Wallgate – Southport – Moorfields –
New Brighton – Birkenhead North – West Kirby –
Hoylake*

'On a tour of one night stands ... A suitcase and guitar in
hand...' Who am I kidding? I'm neither a poet nor a one-man
band. I'm on a bus replacement service from Carlisle to
Appleby and what's more, no one ever wrote a book about
bus replacement services. There again, there was a time
when I slept in a railway marshalling yard outside Carlisle
when hitch-hiking to Scotland. I'm not certain that hobo
cred endures for half a century.

'At Penrith we saw two remarkable pillars fourteen or
fifteen feet asunder, and twelve feet high. The people told us
they were the monument of Sir Owen Caesar, a champion
who exerted his mighty strength to kill robbers and wild
boars.'

According to the plaque on Appleby station, Eric Treacy,
Bishop of Wakefield, died on that very spot in 1978. Perhaps,

despite owning a cathedral and a crozier, he believed that so long as he kept moving he would avoid dying. It may have been a desired consummation as he enjoyed a reputation as a railway photographer. Perhaps God had a little gentle fun with one of his own; just as the double-headed class 45 filled His Grace's viewfinder his heart swelled, literally, to bursting.

John's impressive itinerary and the immutable law of *deja vu* conspired to place us once more on the scenic Settle line. I looked in vain for the crocheted woman who had become our best friend on the first trip, but someone else seemed pleased to see me. A middle-aged man was waving enthusiastically as if I was his long-lost friend. It transpired that he had mistaken me for someone else, but by this point I was sitting opposite him in an aura of shared embarrassment. He was a lecturer at Lancaster University whose mission that day was to convince schoolchildren in Leeds that physics was fun. I failed to disguise my astonishment at this outrageous proposition.

John tried to interest me in a treatise on the formation of the limestone hills through which we were passing and I thought of cavers crawling through the honeycombed rock hundreds of feet underground. Could there be anything worse than being trapped and gently squeezed to death as the light from the head torch is gradually replaced by a crushing eternity of blackness?

It was a relief to feel the sun shining through the glass canopies that are a feature of Hellifield station. In addition, there was song from a flock of tiny birds hiding in the roof. These small pleasures were lost on the old men who were presumably permanent residents in DAVE'S TREASURE SHOP on Platform 2. Dave provides a small display of railway memorabilia and respite care for the locals. 'I can't get warm, I can't get warm,' complained one.

They would have felt more at home, if not warmer, on

245

the train to Heysham. The demographic had visibly shifted. There was a sense that the elderly couples were on their last ever holiday to the Isle of Man. A journey which was now an ordeal. They were tense and anxious. Were their cases still in the rack where they had left them? Were they on the right train?

Their unease was compounded by a young interloper bellowing into his phone, 'No, Marney, I didn't f****** know. Jane told me. I didn't f****** believe it! You are both a pair of f****** ********!' The old people clung to each other in terror, and the conductor did little to reassure them as he pursued one of them down the aisle. 'You got on the train with someone else. Where is he? Tell me!'

The man opposite was reading a magazine article on the rare but nasty phenomenon of wheelchair rage. It occurred to me that it might have been an instruction manual providing advice on how to attach cutthroat razors to the wheels and mow down rivals. This hint of malevolence found an echo in an angry exchange between a senior citizen and the seated young woman. 'Why are you sticking out like that and blocking the corridor?'

'Because I'm pregnant,' explained the victim. 'I can't help sticking out.'

I was not enjoying this train, and John was the same. 'Thank Christ that's out of the way,' was his comment as we left Heysham for Lancaster.

I thought I would try my luck with four old dears cackling conspiratorially round a table. They were returning from holiday and exuding *bonhomie* and general contentment. This all changed when I approached and explained my mission. While three of the women were keen to talk, the senior matron fixed them with a glare that stilled their tongues. Les Dawson's mother-in-law had decided that none of them were to say a word. No secrets were to be disclosed. What goes on tour, stays on tour.

246

I fared better with the twinkly-eyed former compositor with the *Yorkshire Post*. He conjured a lost world of hot type and explained how to pick 'sorts' from a type case with the right hand, and set them into a composing stick held in the left. When the digital world swallowed his skills, he opened a bike shop and now frequently cycles sixty miles a day. He was *en route* to visit his ninety-three-year-old mother. After my encounter with the tight-lipped matron I wanted to wallow in this man's enthusiasm and spontaneity.

Defoe was less impressed.

'Printers! Pah! The spawn of the devil. They'll pirate your work for a shilling. If the mediocre outpourings of a scribbler do not sell, then change the name on the title page. Now it is written by Daniel Defoe. How else could I be held responsible for writing the pithily titled pamphlet *A Continuation of Letters written by a Turkish Spy at Paris: Giving an impartial Account to the Diva at Constantinople of the most remarkable transactions of Europe, and discovering several Intrigues and Secrets of the Christian Courts, especially of that of Paris, continuous from the year 1687 to the year 1693. Written in Arabic, Translated into Italian, and from thence into English.*'

Meanwhile John was describing, in minute detail, the phenomenon that was the Carnforth Squeal. I will provide a flavour of his discourse. 'Although not as pronounced as the squeal that characterises the stretch of line that connects Brewery Junction to Philips Park West, or indeed for that matter, the line that leads into Greetland Junction...'

I executed a quick dumb show suggesting that my bowels were about to collapse, and moved to the next carriage where I spoke to a delightful young woman with the fabulous name of India who was studying English Literature, Philosophy and Media at Liverpool University.

She had just finished writing a picaresque novel about backpackers in America, and was wondering which publishing house she should approach. I suggested Sandstone Press but she thought she would start with Penguin. I suddenly felt very old and cynical in the face of her bright self-confidence. The world was hers for the taking. No obstacle was insurmountable. I offered an unwanted piece of advice: 'never write about what you know,' and attempted a knowing wink but which probably came across as an old man's leer.

Defoe too revelled in the chance to impress. 'Start with a polemical pamphlet, young lady, then progress to fictitious letters, then essays of petition. Next I would urge you to embrace the satirical poem. Finally, works of fiction...'

'John, tell me again about the Carnforth Squeal.'

'No, you should have been listening.'

After the briefest of sojourns in Wigan Wallgate and Southport, we approached Liverpool. As it was a city I had rarely visited, I waited with interest partly inspired by the exhortation on the train's visual display to 'Change here for the U-boat tour.' At that moment we plunged underground. The order to dive had been given by Dietrich von Carlewitz and water poured into the buoyancy tanks.

I had in fact been looking forward to catching a glimpse of the cathedral and the docks but it wasn't to be. So, Liverpool joins Stratford, Oxford and Cambridge on the list of interesting towns and cities that we have passed through, or more accurately, under, but not actually seen. Such is the lot of the maniacal traveller.

Defoe was keen to share details of his first journey into the city.

'From the Wirall, there is a ferry over the Mersee, which, at full sea, is more than two miles over. We land on the flat shore on the other side, and are contented to ride through the water for some length, not on horseback but on the shoulders of some honest Lancashire clown, who comes knee deep to the best side, to truss you up, and then runs away with you, as nimbly as you desire.'

'What! You actually came into Liverpool on piggyback?'
Defoe nodded.

As the next train terminated at New Brighton, I thought it advisable to wake the woman who was sleeping soundly. The protocol is unclear. I could have touched her on the shoulder but touching strangers is not always advisable. Instead I coughed loudly in her direction. She woke paralysed with fear, staring at her father who was trying to tell her she was late for school.

DAY TWO

Hoylake – Bidston – Shotton – Chester –
Liverpool Lime Street – Warrington Central –
Warrington Bank Quay (Walking) – Chester –
Manchester Piccadilly – Wigan North Western –
Liverpool Lime Street – Huddersfield

The previous evening, desperate for fresh air and a semblance of exercise, I had wandered to the sea's edge at Hoylake. As the sun set on the horizon I felt compelled to walk towards it across a vast stretch of wet sand. Caught in its force field, I stepped across ridges and through small lagoons of shallow water, further and further until I felt fearful of the emptiness and mindful that the tide could turn. Remembering the cockle pickers who had been drowned across the bay, like a small boy I turned and ran. I suspect that my fears were groundless and that I would be mocked if I told John. I reached the promenade and turned to watch the sun drop into the sea.

My dreams that night continued the theme of vulnerability. I was in church and was the unwanted recipient of unctuous attention from members of the congregation. They were fawning and pawing at me. Again, I had to run.

Perhaps I was becoming institutionalised. Perhaps I only

felt secure when travelling on trains. I certainly felt at ease again, absorbing bizarre juxtapositions on the journey to Bidston. Each station was advertising a different species of bird associated with the Wirral Coastal Path: Northern Gannets, Common Mures, Razorbills. Then came a fleeting glimpse of the Tetley tea factory which introduced the round tea bag in 1989, and which produces 260 million bags every week with enough tea-bag tissue to cover 128 football pitches. Yes, this was safer territory.

The conductor wore a natty three-piece suit and sighed deeply as if wondering what to say when he gave his daughter away.

We had 38 minutes in Bidston station. The man on the Samaritans poster asked me if I was okay. I was, thank you, despite the odd psychic blip. In fact, I felt fine. I could distinguish the song of a lark from the clamour of birdsong, and the sun was shining. It wasn't exactly an Adlestrop moment but it would do.

John plonked his rucksack between us on the station bench, and a tired looking woman glowered at him until he moved it, so that she could sit down. She was a cleaner with jobs in different towns, now *en route* to West Kirby.

'I finish at twelve. I'm knackered. I can't stop though. The pension's not enough to live on, love, is it? I mean how far does £400 go when you've got to pay the bills? I worked for a while in John Lewis in Liverpool. I loved it but the overseer was horrible.' She asked what we were up to and looked incredulous when I explained that I was writing a book about train travel. 'And what does he do?' she asked, pointing at John.

'He's a retired head teacher,' I explained. After looking him up and down, she obviously had her doubts. I quite liked the way she had referred to John in the third person, as if he were wheelchair bound and she was asking if he liked sugar. If I am honest, I also quite liked being called 'love'.

Having learned that we would spend a night in Blackpool she warned us against such a foolhardy act. I mentally checked that I had said Blackpool and not Sodom and Gomorrah. Apparently, she had had a bad experience. 'Although my late husband quite enjoyed it. The whole place is full of con merchants. We had to pay in advance for the hotel and it was horrible. You could count the cornflakes. And chips. Every night. Straight from Iceland they were. Isn't he cold?' she asked pointing at John. 'In his anorak and jumper?'

John scowled.

'WILL ALL PASSENGERS PLEASE UNDERSTAND THAT THE RED BUTTON IN THE TOILETS IS AN EMERGENCY BUTTON. IT IS NOT FOR OPENING OR CLOSING DOORS. IT IS NOT A FLUSH. YOU MUST ONLY PRESS IT IF SOMETHING SERIOUS IS HAPPENING.'

It felt as if the whole class was getting a row when there was only one culprit. What, I wondered, might constitute something serious in a toilet? A rat floating in the bowl perhaps? A face pressed against the window from outside when the train is travelling at speed?

The platform at Shotton also yielded people of interest. Both were in their eighties. He was eighty-three and rightly proud of the fact. They were Americans from Baltimore. He was an Episcopal priest and she was a social worker. They were spending their twilight years parish swapping. I was intrigued by this ecclesiastical promiscuity. There must be places on the dark web where aging clergy can exchange pictures of pulpits, and then cross the world to taste the novelty of new confessions.

They were enthusiastic about their travels and the pleasures of the UK rail network. He told me that 45% of American men over eighty-five suffer from dementia. His wife gazed at him wistfully. They were currently staying at the Gladstone Library in Hawarden Flintshire, the only residential library in the kingdom. We learned that in 1894, William Ewart Gladstone used his wheelbarrow to haul 32,000 of his own books a quarter of a mile to their new home. He was eighty-five at the time...

She still works helping her contemporaries make the transition into care homes, and expressed sadness at the number of elderly folk who had no contact with their children. 'One girl was feeding her mother cat food,' she confided.

They joined us on the train as their next point of call was Port Sunlight. As gently as we could we told them that the town did not live up to its name, but they were unperturbed. Over the years they had developed an interest in petrochemical works. There was little either of us could think to say. John though, was soon talking knowledgably to them about hooded crows, poison ivy and elderflowers.

Once they left, we settled back into the journey to Chester until I noticed that an angry old man was staring intently from across the aisle at my groin area. I crossed my legs uneasily but his eyes followed my every movement. What was the problem? Had I wet myself? Was I twitching involuntarily? Was he contemplating sexual assault? His grip on his walking stick suggested malicious intent.

The display cabinet on the platform at Birkenhead Hamilton Square station described the discoveries made when the station was renovated in 2014. Historic posters, circus advertisements and old copies of the *Liverpool Echo* featuring the 'Flypaper Murderess' were found underneath the old wall cladding.

My phone told me that in 1889 Florence Maybrick tampered with a Valentine's Meat bottle (which was subsequently found to contain arsenic) and fed its contents to her philandering husband. The story becomes more complex as, apparently, many men took arsenic as an aphrodisiac and a general pick-me-up. In some instances, pursuit of *La Petite*

Mort descended into tasting the more dubious pleasures of *La Grande Mort*. In a bizarre footnote, Florence's son, who became a mining engineer, died in 1911 of accidental poisoning when he mistook a cyanide solution for a glass of water. I felt relieved to slide out of the station towards Lime Street.

'I've got some of the posters from the original film,' declared a man to his girlfriend. '1920s. The Olympics.' He was either an antiques dealer, an art thief, a con merchant or just a common or garden tosser. I couldn't decide.

There was little respite from the surreal as we changed trains. The centrepiece of Liverpool Lime Street is a statue of a black Ken Dodd waving his tickling stick in the direction of Bessie Braddock, the city's former MP. The statue is called *Chance Meeting*. Braddock is holding an egg to acknowledge the contribution she made to society by putting the lion symbol on British eggs.

The sense that my world was falling apart was confirmed by the pixelating of the next train display, which then emitted a noise reminiscent of an ancient typewriter. %$£$£&(*&^%% it said, and I could only agree.

The man in a beige anorak sitting opposite was furtively reading a *Dr Who* paperback. I wanted to assure him that it was OK; we all do odd things. He was not less of a human being because he was obsessed with Dr Who. I wanted to tell him that one of my acquaintances owns an original BBC Tardis but my courage failed me.

Defoe had no such inhibitions.

'My man, you should procure a copy of my Consolidator: or, *Memoirs of Sundry transactions from the World in the Moon: Translated from the Lunar language in which a mechanical but feathered spirit-driven flying machine, the Consolidator, enables various satirical observations to be made from a lunar viewpoint.* The Moon itself is identical to Earth, though it does boast one device, a Cogitator, which, when sat in, connects one's mind with clarity to the work-ings of the world, via a system of gears and springs.'

I found myself hankering for a Cogitator.

Now needing a good encounter, I approached a friendly looking young woman in the next carriage. She looked horrified at my approach and, speaking in a foreign tongue, pointed at her bicycle hanging in the rack. No, I was not about to confiscate it, no, she had not done anything wrong. No, I didn't have the power to throw her off the train even if she had done something wrong. Which she hadn't. Eventually I just moved away.

Increasingly fearful that I had lost my capacity to communicate, I had to try again. Another woman listened sympathetically to my preamble and I started to relax as she opened her mouth to speak. No words came out. Judging by the half words and snatched breathy consonants, she had lost her voice. She may have told me that she goes shopping a lot and loves babies, equally she may have confessed to being a white witch, I had no idea. Someone must talk to me!

It was happening. At last. I relaxed as a young geography student from Durham University told me that he was doing the rounds of interviews with various local authorities hoping for a job as a civil servant. I thought of dissuading him and urging him to get a life, but this would have meant crossing a boundary. I couldn't lead his life for him.

'And what do you do when not attending interviews or studying?' I asked.

'I play rounders,' came the reply, and in that moment I had his soul. In retrospect, I responded with my prejudices firing and grasped a little too easily at the wrong stereo-types. I saw this thin man at primary school trying hard to get invited by the girls to join in their game, offering them sweets from his lunch box. Thankfully I kept these pictures and the associated value judgements to myself and instead learned much about the game.

It thrives at most British universities, has been played since Tudor times and is played at international level. Furthermore, the oldest player is an eighty-one-year-old woman who plays in the Bolton league. She doesn't bat but fields and plays on first post.

Chastened and now better informed, I expressed the hope that his rounders career would be a glowing one, culminating in international honours.

Sticking with young men for the present, I spoke to a Muslim from Luton, a graduate from Hertfordshire University who travels the country for an IT firm. To elicit this much information, I had had to bring my ear close to his mouth which was uneasy for both of us. I am deaf at the best of times and he was softly spoken, impossibly shy and vulnerable in an indefinable way. I wanted to ask him what it was like being a young Muslim in Britain today but I decided that it would be a difficult discussion for us both.

Defoe shook his head as we trundled towards Manchester.

'This great bog extends for five or six miles. The surface looks black and dirty, and is indeed frightful to think of, for it will bear neither horse or man.'

All I could see was mile upon mile of suburban sprawl.

When we pulled into Manchester Piccadilly we witnessed the early days of an exciting new Olympic sport. With astonishing skill and athleticism, five young black kids with attitude managed to board the train while one of their number held the closing door open. The platform wallah faffed and flailed while remonstrating with the door holder. Flying in close formation, the lads managed to glide through the diminishing gap to much applause. The sport, when accepted by the relevant committee, will be known as synchronised leaping.

255

John was becoming irritated with mindless train announcements and had developed the art of embellishment which, I think, added to their import. At Piccadilly, we were urged TO WAIT IN THE LOUNGE ... ALTERNA-TIVELY PLEASE WAIT ON THE TRACK AS THERE IS NO ROOM ON THE WAFER-THIN PLATFORM.

Once on the train to Wigan, he happily improvised ... THIS TRAIN IS FITTED WITH CCTV FOR YOUR PROTECTION AND SECURITY ... IF YOU WOULD LIKE A COPY OF THE CURRENT TAPE FOR YOUR PLEASURE, OR AS A GIFT FOR A FRIEND, PLEASE HAVE A WORD WITH THE CONDUCTOR.

If the carriage had been built with rafters, it would have been crowded up to them. Yet despite the aston-ishing numbers there was virtual silence. It was the end of the day and people had endured sufficient talk from colleagues and bosses. Crosswords, novels and comfort blankets had been dispensed by the train staff who kept a watchful eye on their tired flock. The only noise was being generated by a man stuffing his face with Haribo sweets, consuming them on an industrial scale, packet after packet. He would declare his lapse later when the addiction group met.

At Wigan a man in a wheelchair stared down the carriage steps and into the chasm between train and platform which was truly yawning, and which had provided the original inspiration behind the constant exhortation to mind the gap. Everyone who passed offered to help. 'Thanks Buddy, thanks Buddy', intoned the man. 'I'm just waiting to go to the toilet on the platform.' Eventually the ramp was produced and repositioned once he returned. I asked him if people tended to be helpful. 'People always offer help in the North,' he said. 'Not like the South of England. And I get to go all over for the cricket. Lords, Headingley. It's my life.'

DAY THREE

Huddersfield – Manchester Piccadilly –
Wigan Wallgate – Bolton – Salford Crescent –
Preston – Colne – Blackburn – Clitheroe –
Blackburn – Preston – Blackpool North

The low point of our Huddersfield B & B was accidentally sitting in the sight line of a dozen bald, muscular men staring at football on the TV, cloned zombies who, on receiving a subliminal instruction from their leader, would attack and devour the two nearest OAPs.

This sense of paranoia was reinforced by the conductor on the first train of the day who took pleasure in pointing out that our Rail Rover tickets would not be valid for another half an hour. In the meantime, we would have to purchase separate tickets at great expense. Having extracted a small fortune from us, he showed his softer side and confessed that he too harboured the ambition to travel on every line of track in the kingdom.

At this early hour, personal space was not an option. I found myself only inches away from a young woman who was showing her strap-hanging colleague her arm which had been subject to an infestation of small beetles after she had 'rolled in the garden'. Keen to speculate as to why she had been behaving in such a way, I was distracted by the conviction that my own body was now being violated by a veneer of small insidious insects.

In the comparatively open space of Piccadilly station, I was approached by a young woman dressed in pink with high leather boots and a large black moustache that made her oddly attractive. She thrust something into my hand. I assumed it was either an invitation to a local transgender S&M club or, reading the logo on her chest, a leaflet urging me to check for the signs of testicular cancer. In fact, her sign said not 'Balls' but 'Halls' and I realised that I was now in possession of a packet of cough sweets.

Crawling out of the station on our way to Bolton, we had a good view of a shantytown beneath the viaduct over which we were travelling. One of the squatter's signs read 'Trying to get a deposit for a flat. Any donations greatly appreciated. Thank you xxxx.' Whoever had written it must have been desperate if he/she was willing to bestow at least four kisses on whoever responded. Perhaps I should leave John on the train, and take my chance . . .

I decided to stay and enjoyed travelling through acre on acre of old industrial land that was succoured by swathes of deep green vegetation. Old wounds were being staunched. Ugly brickwork was being hidden by the welcome balm of nature.

Desperate for caffeine and a bacon roll, I left John reading timetables on Bolton station and went to find a café. This was easier said than done, as the hinterland was bleak and café free. Eventually I found a lean-to which, by interpreting subtle signs, I decided might sell food. My hopes rose when I heard a woman screaming for her egg.

Apart from the wailing woman the shop was empty. There was, however, a large ceramic bell on the counter which I duly thumped. A man in Muslim clothing appeared, and I heard myself asking for a bacon roll just before realising that there could be few more insulting requests to make in the circumstances. Expressionless, he disappeared for ten minutes and brought me my bacon roll. I didn't know whether to apologise or just pay and leave. I did the latter and left to the sound of the woman still shrieking for her egg.

The very old couple on the train to Blackburn sat entwined in each other. She didn't want to let him go in case he slipped from the seat, and he just needed her. 'We've got a car,' she explained, 'but since his fall he can't drive. He's got a plate in his leg and a bleed to the head.' He seemed not to hear a word.

'During the war we would go to Blackpool for our holidays. You saved, you see, for Wakes Week and for Christmas.' She glowed with memory. 'The mornings were always bucket and spade. And a show in the evening. During the War you had to take your own food to the boarding house. There wasn't any, you see.

'And I loved the trains. They had such nice pictures on the compartment walls. Places you'd want to visit. And the prickly seats! The fine for pulling the communication cord was only £5 then.' I was about to ask her if she had pulled the cord and suspected the answer would have been yes. She panicked as I had made her forget they were getting off at the next stop. When she stood up the contents of her bag spilled onto the floor. I scrabbled with her and piled her possessions back in: hairbrush, compact, tissues. As they shuffled towards the open door I caught sight of her apple peeler under the seat, retrieved it and gave it to her just before the train pulled away.

John became animated, quite a rare phenomenon. Standing in the narrow confines of his seat, he knocked over a cup of coffee and stared at the landscape through shielded eyes. He was looking for where the former branch line of Calderstones Hospital Railway left the main line and disappeared into the hills to service the newly-built asylum for 'lunatics and epileptics'.

According to M Cornwall's history of the branch line, the locals had been opposed to the choice of location, fearful lest the inmates terrorise passing cyclists. The outbreak of the First World War assuaged this worry as the building became Queen Mary's Military Hospital. At the height of the conflict, the branch line carried up to two ambulance

259

trains per day, and even this was insufficient to carry the wounded. Upwards of seventy locals used their cars to augment the transport arrangements.

The local crematorium was unable to cope with the number of amputated limbs that were delivered to its doorstep. After the War, the building and railway line returned to its original purpose, conveying new inmates to the renamed Calderstones Certified Institution for Mental Defectives.

Cornwall also noted that new patients would be put to work scrubbing bloodstains from the wooden floors, one of whom 'spent two and a half hours on one stain and got nowhere, possibly a reason why he was in the institution in the first place'. There was no sign of the branch line, nothing but deep green foliage.

An elderly man told us that the hills were riddled with tunnels used during the Second World War to hide munitions. He claimed this fact was behind Churchill's boast that, 'We would fight them in the hills.'

Having made an innocent remark to us he was, of course, subjected to a minor interrogation. He was a retired geography teacher and widower, 'Please don't ask me any capital cities.' He was *en route* to hear the Halle Orchestra playing Dvorak's *The Golden Spinning Wheel*.

On the train back from Halifax to Manchester, I spoke to a dapper, middle-aged, well-coiffed Italian with an almost impenetrable accent. Married to an Englishwoman, he'd worked as a barber for television costume dramas and had recently been working on the sets of both *Emmerdale* and *Downton Abbey. Coronation Street* he added for good measure.

He specialised in cutting the hair of people who were appearing in crowd scenes. I told him that as the first series of *Downton Abbey* was not initially shown in Scotland it was some time before I could appreciate his handiwork. He seemed aggrieved that an entire nation had been deprived of the fruit of his labours, and expressed his bemusement by making several theatrical cuts through the air with a pair of imaginary scissors.

'Pray Sir, attend to my wig. Constant travel has left me quite unravelled. Pray, do you possess the new powder compounded of sheep suet, boiled apples, bay leaves and Macassar oil?'

Meanwhile Señor Teasy Weasy explained how, when not actually needed on set, he scoured second-hand shops looking for props that he could sell to the TV companies. Before I could glean more he grabbed his bags and left the train, and my paranoia returned with the thought that, rather than endure further interrogations, my new acquaintances all preferred to leave the train at the next stop.

I returned to John who was celebrating the approach to Rochdale by singing a medley from his favourite Gracie Fields songs. As his rendition of *Sally* had gone down well he embarked on *How are things in Glocca Morra this fine day?* Mercifully we never found out as we had to alight, taking all our possessions with us.

God chose our next train to punish me for listening to other people's conversations. This was payback time for having stolen vignettes from the lives of strangers and speculated inappropriately on a few sentences wrenched out of context. Even by poking my fingers in my ears and singing *la la la* loudly I could not block out the dullest exchange between two solicitors that had ever been held on the planet.

It started out promisingly. 'I've been nominated for the Solicitor's Journal of the Year Award.' I made a mental note not to renew my subscription as the conversation degenerated rapidly into wrist-slitting tedium. They reminisced over a recent meeting to tease out the shades of meaning contained in two clauses. Semiotics, semantics and syntax and all the rest have a place in modern society, but not on a train; not when innocent travellers are subjected to a discussion that would have made a maniacal Jesuit curl up and die.

I distracted myself by admiring the purple rhododendron bushes tumbling down the embankment, but there was no avoiding the drift of verbiage that settled like a damp cloud on the carriage. Eventually the lead speaker tried to elicit sympathy from his comatose female listener by declaring that he basically worked in a hamster wheel. This was an image I could relish. I looked to see if he had protruding front teeth. Not so far as I could see. Did he have bulging cheeks, or particularly muscular thighs from working that wheel all day? I didn't think so but felt he had reclaimed the moral high ground.

Full expiation was only provided by the sight of a semi-naked man lying full stretch on Hindley Station platform, sun bathing. All was well with the world after all. Less edifying was the gang of respectably dressed men baying for blood on Preston station.

The blood they craved would have belonged to supporters of MK Dons. Not being stereotypical football hooligans imparted a real sense of menace. They took it in turns to dip into a bin liner and bring out another bottle of spirits that was passed around until empty, bellowing out songs as if they were in a Nazi Beer Hall, and tomorrow did truly belong to them.

Most disturbing was the way one of the men grabbed another man's jaw tightly and kissed him long and deep on the mouth. This wasn't a glorious celebration of being gay, this was either an attempt to shock passers-by or, more likely, an attempted humiliation by the leader of the pack.

It was a relief to board the last train of the day. Feeling sullied by the odd encounter with the testosterone and drink-fuelled gang, I needed to seek out innocence, and found it in the guise of a young woman sitting on her own with a My Little Princess balloon floating above her. She had been to a party and now wanted to go home and chill. She had no idea that someone had attached the balloon to her back.

DAY FOUR

Blackpool North – Barrow – Carlisle – Preston –
Windermere – Kendal – Ormskirk – Kirkdale –
Kirkby – Wigan – Oxenholme – Windermere – Kendal

I left the Parisienne Hotel, North Promenade, Blackpool (£28 for sea view) early to go for a walk and look at the sea. In the middle of the road, a seagull was picking at the carcass of a smaller bird, and a pair of black tights had been left next to the tram tracks. I hoped it had been a good night.

A large industrial skip blocked the entrance to North Pier, containing a microcosm of all that Blackpool is. It could have been an artist's installation. A whole promenade's worth of faded blue and white deckchairs had been thrown in, their wooden legs awkwardly splayed and their calico dresses ripped. Protruding from their midst was a manikin with chubby thighs and small feet that may have dived in head first from a great height. The final adornment was an assortment of blue collecting tins still attached to chains to deter thieves.

Squeezing past I walked through the deserted ballroom to the pier. I was surprised by the number of plaques attached to the railings, each one a testimony to a dead couple who had enjoyed holidays on the pier. It was too early for the fortune seller to polish her crystal ball and stare into the future. Just as well. 'You are destined to spend all your days travelling the length and breadth of the kingdom, for no real purpose, in company of a large friend.'

Looking down at the beach I saw a tiny girl in a full-length bathing costume, six or seven years old, skipping

263

with bucket and spade through the sand towards the water's edge. She paused, looked up at me through squinting eyes. 'You have to get up early,' she said. It was 1950. The film was shot in black and white. It was the old woman I had spoken to on the train.

John was waiting for me outside The Parisienne. He was talking to an elderly man who had been coming to Blackpool every summer since he was a boy. This time was special as he was going to meet his brother whom he hadn't seen in eighteen years. He had been so nervous he had drunk a whole bottle of Jack Bream the night before.

The young man on the Preston train told me that he had to travel by rail as he had lost his driving licence for drink driving. He had lived in Grange-over-Sands all his days and was visiting his girlfriend who had eventually forgiven him for his conviction. The problem was, he said, that he worked for a vehicle recovery firm. Fortunately, his boss was understanding and was keeping his job open. He had four months to go, but was using up all his savings. He was a part-time rally driver and would often compete in Germany. His family had been furious with him at the time. He travels on three trains a week, which means that he can play games on his phone. Which you can't do when you're driving can you? True, very true.

John and I had a strange Brief Encounter in the refreshment room at Carnforth station. The woman wanted to talk. Staring into the middle distance she told us, 'Suddenly I felt the touch of his hand on my shoulder, and then he walked away. Out of my life for ever...'

I blinked. John was still there, looking at me very oddly. I did my best to console her. She should have got over it now, after all it was filmed here over sixty years ago.

At the risk of sounding like a tourist guide, the Cumbrian coastline is a bit special, hugging Morecombe Bay, skirting tidal estuaries and crossing the Rivers Kent and Leven on major viaducts. Ulverston is overlooked by a lighthouse that has never contained a light. It is a sham lighthouse and should be pulled down immediately. It was built as a monument to Sir John Barrow who must have enjoyed playing with a model of the Eddystone Lighthouse in his bath. One of the highlights of the Second World War was a taunt by Lord Haw Haw that the German bombers were going to use the Pepperpot for target practice.

The ventilation engineer from Sellafield had worked there for twenty years. He was now overseeing the winding down process. He said he was no more than a caretaker who moonlighted as a waste disposal operative. His gentle descent into self-deprecation was accompanied by a twinkly smile. Anticipating my next silly question, he confirmed that he didn't need electricity in his house as he glowed in the dark. We sat in companionable silence, glancing at the boats half sunk in the silt of the Esk Estuary and, on the other side of the train, at a lone shepherd flapping his hands ineffectually at his flock.

Two German students, wrapped around their rucksacks and each other, were happy to practice their English on one of the many eccentrics of whom they had heard Great Britain was full. I decided not to mention Lord Haw Haw. She was a teacher; he was reading mediaeval history. I challenged him to justify such an arcane area of study. He said it was like delving into a mystery, a strange world where lives were short and death featured large. At that moment, cowled monks filed into the carriage, each carrying either a skull or a candle.

The spell was broken by an elderly couple leaving the train. The husband held onto a homemade step that would enable his wife to leave the train without falling into the gap, and being lost to him forever.

I was not prepared for the forbidding approach to Sellafield. The train crept past miles of barbed wire enclosing ominously nondescript buildings. The strangely shaped non-geometric edifices suggest that a nuclear holocaust has already occurred and that the territory, after several centuries, has been reclaimed by aliens with no understanding of architecture.

I felt that I should hold my breath until we were well past the site but I would have expired long before we reached the coastline. Perhaps I was needlessly anxious. After all, there have only been twenty-one serious incidents in the last sixty years, and it is a long time since a ten-mile stretch of coastline was closed and swimming banned. The more recent scandal, when it was revealed that body parts had been routinely removed for analysis from dead workers, was probably no more than media hype. The fact that children living near Sellafield have twice the normal amount of plutonium in their teeth is probably statistically insignificant.

'Admirable satire!'

When it returned, the trackside coast was most welcome. I wallowed in small details: holidaymakers swathed in anoraks; long lines of wooden huts hugging the shore; a slow and gentle tour past the gardens crammed into the tiny space between shore and railway. Someone had adorned their property with shell-encrusted birdcages. An elderly man was tending four full-sized ornamental sheep.

The train slowed to a walking pace that enabled me to beachcomb from the warmth of the carriage. The pickings were predictable: bleached plastic containers, squeezy bottles, a single wellington boot, a blue crate, a green fishing net, a railway sleeper, a wooden pallet and endless acres of grey sea.

It was time to turn back to the carriage, and I was soon speaking to a woman who made the mistake of looking up from her laptop. She was alarmingly messianic about something called Action Based Research, which she claimed was an innovative and subversive approach to gleaning what people thought about a variety of issues. 'It is either research initiated to solve an immediate problem or a reflective process of progressive problem solving led by individuals working with others in teams or as part of a community of practice to improve the way they address issues and solve problems.'

I suddenly wanted to get back to John so that he could talk to me about Morpeth Curves, Dalton Loops or, indeed, anything that he wanted to. Suspicious of my newfound enthusiasm for railway infrastructure, he grunted and pointed out that the conductor had left the train at Corkickle Station and not returned. I could only assume that he had also made the mistake of feigning interest in Action Based Research, and decided to end it all.

Defoe seemed inexplicably restless, and frequently left the pages of the book to pace the carriage. 'Necessity dictates that I return to my dear wife in London. Not well. Pregnant again...'

'If I remember correctly, the last time you weren't so eager to return. Didn't you go missing? One of your biographies says that it took you eight weeks to travel south. What were you up to?'

'Matters of state ... civic duties ...'

'There were rumours that you shacked up with your mistress?'

'Don't judge me.'

'Then tell me the truth.'

'The truth ... the truth ...'

'Yes.'

'I am fearful about paying another visit to Scotland. I fear I will be recognised this time.'

'Because of your work for the Union?' He nodded and looked anxiously around the carriage.

DAY FIVE

Kendal – Oxenholme – Carlisle – Kilmarnock –
Glasgow Central

Apologies if you have been looking forward to wallowing in surreal descriptions of Dumfries and Galloway; apologies too if you regularly travel from Carlisle to Kilmarnock and were looking forward to comparing your impressions with mine.

The truth of the matter is that Day Five was a day too far; I never wanted to see a train ever again; I couldn't face talking to another stranger. I was the sulky tired toddler sucking his thumb and refusing to engage with the world. I just wanted to be home.

'You're meant to be writing a book,' said John unhelpfully. 'Don't just sit there.' But sit there I did. It was as if I was separated from the rest of the carriage by a Perspex wall; I could see movement and could hear muffled sounds but was powerless to investigate.

Defoe also did his best to encourage me but to little effect. He even offered to take over the narrative but he too struggled to find much to say. In fairness, looking out of the window, he seemed downcast as he gazed on a countryside devastated by the endless battles between the English and the Scots. The best he could offer me was a pessimistic comment on the local population.

'In a word, the common people not only are poor, but look poor; they appear dejected and discouraged, as if they had given over all hopes of ever being otherwise than they were …'

He looked at me, and shrugged.

'Melancholia,' he said. 'Scribbler's curse.'

JOURNEY EIGHT

The North of Scotland

DAY ONE
Glasgow – Aberdeen – Keith

We had decided to leave the best until last. We both live in Scotland and both feel passionate about the country and know it well, and these factors made our final journey in some ways more challenging. I would complete the first leg without John, who lives in Keith where we would be reunited. Was I in the grip of Stockholm syndrome, unable to live without my jailer? Would I hanker for increasingly obscure facts about continuous welded tracks?

Familiarity with Glasgow Central station counted for nothing as I walked into a nightmare of Union Flags. Had there been a coup overnight? It would certainly explain why Queen Street station had been closed...

The answer was more prosaic, but arguably more menacing. The sycophantic toadies of ScotRail had decided to emulate the celebrations being held in the Mall to mark the Queen's ninetieth birthday and were throwing a party on the main concourse. A small army of middle-aged women with royal perms competed to offer me a cake. Oh well, perhaps I was no more than a closet royalist after all, whose republican principles could be bought with a slice of Madeira.

Defoe stayed away from the party preparations. I suspected he was trying to work out which monarch was on the throne so that he could couch his loyalty in tones sufficiently convincing to avoid being imprisoned again.

My hackles rose when I was dissuaded from sitting inside the roped-off area. The seats were reserved for VIPs, establishment figures, freemasons and the entire board of Rangers Football Club. Or so I convinced myself, until one of the cake-bearing matrons pointed out that all money raised would go to Dementia Awareness. I was chastened, and reflected that at some point I too might be a beneficiary of this most worthy of causes.

Soon after gliding out of Glasgow Central we passed the charred remains of Dundyvan church which suggested that a second, more violent reformation had swept the country since we had been away.

A quick web search reveals that the doorways were bricked up and the windows covered some twenty years ago. This failed to deter the vandals of North Lanarkshire who broke in and smashed the stained glass from the inside. Nevertheless, an Astrology Society expressed interest in renovating the building, presumably because the roofless church afforded a clear view of the prophetic heavens. A further recent report mentioned that bushes and plants were growing on the wall heads and masonry joints. This, one assumes, would make the building equally attractive to pantheists.

'His Majesty's gift of 1,000 pounds for sending ministers and missionaries to the Highlands, is certainly one of the most needful charities ... A most horrible ignorance has so far spread over this country.'

'You're probably right.'

Meanwhile a man on the other side of the aisle executed

a perfect mime of someone he saw at an airport destroying a suitcase by cramming it into the overhead locker. The veins stood out on his forehead and the muscles in his arms bulged. His companions roared their appreciation.

Defoe though, was staring out of the window at the Ochil Hills.

'In the past we mounted these hills black and frightful as they were, to find the road over the moors and mountains to Stirling.'

'Do you really think they look black and frightful?'

Stirling Castle rose on the right side of the train. It is a real castle, there is nothing namby-pamby or *faux* about it. Its walls are drenched in the blood of Picts, English, Scots, and sundry noblemen. Its rooms have witnessed murder, mayhem and some splendid meals.

'They who built the castle, built it, as the Scots express it, to continue aye, for ever and a day after.'

More daunting, and visible from the train, is Cornton Vale Prison, until recently home to 217 female inmates most of whom were mentally unwell and who had been incarcerated for crimes that, had the perpetrator been male, would have merited no more than a wag of the finger and a gentle admonition from a jovial judge. A quick search of tabloid headlines associated with the institution reveals the extent of the stigma: KILLER MUM WHO CAUSED YOUNG DAD'S FATAL BRAIN INJURY WITH ONE PUNCH IS LET OUT OF PRISON FOR DATE WITH JAILBIRD FIANCEE. Presumably this banner left little room for any other words on the page. KNIFE THUG KIM GRAY FREE TO SIP A COCK-TAIL AFTER HER EARLY RELEASE FROM PRISON FOR ALMOST KILLING A CABBY. And on it goes.

'We too had chapbooks to entertain the rabble. Women prisoners were got with child, those in debt were tortured by their gaolers. Prostitutes mingled with thieves and murderers. Gaol distemper was rife.'

Meanwhile the mime artist was sharing his views on the still loathed football commentator, Jimmy Hill. Unaware of his demise in 2015, the apologist offered a heretical view: 'He's not *that* bad.' Whoever suggested that the Scots are an unforgiving race?

One of their number sported three musical notes tattooed on his neck. They may have been swastikas but, not wishing to stare at him for longer than was conducive to my personal safety, I gave him the benefit of the doubt. What was the tune? The start of a nursery rhyme that his mum used to croon? The theme song of the *A Team* that sustained him through adolescence? A favourite sectarian chant?

Speculation was interrupted by the conductor intimidating an innocent youth cowering in the corner. 'The moment you do that, I think you have something to hide!'

The boy shrunk further into the upholstery. Aware that he now had an audience, the conductor, treading a fine line between the avuncular and the officious, addressed the entire carriage. 'That bloke in first class claimed he was sitting there because there were no seats elsewhere. Of course there are seats, look around you.' We all looked around and nodded our agreement. 'So I tells him, "Give me six pounds, or get off!"' There was little clarity over whether this was an arbitrary fine imposed by this aging bully or a legitimate payment.

At that moment the toilet door swung open revealing the trolley attendant emptying bottles into the bowl. This was strange indeed. It was obvious that, having taken the pledge herself, she was determined to introduce prohibition to ScotRail.

A couple in their early forties slid into the seats on the other side of the table. He was a crane operator on the rigs, she was a nursery teacher. He had worked offshore for sixteen years, and it suited him. 'It pays for the lifestyle,' he said. They had left the kids with the grandparents and snatched a couple of days in Glasgow. Shopping, a few drinks, the casino.

He agreed there were feelings of frustration and impotence when things were happening at home and he couldn't be there to help. Meanwhile he stared at his sleeping wife with doe eyes. It seemed a good time to ask him about dangers involved in his work. He had experienced three bad incidents when in helicopters: two emergency landings and once when the aircraft hovered above the ground and he had to jump. 'We have to show that we can escape from a tank of water every four years.'

'After one emergency landing in Shetland we were led to a free bar and given presents while being urged not to tell the boss ... It's still a good life. There's a great gym on the rig.' His wife woke up and, catching his last sentence, poked him in his over-developed bicep and said that she didn't really like muscly men.

The guard had reverted to avuncular mode and was moving an elderly couple from their snug airline seat to an empty table where he told them they would enjoy more space.

The mime artist was performing again. 'If my wife sees a single hair, she yanks it out.' He skilfully recreated the domestic cameo complete with exaggerated yanking movements and a convincing soundless scream.

As Dundee curved towards us across the Tay Bridge Defoe declaimed, 'A pleasant, large, populous city, and well deserves the title of Bonny Dundee, so often given in its discourse, as well as in song (bonny, in Scots, signifying beautiful).'

'I think we know that, Daniel.'

I realised that my Figment was eying the other passengers with suspicion.

'What's up?'

'We did not find so kind a reception among the common

273

people of Angus as the Scots usually give to strangers. We found it was because we were English men; it was on account of the Union, which they almost universally exclaimed against though sometimes against all manner of just reasoning.'

'I'm afraid these days have come again.'

'You said you would afford me your protection.'

As we drew into Aberdeen, I realised I was smiling. John and I met at University there in 1968. I was now nearly sixty-eight years old. This meaningless alchemy of numbers told me that nearly half a century had passed since then. I unashamedly surrendered to the ache of memory, and then made efforts to resist by reflecting on the nature of nostalgia with its subversive capacity to accentuate the sentimental and erase the painful in equal measure.

With an hour to pass in the city, I gave up the struggle and, on leaving the station, consciously sought out the memories. There was Ed balancing a pint of McEwans on the head of a small boy who made the mistake of pausing outside the Kirkgate on a sunny afternoon. Up above, the raucous gulls applauded. Was that me lying happily drunk in Marischal Quad during freshers' week? And on they flowed.

One of the reasons why Aberdeen is so conducive to nostalgia is that the combination of mist and granite makes the entire city look like a collection of old black and white postcards. If there is the occasional splash of colour, a red raincoat perhaps, it endows the drab with added signifi-cance.

I noticed that Defoe was staring at the feet of passers-by. He seemed particularly transfixed by the heavy boots worn by a trauchled middle-aged woman.

'What on earth are you looking at?' I asked.

'Aberdeen has a very good manufacture of worsted stock-ings, which they send to England in great quantities, and of which they make some so fine, that I have seen them sold for fourteen, and twenty shillings a pair.'

En route back to the station I went into Waterstones in Union Street, sought out several copies of my recently published novel and took them to the counter asking with an authorial swagger if they would like me to sign them. As I flourished my pen in a transient delusion of celebrity, I considered that anyone could experience this particular pleasure. Just wander into any High Street bookshop, pick up novels by an obscure author, claim to be that author and, when lots of people are watching, sign the books with aplomb.

Back in Aberdeen station, I cast my eye down the astonishingly long list of *The men of this company's service who laid down their lives in the Great War of 1914-19*. Recently I read a station plaque in Kreuzberg. According to that apparently innocuous sign, in times past trains departed for Belsen, Auschwitz and Dachau.

As we left Aberdeen for Keith I saw OMERTA written in foot high letters on the side of a house – presumably a reference to the mafia code of silence. Elsewhere in Scotland I had seen GRASS scrawled in red on people's property denoting that an informer was in residence. Was this an Aberdeen variant, a pre-emptive statement of loyalty to whichever criminal fraternity held sway?

I spent much of the journey speaking to an Inverness Caledonian Thistle supporter. He told me that he had had ICT tattooed on his heart when on holiday in Spain for 150 euros. He was a redundant shot-blaster who now commuted to work as a labourer for his brother, but his passion, his sole *raison d'etre*, was to follow his team to every game, home and away. Together we explored an entire gazetteer of football by forging obscure links based on player transfer between clubs. He declared that Fraserburgh FC in the Highland league was the coldest ground in the entire kingdom.

Defoe had been listening to the man's accent.

'Cromwell's soldiers left the citizens of Inverness with the English accent upon their tongues, and they preserve it also to this day, for they speak perfect English, even much better than in the most southerly provinces.'

After an hour of eavesdropping on our conversation, most of the other passengers left to travel in the adjacent carriage, their boredom threshold long exceeded.

I made the mistake of mentioning the officious/avuncular guard from the previous train to my football-loving friend. He knew the man. 'He's an arse,' he declared, and described how he had witnessed the villainous railway employee threatening a girl with prosecution when she innocently proffered her mother's debit card to pay for her ticket. 'He leaves me alone now, after I told him that I have more friends on the railway than him.'

DAY TWO
Keith – Inverness – Wick – Inverness – Keith

It was good seeing John again, but the old doubts returned on leaving Keith as he conjured an apocalyptic vision of a generation of Morayshire farmers dying horrible deaths after ingesting pesticides in their youth.

As I looked through the window I could indeed just make out several sad wraithlike figures dragging themselves out of the hedgerows, desperate for water. Defoe intervened to put things back on track.

'Moray is, indeed, a pleasant country, the soil fruitful, watered with fine rivers, and full of good towns.'

John too attempted to dispel the gloom of his own making by singing 'Straight is the line of duty/Curved is the line of beauty/thou shalt see the curved line ever follow thee.' He has a good voice but that was little excuse. I assume that he was

276

motivated by the curvature of the track and not by any moral imperative. His oddness provided me with the motivation to talk to the middle-aged woman who boarded with her bike.

'I need it to get to my jobs. I've three of them. I'm a cleaner at Moray College and at the police station. I also work in the garden section of B&M. No, I can't tell you what I see at the police station, I've signed a confidentiality agreement. Mind you, the combination of hot weather, BBQs and drink can lead to civil unrest. I will say no more.'

She was also a mature horticultural student at the college and spent much time in her garden, which had previously been owned by a blind man. At the moment she was rebuilding her paths using unwanted bricks from the building section at the college. 'With permission you understand.'

Although I hadn't asked, she told me what she would do if she were in charge of the world. I braced myself. After less than a moment's pause she enlightened me. 'I would make voluntary service compulsory, and make certain that everyone honoured the Sabbath.'

Defoe nodded his agreement.

'There are indeed people here who know so little of religion, or of the customs of Christians, as not to know a Sunday, or Sabbath, from a working day.'

Having made the world a better place, the woman declared that life was for grasping by the scruff of the neck, collected her bike and left the train. Fortunately, it was in a station at the time.

We missed our connection to Wick from Inverness by two minutes. John explained that it was cheaper to send the four of us who wanted to travel north by taxi than for the railway company to pay the fines that would be incurred if the train was late. He then took one look at the taxi and bellowed at the Chinese driver that we wouldn't all fit in. Fortunately, the driver's language skills were poor and he hopefully missed John's more horrible nuances.

I had a dilemma: was it permissible for a book on rail travel to include references to a taxi replacement service? On balance I decided it was, and anyway, it was my book and I could put in it what I liked.

Unsurprisingly, Defoe had thoughts on the preferred means of travel.

'I do confess if I was to recommend to any men whose curiosity tempted them to travel over this country, I would propose travelling with some company, and carrying tents with them.'

John had not been wrong. The physical proximity of three of us on the back seat was proving to be uncomfortable. The man on my left was working 'subsea', and spoke with such authority that I wasn't brave enough to tell him I had no idea what that meant. Left to my own speculations, I saw him as the Jacques Cousteau of the North Sea, or as a character from a James Bond movie propelling an underwater missile towards the HQ of some perfidious villain. He said he had been a pilot in the army and had seen service in Afghanistan and Iraq.

'I was most affected by Northern Ireland. I was seventeen at the time. It was fun at first and then ...' His voice trailed away. He said he had eventually been based at Hereford. It was the first time I had shared my body heat with a former member of the SAS.

He then became a helicopter pilot on the rigs and I wondered if he was the pilot who had caused such problems to my earlier correspondent. He said that there are approximately 800 surplus pilots in the vicinity of Golspie alone. I thought this figure unlikely but murmured my assent. The exaggeration continued as he described how the fall in oil prices had affected the economy in Aberdeen. He claimed there were fields outside Portlethen containing upwards of 1000 ex-lease white Alfa Romeos. This can't have been true.

'Can we go dipping for herring?' asked Defoe like a bored

car-trapped child, desperate for any distraction and, failing that, the toilet. He was pointing in the direction of the Pentland Firth.

'What?'

'I had the pleasure of seeing a prodigious quantity of herring not far from here. The water was two-thirds fish. The operation of taking them could hardly be called fishing, for they did little more than dip for them into the water and take them up.'

By now my neighbour's body heat was imparting a sense of boldness to my thigh. I knew with certainty that if he exaggerated again I would garrotte him, truss him up and throw him out of the car. Sensing the threat, he explained that he wanted to go to Nigg. The cab driver executed a U-turn and stopped in the middle of Invergordon, whereupon the SAS hero meekly opened the door and left. So much for Who Dares Wins.

I was increasingly haunted by the thought that everyone I had spoken to on my journeys had simply made up stories to please me. I was being forced to consider that I was naturally attracted to the delusional and the fraudulent, but realised that I could live with this scenario. It would just lead to a different book.

Our other travelling companion apologised when I asked him what he did and said that he worked for HM Customs in Arbroath. Now, what other professions prompt spontaneous apologies? Undertakers, referees, possibly chiropodists and sex workers came to mind. By way of mitigation, he explained that he worked for the complaints wing of Inland Revenue who took referrals from the voluntary sector and worked with vulnerable people whose tax affairs had become chaotic. I passed him my card.

He became animated describing clients whose accrual of fines for non-payment were greater than the original bills. There were fourteen of these fiscal Samaritans covering the whole of Scotland. Their sole function was to soothe the brows of the easily confused.

Defoe had great empathy for the man.

'Let me quote to you from *The Tradesman in Distress ...*' He drew himself up to his full height, admittedly difficult in a taxi and declaimed:

'Debt is the death of a tradesman; he is mortally stabbed, or, as we may say, shot through his head in a trading capacity; his shop is shut up as when a man is buried, his credit, the life and blood of his trade, is stagnated ...'

This man was unique in more ways than one. He held a season ticket for Arbroath Football Club. I sought his views on the coldest football ground in Scotland. 'Gayfield!' he replied proudly.

When not succouring the bewildered, our man travelled the country seeking CAMRA pubs. He described a hostelry in Sheffield with such relish that we almost asked the taxi driver if he was interested in a thousand-mile round trip.

With time to spare in Wick, I left John at the station and walked by the river. Like Aberdeen, Wick held memories, more melancholic this time. Prime among them was walking fast along the cliffs towards the Old Man of Wick after a funeral, pursued by gulls. I thought of walking along the coast to the sea caves where Robert Louis Stevenson encountered a tribe of gypsies but I had done that before, and I doubted if the travellers had returned.

Back on Wick station, I spoke to an old couple who had moved to the far end of the platform to enjoy the sun. She manoeuvred her Methuselah husband towards the blue earth-filled barrels that were linked together in the form of a train to amuse children. She told me that he had to sit down, and that he loved the sun. He was the colour of parchment. After several laborious three-point turns, she had him positioned so that he could wedge his buttocks between two of the barrels. He turned his face to the sky. What were the

Wilfred Owen lines? 'Move him into the sun/gently its touch awoke him once.'

Despite her husband's lack of mobility, they were on a day trip from Inverness at the end of a five-week holiday from Sheffield. For the life of me I couldn't remember the name of the CAMRA pub. 'I want another life,' she said, 'to fit everything in.' I asked her what she had done with this one. 'I spent eleven years in an office. I didn't want to, I wanted to work in a food factory. And then the kids came along. And then my husband had two heart attacks. I didn't do anything really.' I told her quite forcibly that that clearly wasn't the case. 'Well,' she said, 'I didn't want anyone else to bring the kids up.'

In addition to enjoying the sights they were researching their ancestry. 'My great-uncle designed the Inverness Cape.' The aforementioned garment belongs in the same eponymous pantheon as the Wellington boot and the Mackintosh, and is associated with Sherlock Holmes after Sidney Paget illustrations for *The Strand* showed him wearing one. Equally impressive is the fact that it was the outer garment of choice for Jon Pertwee in the third incarnation of *Doctor Who*.

The sun moved along the platform, and so did they.

It was a relief to board the train to Inverness and head out across the flat lands of Caithness. We would have struggled with another two-and-a-half-hour taxi journey. On the far side of the River Thurso, and through the trees, a funeral was being conducted. The black suited mourners were in stark contrast to the bright sun. Hanging above them were the words, 'Grand day for it.' And the reply, 'Aye.'

Defoe was staring at the sky.

'Tis worth observing that here in the month of June, though indeed the sun does set yet you might see to read the smallest print, and to write distinctly, without any help of a candle. No wonder the ancient mariners believed that the

281

Elysian fields must lie this way; when they found they were already come to everlasting day, they could no longer doubt but heaven lay just ahead.'

I left both John and Defoe to their thoughts and wandered further down the carriage.

'Hello, can I talk to you? I'm attempting to travel on every mile of railway track in the United Kingdom.'

'So am I,' came the unexpected reply. I had met my doppelganger.

The grizzled Australian was in his seventies. His parents had emigrated as 'Ten Pound Poms' under the Assisted Passage Migration Scheme, also known as 'Bring out a Briton', a central part of the 'Populate or Perish' policy. The family decided to stay and avoid the stigma of returning and being dubbed 'Boomerang Poms'. This was quite enough slogans for one day.

'Throughout my time in Australia I was haunted by a childhood memory of travelling at the age of ten on the Vale of Rheidol Railway. I just couldn't get the picture out of my head. Know what I mean? I worked as a banker, but, you know, I hated it. Then I started a business offering driving lessons to the disabled. But I still kept dreaming of those steam engines. They wouldn't leave me. Anyway, I eventually found the courage to tell my wife that I had to return to Wales. I just had to. She didn't want to come, for some reason, so anyway, here I am and while I'm at it, I thought I might as well travel on the whole damn network.'

He promised to stay in touch, which he did, sending me daily pictures of his subsequent journeys.

I then spoke to a retired toolmaker who had freedom to travel as his wife was in a nursing home. His eyes made it quite clear that this was not an area for discussion. For a moment we sat in silence, which he broke by telling me, as several people on this journey had already done, 'There's never enough time.'

If this was an emerging theme then it needed an airing. What is it about rail travel that encourages thoughts of mortality? Is 'time's winged chariot' really a train? Do we equate movement with escape? Does seeing landscape pass quickly equate with living to the full? Do we mistakenly feel that if we keep moving, we will avoid the day of black clothes and the ironically bright sun? In my case, I think the answer to these questions is 'yes'.

John brought me back to earth by pointing out that the line on which we were travelling was floating on a blanket of bog. I thanked him for this unexpected observation.

He was now on a roll and waxed lyrical about the gold rush in Kildonan in 1869 when upwards of 600 prospective prospectors made their way to pan for gold in the Helmsdale River under the avaricious eye of the Duke of Sutherland. Before disillusion and penury held sway, a German called John Peter Dunker (aka Herr Kagenbusch) waved his cloak of fraudulence and alchemy over the region, bewitching the Duke among others. Eventually the furious locals resorted to pouring water down the chimneys of his furnaces. He was subsequently put in gaol.

Next, in full tourist guide mode, John pointed out the monument to the Duke of Sutherland which still attracts attention from Scots who have not forgiven him for his role in the Highland clearances. An attempt to dynamite the plinth was made in 1994 and more recently police have been investigating cases of alleged vandalism.

To introduce a more conciliatory note, he started singing *Granny's Heiland Hame* which makes maudlin reference to Ben Bhraggie:

Far away in the heilands, there stands a wee hoose /And it stands on the breest o' the brae/ Where we played as laddies there long, long ago/ And it seems it was just yesterday ...

I would like to report that his efforts were met with spontaneous applause from our fellow travellers, but this would be far from the truth. Defoe locked himself firmly into Chapter 4.

Annoyance with John was a likely explanation for the qualified welcome I received from the man in running gear behind us. Yes, he had run three marathons but he spent most of his time helping to decommission Dounreay which, he said, was a complex task. His expression changed and I could read the thoughts in his head as if his brow had been a ticker tape machine: Why is this odd man talking to me? Why doesn't he just go away and re-join his singing friend? Which is what I did.

John declared the scenery was good for his soul but I: (a) didn't realise he had one and (b) assumed that if he had at one time possessed one, by now it would have been sold to the devil in exchange for an encyclopaedic knowledge of Scottish topography and railway infrastructure.

Defoe though took his cue from John.

'The mountains are full of deer, harts, roebucks etc. Here are also a great number of eagles which breed in the woods, and which prey upon the young fawns. Here are also the best hawks. Furthermore the rivers and lakes are prodigiously full of salmon ...'

I watched an old man standing mesmerised in front of the toilet door at the end of the carriage. It opened, it shut. It opened, it shut. Just as I was on the point of intervening, it opened. He moved inside. It shut.

A young research and design engineer worked for a firm making diabetic markers. He talked about the dilemmas faced by his organisation, which was committed to ethical engineering but constrained by the need to turn a profit. He was a keen mountain biker, rugby player and rock climber. He also enjoyed building computers and had a four-year-old son. Just when I had decided that he was a thoroughly nice bloke, he spoiled it all by asking where I lived. 'Glasgow', I said. 'I suppose someone has to,' was his cruel and unfeeling reply.

The carriage windows were closed as we approached Invergordon. The town has been plagued with unwanted smells. Four years before a fire had destroyed thousands of tons of fishmeal, leaving the locals retching and clutching nosegays. The firm responsible pledged £6000 to pay for floral displays in the town centre for the next three years by way of apology.

It may have been the smell of rotting flowers that left me gagging when I visited recently but it seems more likely that another fishmeal shed was the culprit. Either way, I was impressed with the alacrity with which the conductor dispensed protective suits with built in face mask as we neared the station.

Unfortunately, we had insufficient time at Dingwall for me to find the plaque (this, my new hobby) which testified to the fact that '134,864 servicemen were given a cup of tea here during the First World War'.

'Wait,' said Defoe before we left the station. 'Wait.' He punched his brow trying to dredge something out of his memory. 'Got it,' he said. 'The Women-Rabblers of Dingwall.'

'Who?'

'I reported it in my review. When the Presbyterians tried to hold a synod in Dingwall, they were besieged in the manse by an angry rabble. And then Isbel Macka, a scandalous person, as being a common notorious whore and vagabond came into the room and addressed all the ministers, telling them that she had about 300 under her command, most part of them women, and that if they went back to preach they would beat and knock them all down. Thereafter, a multitude of women came with batons, and stones and clods, and such was the barbarity of the Women-Rabblers, that they were heard to say that all the Presbyterian women that came to worship would be ravished, and the men-rabblers would lie with them.'

As we skirted the Beauly Firth on the approach to Inverness, I looked for sightings of porpoises but to no avail. I realised then that I was gradually losing my powers of observation. I needed to sleep and, on the final leg of the journey back to Keith, decided that my working day was over. It was not incumbent on me to talk to anyone else, which included John and Danny boy.

DAY THREE
Keith – Inverness – Kyle-of-Lochalsh – (Bus) –
Broadford – (Bus) – Armadale – (Ferry) – Mallaig

After copious amounts of John's whisky, I woke with a slight hangover but renewed enthusiasm. Today I would meet the most astounding people who would tell me tales that would boggle the imagination. As ever, John would be a font of knowledge, generally a great help and, today, wouldn't sing.

I wasn't prepared to be met with gales of laughter from the first person I approached. The young man could barely contain his disbelief when I described our mission. I was the maddest person he had ever met. After this affront to my pride, and rebuff to my early morning aspirations, I just listened. He had applied for a welder's job in Tain and was going for an interview. He hadn't dared tell his current employer so had made up a story about a sick auntie needing attention. His family had moved from Shetland so he felt he had to move as well. There was nothing to do in Shetland apart from hanging about at Tesco's. More gales of laughter. And going to the gym. All his pals were either on the rigs or away fishing. 'And the fishing's a family thing.' Beneath the laughter, his loneliness was obvious.

One of the frustrating aspects of this enterprise is not knowing what subsequently happens to the people I meet. Many of the travellers I spoke to described lives that were on

286

the cusp of change. I wanted to know what happened next. Empathetic curiosity or prurient interest? I don't know. Either way, laughing, lonely man, if you read this, please tell me if you got the job. Have you made new friends? Do you go back to Shetland? Did your auntie get better?

'Pray, what did that young man say?'

'You heard as well as me.'

'I could understand nothing of what he said, any more than if we had been in Morocco.'

'It's no wonder, Daniel, that you were a rotten spy if you couldn't understand a word that was said by folk North of the border.'

'Most of the gentlemen I met spoke French so it was more to our convenience to make the common people believe we were French.'

'Less of the common people. This, remember, is the Socialist Republic of Scotland.'

As we approached Nairn station, the conductor wheeled an upright piano into the carriage. He tore off his uniform, put on a silly moustache and a bowler hat, twirled his walking stick with impressive skill and moved with the staccato jerks of a silent movie. After inspecting our tickets he made them disappear behind his ear.

Charlie Chaplin's biographers are agreed that the days he spent in Nairn were some of his happiest.

John broke the spell by claiming that, until recently, the signalman would cycle along the platform as he was in charge of boxes at either end of the station.

We had both looked forward to the journey to Kyle, one of the most iconic routes in the United Kingdom. As these pages testify, we had endured some astonishingly ugly journeys through the industrial heartlands of England, across dystopian landscapes and through endless nondescript suburban sprawl. This was our reward. The route would take us past Raven's Rock, along the shores of Garve, through the forests of Glen Carron towards the brooding Cuillins of Skye: unqualified beauty followed by more of the same.

John and I were two of the younger passengers on the train from Dingwall. A huge party of OAPs, or, more accurately, VERY OAPs, had commandeered the carriage. The noise level was appalling as communal deafness interacted badly with the need to communicate. Apart from one or two bewildered individuals, the entire group bellowed and roared as they failed to lift their suitcases onto overhead racks. Not one of them was going gently into that good night.

The roaring abated as quickly as it had started. Old bottoms found their way onto seats, and eyes closed. Having failed to interest any of them in her Guide to Interesting Stations Through Which We Will Pass, their leader, a stylish youngster in her late fifties, took her seat. This was too good an opportunity to miss. She seemed pleased to chat to any sentient being, and I quickly fell in love. She had a wild past spent hitch-hiking and backpacking her way across the world. I could only guess at the number of lovers she had left broken-hearted. Her best trip ever had been on the Lima to Huancayo train.

'There were armed guards, and the next day the line was bombed by the terrorist group Shining Path, or Sendero Luminoso. The organisation endorsed Maoism, employed guerrilla tactics and wreaked havoc in Peru in the 1990s.'

She claimed to have read one of my earlier books which endeared her to me still more. I asked how she coped with her currently less stimulating life. She said it wasn't without its challenges, and indeed pleasures. She also led tours through European canals and rivers which kept her sane. All the time she was talking, she kept at least one eye on her elderly charges. 'No George, it's not time to get off yet, sit down love.'

Defoe approached, desperate to charm her, but I told him in no uncertain terms to get back to his seat.

I thought I had best return to John who seemed to have something important to say. I was wrong. His current perplexity was trying to make sense of the configuration of worm casts on the shore we were passing. He reacted to my barely disguised disinterest with a scowl, which in turn was interrupted by the woman opposite as criticism for her using her mobile phone. Once we assured her that wasn't the case, we talked.

She was the daughter of the editor of the *West Highland Free Press*, a left leaning newspaper that commands much respect in Scotland. She had lived on Skye for the last thirty years having moved there with her father when she was twelve. She talked of her passion for the island where she works as a waitress for three evenings a week. We discussed the politics of her father's paper and the extent to which the Gaelic slogan on its masthead said it all: An tir, an Canan 'sna Daoine – The land, the language, the people.

'Would your husband be willing to republish my Essay on *Removing National prejudice against Union with Scotland?*'

A young girl looked up from her colouring book and half listened to our conversation. Her mother proudly told us that her daughter had just won a competition at the Mod. The girl herself made a comment in Gaelic and received a gentle reminder from her mum that the language must never be used to exclude others.

I then introduced myself to an old fellow from Harris who, in his time, had been a linesman to the County, or more specifically, a telephone engineer who held the distinction of replacing the last operator-dependent telephones in Britain. Never again, 'Please wait a moment while I connect you', followed by the suspicion that the operator was still on the line, stealing secrets for the purposes of gossip and blackmail. 'In fact,' he said, delivering a much-rehearsed line, 'I spent most of my working days up the pole.'

I returned to John who shared with me one of his more

interesting facts. The large gap between the two tracks at Garve Station was planned deliberately to ensure that a train carrying a fishing boat could safely pass another. I almost forgave him his unwanted thoughts on worm casts. Strange to think that rail was to be the preferred method for taking the fleet across the country. The gap was never put to the test as the plan was cancelled before the line opened.

Defoe was tut-tutting as he stared out of the carriage window.

'What's the matter with you?'

'It is indeed a frightful country full of hideous desert mountains and unpassable, except to the Highlanders who possess the precipices. Here in spite of the most vigorous pursuit, the Highland robbers, such as the famous Rob Roy, find such retreats as none can pretend to follow them.'

'Highland robber is not the best term to describe a national hero.'

John interrupted to point out that we were passing though the estate that gave its name to the Brahan Seer who was credited with foretelling the day 'when long strings of carriages, without horses, shall run between Dingwall and Inverness.' He also predicted the winners in the Grand National of 1968 and was subsequently banned from Ladbrokes, Betfred and Paddy Power.

A small group of protesters met our train at Strome Ferry. They had been there since 1883 and were still objecting to the unloading of fish on a Sunday. Some of them were heavily bandaged, having suffered in the riots during which 200 of their fellow fishermen occupied the railway station. As a consequence, several men were imprisoned. This explained the threadbare banner being held by one of the protesters, RELEASE THE STROME FERRY TEN.

Some of these facts were stolen from a leaflet purchased from the Friends of the Kyle Line or, more specifically, from the charming daughter of the man who founded the Friends. She seemed quite happy to be exploited as a slave by her despotic father, and even offered me a certificate confirming that I had indeed travelled on this famous line. Why is it that only really attractive lines are supported by Friends, when many lines are much more needy? What about Middlesbrough to Hartlepool or Sunderland to Newcastle? There is no justice.

John pointed out Duncraig Castle and told me that the original owner had built it with the proceeds from the opium trade. James Mathieson would import Opium into China in exchange for tea. To celebrate the dubious source of his wealth, he had his ceilings adorned with plaster mouldings of poppies.

'Didn't you get involved in the opium trade, Daniel?'

'I'd rather not say.'

Now in fine form, John told me that, as in rural India, cattle, until recently, had the right of way in the village of Plockton. After a marauding cow killed a seventy-four-year-old English tourist, measures were introduced in 2003 to curb their freedom to roam.

At Kyle of Lochalsh we took the first of two buses to Armadale on Skye; the only sensible way to bridge the gap between the two rail termini.

Defoe commandeered the front seat next to the driver and stared enraptured at the passing scenery. 'My heart swells,' he declared thumping his chest. 'Why did I neglect to visit this most remarkable of islands? Was it madness that I preferred London to these vistas of unsurpassed beauty?'

DAY FOUR
Mallaig – Crianlarich – Oban –
Dumbarton Central – Bellgrove, Glasgow

Unable to locate the fleshpots of Mallaig, we wandered into a pub near the harbour. The television set was home to a malicious goblin who knew how to turn the screen blank whenever a player looked like scoring in a much anticipated football match.

Further irritation was provided by the landlord's dog which had the unamusing skill of standing on its hind legs and punching a front paw into the nearest male groin. Soon most of the men in the bar were either doubled over or covering their genitals like defensive players facing a free kick. John observed that the dog would be a match for the honey badger. I made the mistake of asking him to explain.

Apparently, the honey badger does not live up to its innocent sounding name. It is among the most vicious of creatures, whose preferred method of attack is to grab the bollocks of its adversary in its teeth. It is a member of the weasel family; emits loud grunting sounds when mating; is one of the few species capable of using tools; can dig a tunnel into hard ground in ten minutes and possesses an anal pouch, the smell of which is suffocating. It was time for bed.

We had been told that the Fishermen's Mission opened at silly o'clock in the morning, and so it proved. What ensured that this was the finest breakfast venue we had sampled so far, was the fact that it doubled as the biggest second-hand bookshop in the west coast of Scotland. Its clientele was equally unexpected, prime among whom was the cowboy with leather hat, bandana, waistcoat and cow print chaps.

On Mallaig station I spoke to an immensely tall American from Seattle. He and his wife were Sinologists who had spent much of their professional lives in China. When I asked him why, he replied, 'Because the Chinese women are so attractive.' This was the cue for the attractive young Chinese women in their party to emerge from the shelter and simper in his direction.

Defoe was jumping on the spot with rage.

'The Chinese people are sordid slaves and wretches. A miserable people oppressed by grasping mandarins.'

'Pardon? You can't just come out with stuff like that.'

'Let me quote my own dear Crusoe: "but when I come to compare the miserable people of that country with ours, their fabrics, their manner of living, their governments, their religions, their wealth, their glories, as some call it, I must confess I do not so much as think it worth naming, or worth my while to write of."'

The rain partly obscured the views of Eigg and Rum, and I failed to locate Ben Knox's shack on the beach at Morar, or see Burt Lancaster dangling his watch over a rock pool in a transcendent moment that marked his acceptance of the languid rhythms of rural life. My own local hero, John, was eager to point out the formerly private station at Beasdale.

More impressive were the glimpses of the Atlantic before we disappeared into the darkness of successive tunnels. Perhaps we had exceeded our quota of beauty and had to put more money into the slot before we could wallow once more in the spectacular vistas.

As the steam-hauled Jacobite train was waiting for us to cross the Glenfinnan viaduct, I felt that we were entering a different reality. This location was so familiar from Harry Potter and tourist literature that we were entering deeper into the land of cliché and the banal. Time to talk.

The young man had just competed in the St Kilda Challenge, having helped crew one of the 27 yachts that crossed to the remote archipelago. He was still glowing from sheer joy. He had responded to an advertisement and been chosen to crew with four elderly Scotsmen whose love of the sea matched their love of whisky. He agreed that the company of elderly Scotsmen was not for the faint-hearted. When he described landing on the island I tried hard to suppress the jealousy I felt.

In the overhead luggage rack something was moving in a black bin liner. Suddenly a single beak emerged and within seconds a host of puffins and fulmars were squawking their raucous way through the carriage. Wiping the bird shit from my arm, I listened again to the far from ancient mariner.

Having a forestry degree, he was employed selling woodlands in North Wales. He had experienced a life-changing motorbike accident in Thailand, and since then had a much stronger sense of his own mortality. He agreed that it was better to have these intimations when young rather than at my age when the pages are peeled from the calendar with an ominous rapidity. He tried to interest me in a small copse but I politely declined.

Oddly, and for no obvious reason, he mentioned having lived in East Grinstead. After our traumatic time in that town, I felt a cold chill and looked at the mariner again. Was he an alien sent by deviant scientologists to capture and enslave John and me?

Just in case, I moved to sit alongside a retired fisherman from Orkney and his wife. He was happy to talk about the dangers he had endured over the years. Being swept overboard was a common occurrence and was usually the result of becoming entangled in the ropes. 'Most of the time we got them back.' The main risk to safety, he said, was tiredness.

'Read *My Humble Proposal to the People of England* in which I mention that it cannot be said and with justice that the Scots fishermen are negligent, and do not improve this fishery to advantage.'

'Noted.'

'Whales in abundance frequent the Islands of Fladden, Orkney, and Lewis; 114 ran ashore on the island of Orkney in the year 1691. Cod, tusk, and ling are caught in vast plenty upon all their coasts. Haddocks, Sturgeon, Turbot, Trouts, Perch, Pike, Scate, Greybeard, Mackerel, Keeling, Whiting, Sea-urchin, Cat-fish, Cock-padle, Lyths, Spirlings, Soles, Flukes, Garvie, Eels, are also caught on the Scottish coasts in great plenty.'

'Thank you Defoe, I think you're showing off now.

Anyway, what sort of fish is a Cock-padle? Would I really eat a Cock-padle supper?'

'Otters, whose skins are useful for muffs, are very numerous in the Isles. Shell-fish of all sorts as Lobsters, Crabs, Oysters are also found in vast Quantities in the Western islands; the latter so large that they must be cut in three or four Pieces to be eaten.'

'Stop it now.'

'Cockles, Mussels, Wilks, Scallops, and Sprats are cast by the tide, in such numbers, on the isles, that the people cannot consume them.'

Meanwhile the Orcadian fisherman was telling us that the strangest thing that happened to him at sea was being beckoned ashore by the lighthouse keeper on Flannan Isle ... In that instant, I shed forty years and was performing Wilfred Wilson Gibson's poem to a captivated (possibly merely captive) audience of first year pupils. The tale of the abandoned lighthouse and the untouched meal is certainly up there with the Marie Celeste.

At Crianlarich station John toyed with the idea of making a citizen's arrest on the young trolley attendant he discovered enjoying a fly smoke between two sheds on the platform. 'It's an offence!' he boomed. The poor girl assumed her end had come, and offered him half of the day's takings before he grudgingly relented and warned her not to repeat the pernicious act. I personally considered that the Japanese tourists excitedly taking pictures of a railing and a sign to the toilet were more deserving of censure.

On the Oban train I took a risk and spoke to a young girl on her own. This was generally against the rules. She was French and, oddly, I felt less embarrassed interrogating her in her own language than in English. She was studying Asian Anthropology in Paris. There again, she could have been studying astrology, astronomy or astrophysics and I may not have picked up on the detail. She was an advocate of *le camping sauvage* and had been walking for eight days.

I abandoned my hugely impressive multilingual discourse, thanked her, returned to my seat, and gazed at the desolation of Rannoch Moor...a country lying as waste as the sea; only the moorfowl and the peewees crying upon it, and far over to the East, a herd of deer, moving like dots. Much of it was red with heather; much of the rest broken up with bogs and hags and peaty pools. At least that is how it appeared to Robert Louis Stevenson as he plotted the travails of David Balfour and Alan Breck.

'Who is Robert Louis Stevenson? My Tour should provide sufficient points of comparison without reference to hack wordsmiths.'

'Are you jealous?'

'My works speak for themselves.'

John, having failed to interest me in the intricacies of cattle docks(?), explained the system of trip wires intended to stop rocks falling onto the tracks from the slopes of Ben Cruachan. The system was known by train drivers as Anderson's piano because of the noise it made when the wind blew. Irrespective of what it was called, and despite it producing the music of the spheres, the system failed to prevent a derailment in 2010.

Meanwhile, a German tourist, camera pressed hard against the window, was cursing the trees for obscuring the views. It was difficult to know to whom he should complain.

The brief stop in Oban gave John and me sufficient time to recover from each other's company. My mood was certainly improved by buying a facsimile of Shakespeare's third folio for a pittance in a charity shop.

We couldn't help but eavesdrop on the two third year boys commuting from Oban to Dalmally. The bigger of the two was teasing the other about his lateness, accusing him of walking a girl home before he got the train. Judging by the ferocious blush that followed this accusation, his friend had hit the mark.

My final victim of the day was a physics student from Glasgow who was returning from having helped a vulnerable man climb Ben Nevis. When not studying, he worked in a karate club in Paisley whose clients all suffered from crises of confidence or mental health challenges, such as a man who wouldn't leave his house after he had been brushed aside, bullied, and sent to the back of the queue in a fish and chip shop.

'After attending the karate club for several weeks, he's a different man. He has friends. He talks a lot. He's now more than capable of holding his own in that, or indeed any other, fish and chip shop,' the student said.

It did feel like a descent into Glasgow as the chrysanthemums and faded CND signs gave way to mile on mile of barbed wire hiding bland, windowless buildings. We were running parallel to the Clyde and Faslane and the river was screened by thick vegetation and trees. I have never thought of Mutually Assured Destruction without seeing the manic eyes of Alfred E Neuman staring from the cover of the American comic. John assumed the role of doomsayer by peeling back the hillside and pointing to the warren of Dr Strangelove tunnels housing nuclear warheads. He also reminded me that this was once the stamping ground of Harry Lauder.

'The defence of the realm is the paramount duty of all patriots.'

Our own sense of unease was compounded by an altercation taking place at the end of our carriage. A man with no ticket but lots of empty lager cans was telling the conductor what he could do with his officious ways. 'I'm not taking abuse like that,' said the custodian of rectitude who returned to his cubbyhole to summon the police. Two officers boarded the train at the next stop. Our foul-mouthed rebel carefully placed the empty cans in the litter bin and surrendered into their welcoming arms.

There was something both familiar and comforting about the red sandstone tenements of Dalmuir. We had been *Roamin' in the Gloamin*; we had *Kept Right on To The End of the Road*; and I did *Love a Lassie* whom I would see soon.

DAY FIVE
Glasgow Central – Stranraer – Kilmarnock – Glasgow Central

John appraised the rolling stock in Glasgow Central: 'Blood and custard'. I assumed he was answering a question I had not asked about his breakfast choice. I already knew that the old Great Western Railway carriages were described as chocolate and cream; this was just something else I had learned.

My next mistake was in assuming the German engineer was Dutch. This never goes down well. He was *en route* to Ayr, 'To take photo of old Victorian seaside resort.'

'Clearly a spy,' Defoe whispered.

We talked about Berlin. 'The city gets younger every year.' Not like Ayr, I thought. 'Soon I will have to leave Berlin as I will be too old. And I will have a cup of tea!' I suggested he try a few pints and get a real sense of a faded British seaside resort. The conversation was just about holding together. And then he said to me, 'I'm looking at landscape. I not have time for talking.' That was me told. I slunk back to my seat while he took a photo of a sign hanging in Kilmarnock station: COMMUNITY RAIL PARTNERSHIP.

'Ayr, a sea-port,' said Defoe. 'Like an old beauty, it shows the ruins of a good face; but it is also apparently not only decayed and declined, but decaying and declining every day, and from being the fifth town in Scotland, as the townsmen say, is now like a place forsaken.'

There were only two other people in the carriage. The first was also German. Already the day was feeling quite odd. He was walking the Southern Uplands and worked in a kindergarten. 'I just need silence in my head after the kids.'

The last man in the carriage was returning to his home in Girvan after night shift at A&E. Ex-military, he hated civilian life. He also had little time for Russians.

Having spoken to everyone in the carriage, it was time to play Defoe at his own game. What would he have said at this point? 'The Isle of Arran was clearly visible, and we could just discern the Paps of Jura in the distant Inner Hebrides. At Girvan we had a commanding view of Ailsa Craig squatting on the horizon like a dumpling.'

Defoe stopped drumming his fingers on the armrest in a particularly irritating manner, and looked up.

'Ah, a pastiche! I approve. Dumpling is very good.'

The bleak countryside south of Barrhill has been compared to the Falklands, which might explain the thin line of soldiers yomping along the horizon. I had never understood this military term, and was now none the wiser. Close to the track we saw several Argentinian boy soldiers cowering in foxholes.

'The common people here not only are poor, they look poor; they appear dejected and discouraged, as if they have given over all hopes of ever being otherwise than what they are.'

It was pishing in Stranraer where we had three hours to spend before the return train. John was more than happy to spend all 180 minutes in the bleak waiting room. Being of a more manly disposition, I strode through horizontal rain towards the town.

Three quick and very wet tours of all inhabited streets were long enough for me to note the prevalence of bored Alsatians growling menacingly from front windows. The exception was the Alsatian being driven up the high street in the passenger seat of a small car. Several strangers smiled at me wistfully, as if they too remembered the day they first set foot in Stranraer. The town does have an ominously large number of voluntary sector organisations offering victim support.

The museum, admission free, promised respite from the deluge. To justify dripping all over the well-appointed municipal space, I feigned interest in several large agricultural implements and a wooden spoon found in a local bog. I met a nice old lady in the education wing who pointed to the children's play area. 'Wouldn't it be nice,' she said, 'to dress up as a lion?' I knew exactly what she meant. While I have neither sympathy nor understanding for grown men who want to be dressed in nappies, I knew what she meant. Then it occurred to me that her husband, who was lurking in the background, would probably hit us with his walking stick unless we stopped.

The next refuge was the public library where I tried to buy a booklet on Stranraer in the Second World War. The librarian handed my not insignificant change to someone else in the queue. After a brief exchange about the redistribution of wealth he relented and returned my money.

As all cafes were packed to the gunnels and well beyond the plimsoll line, I made the mistake of going into a Wetherspoons look-alike pub for a coffee. Before I reached the bar I was aware of a man talking loudly, while nursing a midday pint. I assumed he was talking into a Bluetooth device, but no, his surreal monologue was addressed to me. 'It's 540 miles, and that's from Keswick. I'm no Button or Schumacher but no one overtakes me, know what I mean? That's at least five gallons of diesel. Do you know that place on the outskirts of Bo'ness?' There was a difficult moment as he waited for me to respond to his direct question. 'I know the place well,' I lied. Our encounter continued in this vein until the arrival of my coffee gave me an excuse to forsake his company.

I trudged back through the rain. I don't think I was yomping by any stretch of the imagination. The seagulls screeched at me: 'What did you expect? What did you expect?'

JOURNEY NINE

The Scottish Borders and Fife

DAY ONE
Glasgow Central – Haymarket – Dunfermline Town –
Glenrothes – Inverkeithing – Perth – Stirling – Alloa –
Stirling – Waverley – Tweedbank – Waverley –
North Berwick – Waverley – Bellgrove

The day didn't start well. Because of the weather, John and I took a taxi from my house to Central Station. 'Glasgow has become a shit hole, so it has,' was the taxi driver's idea of a friendly greeting to his first customers of the day.

'It's manky. It's a disgrace! Look at the f****** pavements, man.' John and I peered out. 'All they pensioners, they pay into the fund all their days, and what do they get? F*** all! A've left Glasgow. I live in Balloch. I'm not bringing my kids up here. And they street lights, for f**** sake! Hauf of them are switched off at night. It just needs one wee girl to be raped. Building all they homes for foreigners ...'

The exchange coloured my outlook on the day. I became aware that I was obsessively checking that my phone, note-book, spectacles and pen were in different pockets. This involved me patting each pocket in sequence, which wasn't a good sign.

'I don't think Glasgow is a shit hole,' said Defoe who had been reflecting on the taxi driver's judgement. 'Glasgow is, indeed, a very fine city. 'Tis the cleanest and beautifullest, and best built city in Britain, London excepted.'

Despite his enthusiasm for Glasgow, Defoe, once again, wanted us to spend more time in Edinburgh than our schedule permitted.

'Can we not visit the Chamber of Rarities where they have several skeletons of strange creatures, a mummy, and other curious things?'

'No,' I said. 'We will see many strange creatures in Fife. Trust me.'

'Humpff.'

As we crossed the Forth Bridge, I peered down to the concrete building on the Island of Inchgarvie with its black spaces for windows, and staircases that lead nowhere. 'Why didn't you mention the islands in the Forth in your Tour?' Defoe was disconcerted by the question and whistled tunelessly under his breath. 'Is it because of its history? It was a prison, wasn't it? Did you visit when you were recruiting informers in Scotland prior to the Union?'

There was suddenly no sign of Defoe; it was as if he had merged into the upholstery.

On the other side we could see the two halves of the new Queensferry Crossing leaning towards each other, fingertips outstretched in a parody of Michelangelo's Creation of Adam.

The Fife Circle is not the one that Dante forgot. Rather it is the configuration of lines that links the faded resorts of Burntisland and Aberdour to the former mining communities of Cowdenbeath and Cardenden, with the historic town of Dunfermline thrown in for good measure.

John was at his best peeling back the landscape to reveal an industrial past and significant rural poverty. His specialist area was identifying overgrown railway sidings

302

that previously carried coal and troops. My flagging concentration flagged further when he waxed lyrical about a new coupling system developed by the Germans.

Defoe's mood had also deteriorated since my untactful reference to his career in espionage. He stared at Dunfermline and muttered.

'A town in its full perfection of decay ... There is a decayed monastery ... here is a decayed court. The palace is sinking into its own ruins; the windows are gone, the roof fallen in ... here is a decayed town.'

The main point of interest at Stirling station was the absence of a platform numbered 1. Platform numbers 2-10 were well signposted but of 1 there was no sign. Had it been sold?

A small exhibition paid tribute to John Grierson, a Stirling man, and father of documentary film-making who produced *Night Mail* as an advertising feature for the Royal Mail. The clickety-clack of W H Auden's voice-over must be imprinted on the frontal lobes of a generation that was in thrall to the railways. Did he stand on Platform 1 as the mail train steamed its way through Stirling in the 1930s?

All Scotland waits for her: In the dark glens, besides the pale-green sea lochs Men long for News.

John had been looking forward to travelling on the newly opened Edinburgh to Tweedbank line. Judging by the commotion, so too had the party of pensioners. For some reason one of their number was manoeuvring his Zimmer backwards down the corridor. Next an old boy in a cap stood up and, to much laughter, told Maisie that she was not to strip on the train. Whether train travel usually had this effect on Maisie, we never discovered. Perhaps her care home overlooked a track and when dusk fell, she would pull back the curtains and whip off her drawers for the benefit of tired commuters. Good on you, Maisie.

'How many books have you written?' was the elderly man's response to my usual preamble/excuse for interrupting strangers.

'This will be my fifth.'

'Ha! I've written eleven!'

What was this, an authorial competition? Would he challenge me to arm wrestling? Or a who-can-pee-highest-up-a-wall competition? Donald C.B. Cameron, according to christianstogether.net, is a former Council Member of the Soldiers' and Airmen's Scripture Readers' Association and Prophetic Witness Movement International. I had met my match.

'Well, I have 241 publications to my name, and countless other works wrongly attributed to me...'

'Now, don't you join in.' I was, however, pleased that Defoe's spirits had revived.

The eighty-one-year-old ex-Russian translator had the demeanour of an Old Testament prophet, which must help when that is your chosen topic. I thought it best not to raise the issue of Ezekiel's vision of a new temple or indeed Zephaniah's view that the day of the Lord will be 'a day of wrath – a day of distress and anguish, a day of trouble and ruin, a day of darkness and gloom, a day of clouds and blackness.' Goodness knows, I had endured enough of those on my travels.

I was on safer ground with rugby players of whom there were many on this train. The trouble is, the players I spoke to seemed unfamiliar with the concept of putting one word in front of another and seeing where that leads. Perhaps they were all harbouring concussions and needed time to remember their names.

The exception was Fraser Renwick, a bright young member of the Scottish under-20 squad. He and his girlfriend were returning from an international competition in Manchester, and looking forward to a night out in

Edinburgh. 'England won,' he said with bitterness. She commented that his hunger for success led to him becoming marginally obsessed, but she accompanied this with such a doting smile that you knew she was proud of him. He was modest and passionate, and I will look out for his name on future international team sheets.

'Excuse me, aren't you the fellow travelling on every mile of railway in the United Kingdom?' The man had followed me out of his seat and down the aisle. I recognised him instantly. It was the lovely poet I had met several months previously on the train in South Wales.

I remember you well,' I said. 'You're David Whitmarsh, the man who has a house, who has friends, who has enough.' He told me he was taking a fortnight's holiday from his duties as unofficial bard to the County of Worcestershire.

He returned to his seat where he spent a moment scribbling. 'Not finished yet,' he said, 'but it's a start.' He handed me a leaflet advertising the John Buchan Museum. On it he had written:

The Spell

Tender words spell out a smile
Through blushing lips
The worried brow no more conceals
An aching heart.
Thoughts encrusted;
A vibrant portent manifest
By a sorcerer's wand.

'I will put it in the book,' I said.
'Will you really?'
The encounter was the highlight of all my journeys. Perhaps it was a portent. Perhaps a sorcerer was responsible

for this most extraordinary of coincidences. Who knows, perhaps the encounter had been foretold somewhere in the Old Testament.

When we passed through Drem, I thought I would treat John to a dose of his own medicine by passing on a completely useless piece of information. 'Ah, we are near to the flag museum.' Better that if you can.

'Athelstaneford,' he replied promptly. 'The flag heritage centre lies to the rear of the church in a lectern doocot built in 1583.'

I knew when I was beaten.

DAY TWO

Bellgrove – Springburn – Cumbernauld –
Motherwell – Lanark – Cambuslang – Larkhall –
Hamilton Central – Glasgow Central – Whifflet –
Glasgow Central – Neilston – Cathcart –
Glasgow Central – East Kilbride – Glasgow Central –
Partick – Balloch – Westerton – Milngavie –
Hyndland – Queen Street – Bellgrove

Of all our itineraries, this felt the most daunting. John had organised a series of forays along the many arteries that flow from Glasgow's heart. It felt like a punishment for some seriously bad sins.

Initially we hugged the Forth and Clyde canal before being sucked into a dark green corridor; a lush sleeve of vegetation through which we were permitted glimpses of sandstone tenements, modern estates and fields of tan coloured cows.

Defoe was delighted to see the canal.

'I knew it!'

'What?'

'I always knew how easy a work it would be to form a

navigation of art from the Forth to the Clyde, and so join the two seas.'

Cumbernauld has had a bad press. The town has won the *Plook on the Plinth* award on two occasions, and was runner up to Aberdeen in 2015. This may suggest that things are getting better. *The Daily Mirror* took delight in nominating Cumbernauld as the worst place to live in the United Kingdom. These awards are unhelpful. No captain of industry, or indeed cabin boy, will wake from a dream shouting, 'We will relocate to Cumbernauld. The angels have told me!'

By the same unwritten law that had applied to all our journeys, we had a lengthy period to test the legitimacy of these unwanted accolades.

In the absence of any signage, I turned left outside the station and followed a thin tarmac path into a dead end. It might not have been a dead end. It was possible that the path had surrendered under the weight of weeds. Beyond this jungle, several semi-derelict business premises leaned against each other for mutual support. If this was a maze I had failed to find either the Minotaur or the way out. Putting this dystopian foray to the back of my mind, I returned to the station and started again. John was sitting where I left him, sunk in torpor and inertia.

I followed an underpass that promised to lead me to the town centre which was only fifteen minutes away. I was soon hopelessly lost which was quite an achievement as I had been directed along an elevated walkway from which there was no escape. After fifteen minutes I was standing with a group of parents outside a primary school, all of whom were staring at me suspiciously.

Back on the walkway, I asked a woman for directions. She was helpfulness personified and I felt would have led me though fire to put me on the straight and narrow. Her two large dogs were less keen. They both reared onto their back legs, risking strangulation, salivating at the thought of sinking fangs into slightly tough pensioner flesh.

The streets were carless, bleak and oddly quiet. Tight terraced houses opened directly onto the street and must have been modelled on sepia representations of community life in the 1950s. But there were no women in curlers and housecoats, gossiping as they brought in the milk. There was just a sense of sadness.

Ubiquitous grey pebbledash suggested the pallor of sickness. Two council workers aimed their weed guns at tiny plants emerging hopefully from retaining walls, and ignored the broken windows and doors hanging drunkenly from lock-ups. My stint of investigative journalism was over. As the town centre remained elusive I wouldn't presume to comment on its beauty or otherwise.

Behind the station, a black corrugated waste disposal factory moaned as things were ground, compacted and crushed. For a moment my spirits joined them.

The train to Motherwell was empty, another manifestation of the alienation that had characterised my day. John, however, informed me that we were experiencing the rebalancing-stock movements which were common practice after rush hour.

A marshalling yard was swamped with bright red shipping containers proclaiming their loyalty to HAMBERG SUD, and I assumed that the entire German city had been bought and would, any day now, be reassembled somewhere in the central belt of Scotland. I caught myself idly visiting bierkellers in my head, before walking to St Pauli's football stadium. This impression of demolition and relocation was reinforced by the sounds of pneumatic drills which provided the aural backcloth to every station.

In Lanark our carriage stopped at a ninety-degree angle to a narrow street at the end of which was the biggest crucifix I had ever seen. CALVARY screamed a sign attached to the adjacent church building. Religion mutated into Death in Cambuslang station. Platform 2 is overlooked by several haphazardly leaning tombstones, overspill from the ornamental stonemasons that have a property in the High Street. I left the station and took a moment to inspect their products.

Why, I wondered, had so many of the headstones already been engraved with precise names and dates? There were at least five possible explanations: First, the intended recipients, having notified already grieving relatives, decided not to die after all and recovered. Second, the names of various creditors had been carved into the stones as a warning, the Lanarkshire equivalent of waking up next to a horse's head. Third, they had been rejected by the grieving family for whom no memorial would ever be good enough. Fourth, the stones had been stolen from the local churchyard and were waiting to be recycled. Fifth, the firm was wonderfully prescient and knew exactly which of the residents would be next to shuffle off. All other suggestions welcome.

One of the strangest statues (clearly visible from Platform 2) is of a young footballer circa 1950 with bronze hair plastered flat. One of the boy's hands is bent backwards at an unnatural angle suggesting that his death was preceded by an act of torture.

As we climbed down the steps to Platform 1, Defoe was eager to talk. He had seemed nervous all morning. I think he too had a sense of our journey ending. His chosen topic was swearing.

'Far from what it is in England, you hear no oaths or profane words in the streets here.'

'You must have been asleep when we got that taxi yesterday morning.'

'If a mean boy, such as we call shoe-blackers, or blackguard boys, should be heard to swear, the next gentleman in the street, if any happened to be near, would cane him and correct him; whereas in England, nothing is more frequent, or less regarded now, than the most horrid oaths and blasphemies in the open streets.'

I was still mulling over these observations when a lad in his late teens roared into his phone as he paced the platform, 'I'm no taking you f****** shopping the first time we meet.' I assumed he was negotiating the ground rules for a first date.

'I went shopping with ma maw once, but no again. She'd been awfy good to me, mind. I wanted to give her a wee treat. I'm off to see my uncle in Blantyre. Ye can come wi' me if you want. You cannae walk down the street without meeting a f****** bampot. The town's hooching with them. Last time I seen him, was in a pub wi' that woman. Aggie, ken, Saggy Aggie... Shaggy Aggie. She wis mingin'! "Who's that?" I asked. "That's ma bird," he said. F*** me, I thought.'

Agnes, whoever and wherever you are, I hope you have not bought this book.

Strict adherence to the itinerary meant that we were crisscrossing the Clyde. Every time I see the river I instinctively look for the Humane Society's rowing boat. The organisation was formed in 1790 to meet a specific need. At that time, suicide was a criminal act, and anyone who went to rescue a drowning person from the river could be tried for being an accessory to a crime. There can be few more satisfying jobs than saving people from drowning or indeed bleaker tasks than rowing endlessly up and down the filthy water looking for bodies, pulling them aboard and returning them to the authorities or distraught relatives. The latest incumbent is George Parsonage. Now in his 70s, George has, over his lifetime, rescued more than 1500 people including the woman he eventually married.

'If a man were drowning, and another came to his aid, would the drowning man ask his helper's religion before sticking out his hand?'

'Not even in Glasgow, Danny.'

The train moved through a succession of tunnels as we

approached Central Station. Glimmers of light shone from subterranean alcoves; a teasing strobe effect that left no clear images, only a sense of forgotten vaults. At one point the vaults merged to reveal an abandoned station, but in an instant it was gone.

On Milngavie station I spoke to a woman with grandson and guide dog. She was entertaining the former and training the latter. She explained the training process which takes at least two years. Not all dogs make the grade. However, rather than being shot for failing, or humanely put down, most become assistant or mentor dogs.

Defoe wanted to pat the dog. He looked sad.

'What's up, Daniel?'

'Nothing.'

'Didn't you go blind towards the end of your life?'

He looked away.

The woman explained that her grandson had autism and loved trains and railways. He enjoyed memorising station names and the numbers on carriages. Speaking as someone who could probably live quite happily at the end of several spectrums, I hope his gift brought him pleasure.

I always enjoy the approach to Balloch and the journey parallel to the Clyde basin. The approach to the harbour still functions as a ships' graveyard. Wooden rib cages stick out of the silt, and trawler deckhouses tilt into the water. I realise this is not the first time that I have attempted to wax lyrical about half-sunken boats viewed from railway lines and, to be honest, it is a fascination I don't fully understand. The basin features prominently on the Urban Ghosts website. I just wished we could have got the train fifty years earlier and been able to gawp at a steam trawler, a World War Two minesweeper and a torpedo boat.

Meanwhile Defoe had leapt to his feet and clutched at his brow.

'Inspiration!' he cried. 'It was something you said ... I see him now, my man. I will call him Crusoe. He is shipwrecked. Yes ... but the ship struck upon a sand, and in a moment the sea broke over her in such a manner that we expected we should all have perished immediately ... a raging wave, mountain-like, came rolling astern of us ...'

Back in the present, I spoke to my second young French woman in as many days. She was also a student walking through Scotland on her own whose ambition was to open a hostel in the Highlands. These spasmodic encounters with young enthusiastic travellers were emerging as a highlight of our pilgrimage across the kingdom.

In the interests of balance, I approached a grizzled, dishevelled and rain-soaked man in his forties. He was instantly deferential and called me Sir. I wish people wouldn't do that. It speaks of a personal history characterised by sadness and ultimately by dependence on professional staff for guidance and practical help. He was *en route* to see his support worker in Dalreoch. He couldn't work, health issues, he said. 'No jobs in Alexandria unless you're good with computers.' I wished I could take a tiny bit of the French girl's hope and give it to this man. She had plenty and wouldn't miss a soupçon.

Earlier, I had seen him being harangued by the conductor over an anomaly with his ticket, a recurring feature of this train. Mother and daughter, both ravaged by time and poverty, produced a whole fistful of cards with which they attempted to pay for their ticket. Card after card was inserted and rejected. Eventually the conductor lost the will to argue, shrugged and moved on.

John, who had been surprisingly quiet on the journey so far, showed renewed signs of life as we passed through Pollokshields East. The source of his animation was a malevolent plantation of hogweed with flowers the shape and size of satellite dishes. 'Nasty blisters,' he said, 'they should do something about it. It's dangerous stuff. You could seriously hurt someone with one of those stalks.' This brought such a bizarre thought to mind, that I had to give it an airing.

'So,' I ventured, 'you could chase your worst enemy through the streets with a stalk of hogweed, catch him, debag him and beat him across the arse until he blistered.'

'That would work.'

Perhaps we had spent too long in each other's company. We both stared out of the window at Hampden Park, a field of dreams and nightmares in equal measure for most men in Scotland.

DAY THREE
Glasgow Central – Largs – Ardrossan South Beach –
Ardrossan Harbour – Paisley Gilmour St – Gourock –
Port Glasgow – Wemyss Bay – Glasgow Central –
Paisley Canal – Glasgow Central – Anniesland –
Springburn – Glasgow Queen Street

The last day of travel. The culmination, the climax, completion. The day on which the rail network would finally surrender its secrets leaving us both sated and fulfilled. A day worthy of celebration as John and I had, apart from a few moments, stayed friends.

Defoe too seemed on good form.

'The country between Paisley and Glasgow, on the bank of Clyde, I take to be one of the most agreeable places in Scotland, take its situation, its fertility, healthiness, the nearness of Glasgow, the neighbourhood of the sea, and altogether, at least, I may say, I saw none like it.'

This mood of positivity seemed at odds with the man opposite, staring ahead with haunted eyes. What was he seeing? What fears did the day hold? What had been said last night? Was the situation retrievable? And then he fell asleep.

A red car with two eyeholes punched in its pixelated

313

windscreen stood in the middle of a scrap yard. Had the driver and passenger both survived? Had they been attacked by enemies? Was there blood on the upholstery? No, this didn't feel like a day of epiphany and fulfilment.

Nevertheless, the first person I spoke to smiled when I told him my reason for travel, and his eyes sparkled. He was on his way to Kilwinning where he worked valeting cars. He used to work in the building trade. 'But you've got to pay the bills, man. I've got two kids, nine and three with my partner. I've got no real interests. I follow the football a bit. There's no time for anything, man, not with work and the kids. I don't have pals, man.' I asked him where they had gone, but he didn't know.

Each station at which we stopped was displaying a poster with the face of a frightened young boy in front of the words, *140,000 children go missing in the UK every year. Help us bring them home.* This was a stark and disturbing thought. How many of these children had John and I glimpsed on our travels? Where had they gone? Abducted, murdered, sold? Why hadn't we helped them? Seeing me distracted, John told me of a time when he had been with a party on Cumbrae whose main pastime was hitting golf balls at the passing ferry. When this failed to dispel images of lost children, he described with much relish the celebrated Largs railway accident, which ended when the train demolished several buildings before parking itself in the taxi rank.

As we entered Ardrossan, I noticed the outline of the castle squatting in a housing estate. Our itinerary meant that we had fifty-two minutes in the town before catching the next train. By idly googling the castle I discovered that it was reputedly haunted by William Wallace, had associations with the devil who left an imprint of his hoof on one of the rocks, and had a scary crypt nicknamed Wallace's dungeon. Believing, not unreasonably, that this must be the place where many of the 140,000 children were being kept against their will, I decided to play the tourist. Time was tight but it could be done if I ran. I crossed the links and was nearly squashed flat by an over-enthusiastic bus driver who thought that I wanted him to stop. I declined graciously, reassembled my limbs, and jogged into the estate.

The castle was looming ever larger, but the railway line was between us. Now, a little obsessed with my mission, I ran back to the station. An elderly Dutch couple gave me directions far too long to memorise. The postman did likewise but accompanied his words with some helpful pointing.

Curtains twitched as alarmed residents noticed that an old man had escaped from his care home and was running down their street. I found myself in the Parkhouse Community Garden, which, while admirably well-tended, was not where I wanted to be.

Another sprint and for the second time in as many days, I found myself in a primary school playground. This was not going to plan. Perhaps this was what yomping meant.

Two more streets and I was in the car park of Ardrossan Winton Rovers Junior Football Club. For the record, and for followers of minor football, it is a neat little ground but the team finished twelfth and were relegated from the West of Scotland Super League in season 2015-16.

I was completely bloody lost.

Ardrossan Castle had been spirited away by the devil, it had sunk into the ground. It was as elusive as Brigadoon. It was the Holy Grail of our pilgrimage across the whole of Great Britain and I had failed to find it or, indeed, rescue any of the missing children.

Pouring with sweat, I made it back to the station with two minutes to spare. 'Where on earth have you been?' asked John.

I settled back on the train and was looking forward to a period of reflection, during which I would attempt to put our thirty-seven-day journey into some perspective and work out what it all meant, but that was not an option. The two men behind us were bellowing at each other.

'There's never a dull moment, Big Man, a've jist got a summons to appear in court tomorrow. F***'s sake, what a load of s****! Have to talk to my lawyer this evening. She's just dug herself into a hole, ah'm telling you, man. And ah say to her, "what about my rights?" And she's s****** some bloke. At least that's what one of the boys said after a recent visit. I thought she was out jogging, or visiting a pal ... The dog was the only thing she left me. She took the laminate floor, she smashed up the kitchen, took all the light bulbs. Her dad was allergic to the dog. That's why she left it. I was offered a job at sea, but I couldn't take the dog. Turned the job down.'

'If you lock a dog in the boot of a car for five hours, when you open the boot, the dog's pleased to see you.'

There was a lot to think about here. Meanwhile John did his best to dispel some of the dark clouds left hovering by these revelations. He reminisced about his time in Greenock, and described how he and a pal would regularly row across the water to Kilcreggan to get to the pub. 'We had fun avoiding the large ships in the dark on the return journey ...'

'Greenock. The town is well built. It is the chief town on the west of Scotland for the herring industry ...'

'Now, don't start giving me lists of fish again.'

As we wandered through the rail terminus at Greenock, John expressed surprise that I had never heard of Operation Mincemeat which had its origin in the vicinity. As a jape to confuse the rotten Huns, a dead tramp named Glyndwr Martin, who had died after injecting rat poison, was taken by submarine to Spanish waters and left to float about until discovered by local fishermen, who assumed that he had been involved in an air crash. Glyndwr's pockets had been filled with secret orders from on high, and other items intended to mislead any suspicious authorities. These included the photograph of an imaginary fiancée, love letters, an engagement ring, a pompous letter from his 'Dad', and a message from Lloyd's Bank demanding payment of an overdraft of £79 19s 2d. As far as we know, no other dead Welsh tramp made such a contribution to the war effort.

On the train back to Glasgow I asked John if my copy of *The Tour* had fallen off his side of the table.

'Christ!' he said. 'It must have been with the papers when the man came collecting rubbish.'

'What!' I said.

'I must have bundled everything up together.'

I felt a profound sense of loss. It was only a paperback but I was bereft. My Figment had left me. 'I don't believe it.'

The final overheard conversation of our nine journeys echoed my mood.

The downtrodden restless man across the aisle turned to his partner. 'Ah just hate him. He jist beats his wife for no reason.'

'And ah dinnae like the young girl, she's using…' replied the woman.

And then our adventure was over.

EPILOGUE

We stood on the concourse of Glasgow Central station, looked at each other and shook hands. We had spent a huge amount of time together. We had travelled well over 15,000 miles of railway track; we had passed through over 3,000 stations. If you live near a railway line, we probably saw your house and your washing hanging out; if you work near a railway we probably saw your office or factory, we may even have seen you outside snatching a smoke; if you watch football we probably saw the ground you visit; if you commute by train we may have seen you reading your paper. If your luck was out, we may even have spoken to you.

We had poked our noses into every part of the kingdom; I had the privilege of speaking to cleaners, ex-soldiers, surgeons, social workers, rat catchers, poets, students, security guards, builders, bouncers, tax lawyers, house painters, landscape painters, folk singers, clock makers, rubber testers, holidaymakers, printers, welders, equine therapists, fishermen, the retired and the unemployed.

Surprisingly, John and I were still friends, and, by way of a bonus, I had developed an even greater fondness for a long dead author.

I knew that if Defoe had not been swept into the bin, he

would have drawn himself up to his full height and asked, 'In this account of your Tour, do you think you have succeeded in rendering the Present State of Britain?'

That is a difficult question. As I explained in the prologue it was never my intention to pass comment on The Publick Edifices, seats and palaces of the NOBILITY and GENTRY, nor indeed on The Produce and Improvement of the Lands, the Trade, and Manufactures, as Defoe did so well three hundred years ago.

My journey was always going to be about people. Despite my initial shyness, I spoke to at least 250 strangers, only two of whom chose not to talk to me. With hardly any exceptions, people were open and friendly. I was privy to their thoughts about family and work; I was granted insight into their enthusiasms and obsessions; I was given a sense of what worries them, and equally what sustains them; I was granted privileged access to a raft of memories and regrets.

I still think about the people I met. Has life improved for the Welsh woman who was nursing her dying dog? Was the distressed passenger ever reunited with her luggage? Does the young man suffering with depression still manage to visit his sick father?

Given my background it was not surprising that many of my encounters were seen through the prism of mental health. Although it would be arrogant to pontificate on the well-being of a whole nation on such scanty evidence, I would be less than human if I had not emerged with some new perspectives. If poverty is a risk factor for mental ill health then it must be conceded that most, but far from all, of the people I spoke to had at least sufficient funds to buy exorbitant train tickets. Even so, a handful of my encounters were with very vulnerable and arguably unwell travellers. Many who shared their stories with me also revealed a patina of anxiety or sadness that could be an indicator of difficult times ahead. The majority however showed an enviable, life-enhancing resilience, humour and a sort of quirky stoicism that will stand them in good stead.

If I were asked which stranger made the greatest impression on me, I would unhesitatingly nominate David, who I met twice: in Wales and in the Scottish Borders. This in itself still strikes me as beyond a coincidence.

Since finally returning home I have frequently found myself repeating his mantra:

I have a house, I have friends, I have enough.